Pelican Books
A Farewell to Arms Control?

Elizabeth Young took a degree in Philosophy, Politics and
Economics at Oxford. She has written widely on disarmament
topics during the last ten years for the British and American press,
including articles for *The Times*, *Guardian*, *Sunday Times*,
Foreign Affairs, and *The World Today*; she has also been a
regular book reviewer for the *Bulletin of the Atomic Scientists*.
Her publications include *Old London Churches* (1956, with
Wayland Young), *Nations and Nuclear Weapons* (1963), *The
Control of Proliferation: the 1968 Treaty in Hindsight and Forecast*
(Adelphi Paper, no. 56, 155, 1969) and a book of poems, *Time is
as Time Does* (1958). She has also edited with Lord Ritchie
Calder and contributed to *Quiet Enjoyment: Arms Control and
Police Forces for the Ocean*, a collection of background papers
for the 1970 Pacem in Maribus Conference (University of
Malta Press, 1971).

Elizabeth Young is married to Wayland Young, Lord Kennet,
who was a Minister in the last Labour Government, responsible
for planning and environment. They have six children and live in
London.

Elizabeth Young

A Farewell
to Arms Control?

Penguin Books

Penguin Books Ltd, Harmondsworth,
Middlesex, England
Penguin Books Inc., 7110 Ambassador Road,
Baltimore, Maryland 21207, U.S.A.
Penguin Books Australia Ltd, Ringwood,
Victoria, Australia

First published 1972
Copyright © Elizabeth Young, 1972

Made and printed in Great Britain by
C. Nicholls & Company Ltd
Set in Monotype Times

For Zoe

Contents

Acknowledgements

My thanks to Yale University Press for permission to quote from Thomas Schelling's *Arms and Influence*, and to the International Institute for Strategic Studies for permission to quote from their annual publication, *The Military Balance*.

Judy Beetham I want to thank for typing the manuscript: her ability to decipher the undecipherable far outpaces the thinking about the unthinkable which is traditional in this gloomy field. I want also to record the kindness of the librarian at the United Nations office in London, Miss McAfee, and the usefulness of the BBC Monitoring Service's 'Summaries of World Broadcasts', published daily from Caversham Park, Reading, Berkshire, which are frequently referred to in the text which follows.

1

Introduction

The end of the world has now been at hand for twenty-seven years. This is not unusual. It has often been at hand before, expected by large numbers of people, and if they conceived it in terms of the wrath of God, and we conceive it in terms of blast and fall-out and the greenhouse effect, they believed in miracles and we believe in material causality. It is not our apprehensions which are different from our forefathers', but our theories of knowledge.

The United Nations has also been with us for the same length of time. Nations, however, though increasingly united in experience and needs, are not so in cooperation; they continue to generate and multiply the means to species extinction. Theoretically, nations could settle their disputes, or at least refrain from threatening each other's security, and consent to disagree. But the difficulties of identifying security, of defining it except as the ability to threaten an opponent, regularly overwhelm the fragile concept of international peace. Alternatives to national governments all appear worse than the system we know. Meanwhile, governments large and small progress through endless games of military and diplomatic snakes and ladders, each ladder regularly turning into a snake, and each snake into further escalation of weapons acquisition. Strategic theories are worked out, are accepted, and with several years' delay weapons systems are procured, to reach final deployment when the theory they embody has been abandoned and the world transformed: the political and economic landscape is littered with obsolete strategies and hand-me-down weapons systems. We look back, not knowing how to combine the lessons we draw from tragically unsuccessful appeasement in the thirties and tragically unsuccessful intervention in the sixties.

And yet a kind of gloomy stability obtains: there have been many wars since 1945, but nuclear weapons have not again been used; indeed, nuclear threats no longer seem particularly effective – if ever they were: the most recent, those made to China by Russia during 1969, had no obvious effect at all. To match the gloomy stability, there is a gloomy consensus that arms control would probably only be fire to this frying pan: the world of the arms race is familiar, even if not very well understood and heading God knows where; a disarmed world is not only unfamiliar, but as inconceivable to us as marriage is to a ten-year-old. So the nuclear threat continues, and impels most governments who have the resources and the technology to assure themselves of an option on nuclear weapons regardless of the Non-Proliferation Treaty (NPT) which many of them have signed, and regardless of such alliance guarantees as they may appear to enjoy. The superpowers talk in a desultory way without wishing to risk their supremacy and negotiate only with each other. Neither gives, perhaps neither can give, halting the arms race very high priority, though as a change from ten years ago the United States appears to set disarmament higher now than does the Soviet Union, and the Soviet Union is the more entangled in ideological fantasy.[1]

One confusing factor is the mounting evidence that conventional wars are not, as they used to be, terminable by military means (except perhaps for the 'overnight swat', in circumstances as rare as those of Czechoslovakia in 1968).[2] The 'conventional option', the ability to fight 'limited wars', and by these to achieve limited aims, was the Kennedy administration's principal contri-

1. Compare President Kennedy's inaugural declaration, that the US would 'pay any price, bear any burden, meet any hardship, support any friend, oppose any foe, to assure the survival and the success of liberty', with Mr Kosygin's remarks in Ulan Bator on 10 July 1971: 'The strength of the socialist community is determined . . . by unity of ideology. . . . The socialist gains of the peoples are inviolable and it is the common internationalist duty of all socialist countries to defend them.' The style is different, the meaning like.

2. Current Chinese, Albanian, Romanian, and Yugoslav arrangements for a 'people's defence' seem aimed at demonstrating that Czechoslovakia's fate is not for them. Hungarian 'civil defence' seems not dissimilar.

bution to the United States' war-making capacities and, by example and second-hand trade, to the world's. The Indian incursion into East Bengal at this moment appears as conclusive as the Israeli victory of 1967. But the war in Korea (staunched by a rather insecure armistice), the war in Indochina, the war in the Middle East, all 'limited wars', show no sign of termination. (France did not, as her government had intended, by summer 1971 get all her troops out of Chad, where they are 'assisting' the government against rebels.) Because the nuclear super-powers do not propose to allow their clients to be defeated, local military victories do not lead to the other side's political defeat. On the other hand, the super-powers themselves will not seek to settle any of these issues by making war on each other, because in general nuclear war victory is inconceivable. Although 'limited' geographically and in political or military scale, wars may be 'unlimited' in duration, each client kept going artificially and indefinitely by military aid from its supporters. Because it was a breakdown in the political situation that led to war in the first place, and in each of these cases the political situation remains unresolved, it is hard to see that they are politically terminable either.[3] These wars are haemorrhages and ever increasing treasure is draining away into the acquisition of arms with which to fight them.[4] Up to now[5] arms control and disarmament policies and

3. The North and South Korean Red Cross began, in September 1971, to talk to each other about procedures which might lead to actual conversations. As the North Korean Radio put it, 'they laid a telephone line to link the severed nerves between the North and the South.' (KCNA, 29 September 1971). In January 1972, after fourteen meetings, virtually nothing had been agreed.

4. The massively authoritative SIPRI volume on *The Arms Trade with the Third World* (Stockholm, November 1971) establishes that 'The gross national products of all developing countries have grown at an average of five per cent a year since 1950. Their military expenditures have grown at a yearly rate of seven per cent, while their major weapons imports have grown at a rate of nine per cent', and points out that the few recent proposals for regulating or supervising the arms trade have been neither well-formulated nor serious. The French Government believes the developing countries military spending to be nearly double what they receive in economic aid.

5. Except for the weapons cut-off in 1965, when fighting broke out in the Indian subcontinent. Both sides had acquired their weapons from Western

negotiations have had no bearing on them: indeed most of these policies and negotiations have had about as much bearing on the life of nations as a Mafioso's crossing himself as he loads his gun, has on his hopes of heaven.

This book will seek to substantiate that rather harsh statement, to account for the present state of affairs which is expensive and dangerous, though not incomprehensible, and, because it may still be open to improvement, to suggest some directions in which that may be sought or hoped for.

This is worth attempting at this time partly because of the morass that traditional war-making cannot get itself out of; partly because the strategic balance is having to re-form with the return of China to active international life, and partly because the tip of the arms race is due for another technological metamorphosis, perhaps for two. The first of these is probably not the often-cited action-reaction phenomenon[6] of Anti-Ballistic Missile (A B M) and Multiple Independently Targetable Re-entry Vehicle (M I R V). What is much more likely to alter the course of the arms race in the next few years is the increase in long-range accuracy of missiles which may well be within about thirty metres at intercontinental range by the end of the seventies.[7] Allied to multiple re-entry vehicles launched from either ballistic or orbiting missiles,[8] and to highly accurate photographic information, this would make all land-based targets (including retaliatory and anti-ballistic missile related radar sites) excessively vulnerable. The

---

governments which were not concerned to back either side to win. By 1971, India had a treaty with the Soviet Union, who massively supplied her and backed her to win.

6. American Secretary of Defense Robert McNamara's phrase for the likelihood that further deployment of the one would trigger further deployment of the other. Because of fall-out there is a limit to the number of anti-ballistic nuclear weapons a government can envisage letting off over its own territory or in its own hemisphere, even if it has a massive civil defence programme such as the Soviet Union organizes. That the phenomenon is currently over-cited, see Chapter 10.

7. See David G. Hoag, *Ballistic Missile Guidance*, Pugwash Symposium on *New Technology and the Arms Race 1970* (copyright MIT). Mr Hoag was Director of the Apollo Guidance-Navigation Programme at MIT.

8. The Soviet Union currently deploys an Orbital Bombardment System.

possibility of moon-shot type accuracy will probably make the strategic arms race change course and take entirely to the deep sea, where so much of it is already. This might provide an occasion for dismantling it, before China too acquires deep-sea technology.

The second metamorphosis would occur if thermo-nuclear weapons could be set off by something other than today's fission trigger. Such a development – which lasers or small-scale fusion bursts might provide – would not only shatter the provisions of the N P T, which are devised to control only fissionable material; it might also reduce the technological and financial threshold for acquiring nuclear weapons. By definition, the more nuclear buttons, the more risk from accident or raving folly.

There are the other, not quite events, but perhaps rather slow happenings which make this a time for re-appraisal. One of these is the growing crisis in Russian orthodox Marxism–Leninism.[9] A peaceful solution of this might bring a Russian government which was aware that co-existence is for keeps, and has to cover ideology as well as everything else, that the downfall of capitalism and universal victory of socialism anticipated by the orthodox Marxists will neither soon nor automatically solve all international problems, and that when it comes 'socialism' is quite unlikely to be *à la mode de Moscou*. The second happening is the environmental crisis, which is bringing home to the human animal that he cannot indefinitely foul his spaceship nest. If our co-existence, indeed if our existence, is to continue at all long, it will be cooperatively as we realize that more and more of the resources and facilities we had assumed were infinite are scarce and have to be shared: economic analysis too is due for another breakthrough. The third happening is in the sea, last and largest of all commons, that we are now beginning to enclose; there too we shall not avoid cooperation.

9. Defining crisis, with the *Concise Oxford Dictionary*, as a 'moment of danger or suspense'. There is no reason to suppose that the Soviet Union, now virtually the last of the great nineteenth-century empires still territorially intact, will be spared the problems of withdrawal from empire just because of the colour of its government. Nor that the recently formulated doctrine of 'proletarian internationalism' will make these problems anything but more difficult to solve.

This is an essay, an interpretation of events and attitudes which themselves are more or less common knowledge. Some of the generalizations are inadequately supported, particularly in 'Hunches' (Part Two): there I am advancing hypotheses (which I do not expect to see survive intact) about the state of affairs at the margin of three specialities: Soviet studies, arms control studies, and philosophy.

The nub of the historical interpretation – which I advance more confidently – is this: although there has been no disarmament other than unilateral since 1945, there have been several perfectly serious, some more or less successful, attempts at nuclear arms control within the two major alliances. For the most part nuclear weapons policies (procurement as well as arms control policies) have not been either coherent within themselves or fully integrated with the general conduct of foreign or defence policy. The United States has pursued a policy of non-proliferation for others since before 1945, and the Russians have since the middle fifties, each showing meanwhile no comparable inclination to curb its own nuclear competition with the other super-power. It is part of the argument that this pursuit of 'horizontal' non-proliferation by the United States and the Soviet Union, while they themselves engaged in the 'vertical' proliferation of nuclear weapons, has been counter-productive, that it has been grounded in the (by no means obscure) native misapprehensions of those two great countries about the rest of the world, and that these policies and misapprehensions have prevented the emergence of a more convenient world system than the present one. The misapprehensions, I suggest, may well be rooted in the philosophies prevailing in Russia and America and shaped by largely self-generated bursts of intellectual fashion. All along, there has been the makings of another, altogether more plausible disarmament programme, described and advocated beyond the earshot of the super-powers.

The realization that we could eliminate our civilization from the world by nuclear war had a mesmerizing effect on governments, and contorted the international system of the fifties and sixties into some absurdly 'bipolar' positions. We can now see that our environment, natural as well as man-made, is being overtaken by not one but a whole series of threats equally menacing, and that rushing into opposed camps was an inadequate reaction. That we can do something better we proved with the Partial Test Ban Treaty – the first international Clean Air Bill – which was achieved by a combination of public pressure, scientific demonstration, and governmental good sense. As a clean air bill it has worked rather well (even though as an arms control measure it was almost useless): perhaps it is as polluters that we can most sensibly realize that we are fellow passengers in Spaceship Earth.

In what follows, some of the events in the American and Russian non-proliferation policies are briefly examined: first, intra-alliance attempts to prevent proliferation (Anglo-American, French-American, Russian-Chinese relations); and then the international negotiations, of which those leading up to the Non-Proliferation Treaty are examined in some detail. These have been by far the most interesting, because it was during the years of their duration that the super-power governments at last came to understand that, if there were ever to be limits to the horizontal proliferation of nuclear weapons, the vertical proliferation of their own nuclear weapons would have to be subjected to limitations too; that unless they first curbed their own proliferation, proliferation would continue. In the last two or three years, the pertinacity of the unaligned governments in negotiating the NPT has already led to provisions in the Seabed Nuclear Non-Emplacement Treaty which may have interesting implications for verification in subsequent agreements, and to some sessions of the Russian/American Strategic Arms Limitation Talks (SALT). Discussions about verifying an underground test ban and about the control of chemical weapons go on in Geneva at the Conference of the Committee on Disarmament (CCD), and it is now agreed that biological weapons should be banned. During the spring of 1971 Mr Brezhnev recapitulated several other familiar topics for discussion, in Geneva and elsewhere. Agreement so far is insignificant, but that discussion, after several years of bored dearth, begins to show signs of liveliness again is itself news.

It is not that the Mafiosi over the years have been entirely hypocritical. The Geneva Disarmament Conference has developed some genuinely ritual functions: the people who are despatched there by their governments are many of them above average able and talented; there is admirably little cynicism or impatience among them, despite the abysmal lack of interest at home and the artificiality and irrelevance of the words they are so often given to speak. There is a lot of mutual support and some pretty whistling to keep the spirits up. The routine of twice weekly meetings is priestly in its regularity and a flame of sorts is evidently being tended. Only the French Government is taking the spiritual risk of staying away. The offerings so far have been quite unreal, but there is a feeling about that, when the not quite unanticipated change of heart takes place, the priesthood, the altar, the temple, will all be ready for use. Or not.

In August 1970 a very limited arms control arrangement was in some sort of operation between Egyptians and Israelis along the Suez Canal. It was an American invention, and no more than 'an oral agreement',[10] but having first appeared to accept it the Russians then took part in circumventing it. It demonstrated, in small but acute form, several of the traditional unsolved problems: particularly those concerning the verification and enforcement of agreements and the degree of certainty a government may require if it is to agree to, and to carry on observing, a measure of arms control. At one point, Mr Riyad, the Egyptian Foreign Minister, inquired of the world at large: 'We have a long list of Israeli violations, but to whom do we submit it?' Article III of the Seabed Nuclear Non-Emplacement Treaty[11] suggests the Security Council as long-stop, but no government is going to repose the security of its people on that veto-prone lap yet a while. How will the near-nuclear weapons states acquire enough certainty that any arms limitations agreed privately in SALT are being observed by the super-powers for them to ratify the NPT? Arms control and disarmament depend on certainty. Certainty is based on evi-

10. Mr Rodgers's, US Secretary of State's words, 17 March 1971. See p. 220, fn. 45.

11. Endorsed by the United Nations General Assembly in December 1970 and now open to signature.

dence. The subject is not much talked about at Geneva. Or else-where.

The Strategic Arms Limitation Talks, begun in November 1969, are the first arms control negotiations to deal with the live centre of the Russian/American arms race, and if any agreement were achieved, particularly about international verification, it would affect political and military affairs the world over. It could at last mean the beginning of a real disarmament process and of a new international system. Even if once again nothing substantial is achieved, there is still a chance that nuclear war will be avoided: the nuclear weapons and other weapons of 'mass destruction' are constantly being overtaken by their own irrelevance to the kinds of war, if any, that it remains plausible to fight. The galloping obsolescence of weapons systems not only fuels the technological arms race, but at the same time makes its *de facto* supercession as an international system more likely.

But even if their military function were to become scarcely more than formal, the huge military machines cannot conveniently be allowed to grow unchecked: with their continued existence and development go vast expenditure of treasure, and the brain drain into military work which that expenditure sucks into itself, both internationally and within each state; the distortion of scholar-ship and science by research at military expense or for military purposes; the fouling of international relations by secrecy and of international commerce by the arms trade; the acceleration of that trade by the requirement of large-scale production and of the balance of payments; the continued and increasing debilitation of developing countries by their local arms races and the feeding of these from outside by first- and second-hand arms traders, and by seekers after ideological or military influence. The impetus of the great Russian-American technological arms race, now further complicated by the availability for military purposes of two entire new elements, space and the deep ocean, is geared to the daunting uncertainties and responsibilities of the politicians, to the rival and incompatible epistemologies of the analysts, to the danger-ously hectic fashions among educated but often uninformed or cowardly elites, and to the professional pessimisms of military men whose job it is to foresee and to prepare for the worst. The worst is now the extinction of human society, and for that there is no useful preparation, except prayer. The military have been seeking, without success, for alternative, non-lethal, types of war in which victory or security, the traditionally expected products of their trade, could still be achieved. Perhaps in fact the only usable forms of coercion that remain are the unconventional, but inexpensive, methods of the guerrilla, the kidnapper, the hijacker, and the secret police. Perhaps the organization of authority and of power is being dissolved into an atomism of violence. But violence is like pain: it indicates that something is wrong, and heals nothing. Can we conceive another healthier atomism?

The specialist in disarmament and arms control is not yet out of business: his function is still to understand, and to discern ways of dismantling, with words the only tool, the impacted edifice of weapons, industries, attitudes, ideologies, anachronisms, momentums, inertias, which, though increasingly unusable, is increasingly an integral part of the world system. Perhaps in 1945, when nuclear weapons first appeared, it might have been possible to extract them, like a thorn, from the international body politic. By now their existence is symbiotic with that body's, yet it – we – are still trying – or pretending – to deal with them as if they were a single thorn, at highly specialized, carefully isolated 'disarmament conferences'. We refer to our cancer with a new language of devotional optimism. But our problem is not the disinfection of a superficial and local wound; it is the cleansing of a bloodstream into which we continue to pump infection, to control and eliminate the disease without destroying the body politic of a still divided world.

Part One: Histories

2

Proliferation and the United Kingdom 1939–46

The next chapters of this book are concerned with the anti-proliferation policies of the United States and of the Soviet Union up to 1970, when the Non-Proliferation Treaty they had promoted came, if not into practical effect, at least theoretically into force. Each of the three other nuclear powers, the United Kingdom, France and China, was, at the time its government determined to acquire nuclear weapons of its own, a member of an alliance headed by a nuclear super-power, which purported to guarantee unambiguous protection, nuclear and all other, in case of attack. It is instructive to see why the third, fourth and fifth nuclear powers were dissatisfied with the guarantees they enjoyed, and to see how difficult the two super-powers found it to discern in this dissatisfaction anything beyond negligible, chauvinistic yearnings.

In each case the discussion will concentrate on the nuclear strand: this is partly artificial, for convenience and brevity's sake, but partly it reflects a true state of affairs. Nuclear policy has always been special, apart, unintegrated. The weapons themselves were invented and are made and stored in utmost secrecy; the contemplation of their use in war is disheartening and militarily unsatisfactory; their political usefulness is indescribable and incalculable. As far as the three proliferatory governments were concerned, the acquisition of these weapons offended their respective chief ally, not only going against his policy and wishes and interests but also publicly embodying doubts about his pledged word. In the fifties the United Kingdom, France and China all conducted their nuclear affairs quietly and unobtrusively. The Conservative governments of the United Kingdom, demurely ogling the restoration of nuclear cooperation with the United

States, carried unobtrusiveness so far as not even to consider using the occasion of the first British thermonuclear test in 1957 for the launching of any kind of arms control or disarmament initiative. In those days Mr Macmillan found himself able to go along with United States anti-proliferation policies (then particularly directed against France) while at the same time, thanks to the Americans, continuing to finger some of the joys of an independent British nuclear capability. This posture earned Britain no respect (on the contrary). The United Kingdom's situation ever since has been one of singularly overt humbug, which prevented us from playing any serious role in the field of arms control and disarmament. The humbug lay not merely in preaching non-proliferation for others while ourselves explicitly seeking to retain independent control of nuclear weapons; but also, and perhaps more seriously, in appearing to cooperate with the super-powers' anti-proliferation policies while remaining entirely silent about those super-power policies which, we knew well from experience, made proliferation more likely. During the halcyon days of the special relationship, America's best friend did not tell her that she, and France and China and other powers too, were acquiring the nuclear option as an insurance we could not but take up, in view of the super-powers' own possession of nuclear weapons, of the political use they were making of them, and of their apparently adamant unwillingness even to discuss curbs on their own arms race. The Labour Government of 1964 was sucked straight into the humbug, and, as a national issue, disarmament and arms control died. Resuscitation is now due.

American non-proliferation policy developed *de facto* during the Second World War and achieved *de jure* status in 1946. Passed into law on 1 August, the Atomic Energy Act of 1946, better known as the McMahon Act, drastically curtailed the administration's discretion in all matters concerning nuclear energy. It was drafted and went through Congress without anyone there knowing very much about the history of Anglo-American wartime collaboration and, in particular, anything whatsoever about two agreements reached by President Roosevelt and Mr Churchill, at Quebec in 1943 and at Hyde Park in 1944. These agreements had formalized the wartime leaders' intention that Anglo-American nuclear cooperation should continue after the defeat of Japan, until terminated by joint agreement, and they gave each party a veto over the use of nuclear weapons by the other.

The possibility of an atomic bomb[1] had been explained by far-sighted physicists to both the British and the American governments in 1939, and the topic had immediately been blanketed in secrecy. Early in 1940 Otto Frisch and Rudolph Peierls, working in Birmingham, outlined to the British Government, and for the first time in the world, an actual programme for making an atomic weapon. On the strength of this outline, well before Pearl Harbor, Mr Churchill and President Roosevelt settled between them that research in their two countries should be conducted on a basis of pooled information and highest secrecy.

By 1941 Roosevelt was suggesting that the whole enterprise should be conducted jointly. Churchill too had been thinking that not only information should be pooled, but work and results. 'We conceived ourselves at least as far advanced as our ally. . . . If the Americans had not been willing to undertake the venture, we should certainly have gone forward on our own power in Canada, or, if the Canadian Government demurred, in some other part of the Empire', he later recalled.[2] Roosevelt was indeed willing and cooperation between the United Kingdom, the United States and Canada at first worked quite smoothly.[3] But as

1. Unattributed American quotations in this chapter come from Hewlett and Anderson, *The New World: 1939–1946*, vol. I of the official history of the United States Atomic Energy Commission, Pennsylvania State University Press, 1962. Unattributed British quotations are from Margaret Gowing, *Britain and Atomic Energy 1939–45*, Macmillan, London, 1964.

2. *The Second World War*, vol. IV, pp. 339–42.

3. The Russian decision to launch a nuclear programme was taken in June 1942. According to Marshal Zhukov, Stalin interpreted as an attempt at 'political blackmail' Truman's disclosures to him at Potsdam (24 July 1945) about the 'new weapon of unusual destructive force'. Quoted by Chalmers Roberts, *International Herald Tribune*, 31 May 1971. A history of nuclear technology in the U S S R has recently been published, which, according to *Tass*, 'notes that the controlled chain reaction and the explosive reaction

the research stage came to an end and as, with the 'Manhattan project', actual production began, the Anglo-American interchange dwindled, in spite of the substantial number of 'British'[4] scientists actually engaged in the work. The Manhattan project was directed by General Groves of the United States Corps of Engineers, and what he considered himself responsible for was the production of weapons for the United States. During the spring of 1943 a stream of complaints began to cross the Atlantic: from Churchill to Roosevelt's confidant, Harry Hopkins, from Sir John Anderson, the responsible minister in the British Cabinet, to his American opposite number, James Conant; to which the Americans replied with what Conant described as 'masterly' evasiveness. In April, Churchill declared that if the flow of information ceased the United Kingdom would take the 'sombre decision'[5] of going ahead separately. Conant, and other Americans connected with the nuclear programme, had become convinced – it is difficult to see how – that the shopkeeper British were really interested not in the military application of nuclear energy, but 'solely [in its] post-war industrial possibilities'. In fact, Churchill himself had always assumed that the post-war military aspects were more important than the commercial, in which, obviously quite genuinely, he disclaimed interest; when Lord Cherwell put this to Conant, Conant found it hard to believe and did not change his mind.

After considerable badgering by the British, Roosevelt gave Churchill what appeared to be a firm commitment that interchange would be fully resumed. This was in May 1943. In Quebec, in August, Churchill was able to write, 'We have secured a settlement of a number of hitherto intractable questions' including 'Tube Alloys', the code name for work on the atomic bomb.

---

had been recognized as theoretically possible by the time of the outbreak of the Great Patriotic War. However, the Nazi attack had prevented the ideas of Soviet atomic physicists for being put into practice for many years.' (*Tass* 7 December 1971, SU 3862/B/2.)

4. Many were refugees from Central Europe, with British passports.

5. R. E. Sherwood, *White House Papers of Harry L. Hopkins*, vol. II, pp. 700–701.

'Articles of Agreement governing collaboration between the authorities of the United States of America and the United Kingdom in the matter of Tube Alloys' were signed on 19 August,[6] and a practical system of joint enterprise emerged which, although it was detested by some of the Americans, worked reasonably well.

In the following summer, the minds of the few who knew anything about it turned to the question of the post-war aspects of atomic energy, and Roosevelt and Churchill discussed this in September at Hyde Park, Roosevelt's country house. There they initialled an *aide mémoire* which included this sentence: 'Full collaboration between the United States and the British Government in developing Tube Alloys for military and commercial purposes should continue after the defeat of Japan unless and until terminated by joint agreement.'[7]

Suspicions had arisen over interchange with France. In 1944 and early 1945 some of the Frenchmen working on Tube Alloys wanted to return to France (among them, Pierre Auger, later head of French space research). General Groves wished to have them followed by American security agents and the British refused, claiming this would be to treat them like prisoners. In the British view, moreover, France had, from the 'pioneering researches of her scientists and their help during the war, a better claim than any other fourth country to participate in post-war arrangements'.[8] The president's advisers told him that the British were 'allowing information to leak to the French', and his reaction was to ask what the French were after and whether Churchill was in on all this. Sir John Anderson was thought to have the 'imperial instinct'. The Americans' firm intention was not to enter into any kind of undertaking towards France. In the words of the American Atomic Energy Commission's historians, Hewlett and Anderson, the affair 'added tension to the mistrust and misunderstanding that had accumulated through the years.

6. Cmnd. 9123, April 1954. Text also in Gowing, op. cit., appendix 4, p. 439.
7. Text in Gowing, op. cit., appendix 8, p. 447.
8. Hewlett and Anderson, op. cit., p. 332.

It made it more difficult for the wartime partners to face the future in wisdom as well as in strength.'[9]

Real guidelines for post-war planning and cooperation, either within the tiny knowledgeable group within the United States administration, or between it and the equivalent group in the United Kingdom, had been ventilated but not decided when Roosevelt died. In fact, on Roosevelt almost alone, and on Churchill's relationship with him, had depended Anglo-American cooperation in Tube Alloys, and with the president's death the only real link snapped. As far as the United States was concerned, the spirit of the Quebec and Hyde Park agreements died with him.

For a moment in the summer of 1944, during the preparation of the Hyde Park meeting, there had been the possibility of a joint Anglo-American internationalist policy being developed – even discussions with the Russians about control and use had been contemplated.[10] In the event, Roosevelt and Churchill had decided on the continuation of rigid secrecy, and perhaps to use the atom bomb against the Japanese when it became available.[11] After Roosevelt's death the same issues were again considered in Washington, but this time, significantly, without British participation (although formal British approval for the use of the bomb on Japan had been sought and obtained). Disagreements within the United States were now crystallizing, and British concerns must have dwindled into comparative insignificance. The scientists working on the bomb were increasingly worrying about the use to which they feared it was to be put, now it was clear that Nazi Germany had no nuclear weapons. They were also concerned about the possibility of a nuclear arms race with Russia. Specifically they wanted an end to secrecy (which they knew could anyway not long be maintained),[12] an end to military direction of nuclear research, and a beginning of international control. Some

9. Ibid., p. 336.

10. Gowing, op. cit., p. 358.

11. At this stage none of the politicians knew of any secondary effects the bomb might have.

12. Official opinion was ranging from Conant's judgement that the Russians would catch up in three or four years to General Groves' that it would take them twenty. Some of the Chicago scientists gave them two years.

of them were pointing out that other great powers would never permit the United States to enjoy a monopoly, but they seem rather to have had the Soviet Union in mind than the United Kingdom or France.

The new President was very much in the hands of his advisers. Those of them who favoured an international system of control assumed that any such system was absolutely alternative to Anglo-American cooperation. They thought such cooperation would lead to a nuclear arms race, and that an international system could somehow be enhanced by American monopoly. The Churchill/Roosevelt agreements, although the Truman administration had acted in accordance with them in getting British agreement to using the bombs against Japan, legally could be deemed not binding on Roosevelt's successor because the requirements of secrecy had prevented them from being submitted to the Senate.[13] When it became clear that cooperation with the Russians was impossible – it had begun to seem unlikely in the winter of 1944–5 – the original belief in international control metamorphosed into a belief in American monopoly.

Mr Attlee, when he became prime minister, was almost as much in the dark about atomic affairs as Truman had been when he became president. Churchill seems hardly to have briefed his successor on these intricate and weighty issues; nor even to have flagged the Quebec and Hyde Park agreements as particularly delicate and deserving notice and care. In August 1945, with British agreement, the two available bombs were used on Hiroshima and Nagasaki; Group Captain Cheshire and Dr Penney (later Lord Penney) were present on Tinian Island, from which the first nuclear bomber took off on 6 August 1945. Probably the war was over in any case, but as Admiral Lewis Strauss, later chairman of the American Atomic Energy Commission, put it,

13. It is sometimes suggested that President Truman was unaware of the agreements. Richard Neustadt for instance writes that 'Truman severed our initial partnership in ignorance that F.D.R. had pledged continuation' – *Alliance Politics*, Columbia University Press, 1970, p. 31. Harry Hopkins in fact told him all he knew about Anglo-American nuclear relations, which included the Quebec and Hyde Park Agreements, on 4 September 1945. *The White House Papers of Harry L. Hopkins*, ed. R. Sherwood, vol. 2, pp. 700–701.

slightly misquoting Emerson, by then 'events were ... in the saddle, riding the decision-makers'.

To the surprise (and against the advice) of the British, the otherwise so security-conscious Americans now published a technical account of the Manhattan project, the Smyth Report,[14] one purpose of which was to educate Congress into understanding what they had already paid for and would soon have to legislate on.

During September, the new British Government and the Canadian Government suggested discussions at which a joint policy could be worked out. The President's mind was then beginning to harden not only against alliance arrangements but against international control, and no real answers came, even to Mr Attlee's proposal a few weeks later for an immediate meeting. What Conant had earlier called 'masterly' evasiveness started up again. The American Secretary of State, James F. Byrnes, was firmly against both international control (the Russians who were not allowing Americans into Poland could hardly be expected to allow inspection of their atomic plants) and close cooperation with the British, and with Mr Truman's approval Mr Byrnes effectively recommended procrastination.

In London, Lord Alanbrooke, Chief of the Imperial General Staff, was aware that 'any international agreement that was not thoroughly efficient was, on the whole, worse than no agreement at all'. He was referring to a possible new world-wide agreement, but he may well have had Anglo-American agreements in mind as well. Mr Attlee, noting that no one in Washington was even considering reviving the Quebec and Hyde Park agreements,[15]

14. Henry D. Smyth, *General Account of the Developments of Methods of Using Atomic Energy for Military Purposes.*

15. The American copy of the latter had anyway disappeared, to turn up again only some years later. Mr Churchill later told the House of Commons that Mr Truman had 'strongly appealed' to him not to raise the agreements in public (Hansard, 15 April 1954, col. 53). Neither he nor Mr Attlee thought it proper to bring them to the notice even of Senator McMahon, chairman of the special committee which drafted the McMahon Act. Nor did anyone else, and Senator McMahon later claimed he knew nothing about them. See below, p. 32.

now that the war was over, and that the flow of information had virtually ceased, interpreted the American attitude as a 'relapse into isolationism'. He wrote later: 'We had to hold up our position vis-à-vis the Americans. We couldn't allow ourselves to be wholly in their hands, and their position wasn't awfully clear always'.[16] He announced the setting up of a British Atomic Energy Authority, with an establishment at Harwell, on 29 October 1945.[17] This was to be under the Ministry of Supply, which implied military objectives, and its activities would provide the foundation for eventual manufacture of atomic weapons. A positive decision about weapons did not have to be taken there and then, but even if the Americans had chosen to revive the full cooperation for which Mr Attlee was still asking, he would not have discarded all option on a British nuclear weapons programme, experience of fluctuations in Washington opinion had over the years been so severe. Lord Waverley, as Sir John Anderson had become, provided continuity with the wartime arrangements, as Chairman of the Advisory Committee on Atomic Energy.

Anglo-American policy cooperation in the international nuclear field could still have been secured during the winter of 1945–6; the possibility was rejected in Washington by default. American domestic concern was now fully occupied with the debate between, on the one hand, the scientists who maintained that research, including specifically nuclear research, could only flourish unshackled by security and that only international arrangements were compatible with this; and, on the other, the *real-politik* monopolists, who intended the United States to win the nuclear arms race they were now foreseeing as inevitable. Neither of these parties saw any glimpse of desirability in Anglo-American cooperation. Representative Andrew May, Chairman of a Congressional Joint Committee which was examining the issues, put it quite simply: 'the War Department discovered the

16. Francis Williams, *A Prime Minister Remembers*, Heinemann, 1961, p. 118.
17. The French Commissariat à l'Énergie Atomique was set up on 8 October.

weapon. Why can they not keep the secret?' General Groves refused to let Senator McMahon's Special Committee examine the full record of Anglo-American relations during the war, which remained top secret information, and Senator McMahon himself had no inkling of the Quebec and Hyde Park agreements before the bill bearing his name was finally passed into law. He later told Mr Churchill, in 1952, that 'if we had seen this agreement, there would have been no McMahon Act.'[18]

In retrospect, it seems likely there would have been an Act very like it, because the Churchill–Roosevelt agreements were only 'executive documents', constitutionally no more than morally binding on Roosevelt's successors, and in the atmosphere of 1945–6 neither Mr Truman nor Senator McMahon would have had much incentive to maintain or revamp them. American external concern was overwhelmingly not with the British (let alone the French or the Canadians), but with the United Nations and with the Russians. A not particularly wide-ranging agreement about cooperation between the United States, the United Kingdom and Canada which had been reached in November 1945 was the next spring being so interpreted in Washington so as to rule out any exchange of information about actual production of nuclear energy, on the grounds that this would be incompatible with the Charter of the United Nations, and so with any system of international control. In fact the President had 'resolved not to allow too close a relationship with Britain to spoil' the chance of

18. *Hansard*, 5 April 1954, col. 52. This issue of the bindingness of the Quebec and Hyde Park agreements has been subjected to a certain amount of fudging. Thus, for instance, Mr Acheson, President Truman's Secretary of State from 1948, in a BBC interview printed in *The Listener* of 8 April 1971, speaking about the possible British veto on American use of nuclear weapons during the Korean War: 'This was at one time in the Quebec Agreements [sic], and with great difficulty we had found out that the Senate would not go along with this and had gotten it out.' Even Mr Macmillan remembers the story wrong: 'After the Fuchs and other security disasters, the Americans – not, I think the Government so much as the Senate – insisted on passing a law called the McMahon Act by which the President was precluded from giving us information concerning scientific advances.' (A BBC interview with Robert McKenzie, reprinted in *The Listener*, 13 May 1971.) Klaus Fuchs was not picked up as a spy until late 1949.

such a system,[19] on which in fact he was pinning very little hope. The Atomic Energy Act which Senator McMahon steered through Congress during the spring and summer finally precluded any real relationship with Britain at all, except of course for that residue of silent and gentlemanly bitterness which was to explode first at Suez and later over the *Skybolt* cancellation with a quality of hysteria Americans found difficult to understand. A recent examination of Suez and *Skybolt* by Professor Richard Neustadt[20] scarcely refers to the original trauma (and then not too accurately). This book is not so much *Hamlet* without the prince as *Measure for Measure* without the duke.

The Soviet Union was not in fact prepared to accept international control on the terms the United States was prepared to offer, and the nuclear arms race between them, which later came to be seen as the 'vertical' proliferation of nuclear weapons, became overt.[21] So did the 'horizontal' proliferation of nuclear weapons: it never occurred to the British Government at the time that Britain had any less right to atomic weapons or atomic plants than had the United States. The British programme was merely a matter of carrying on in spite of the faithlessness, as it seemed, of the American ally.[22] Public interest anyway was minimal. In April 1946, when President Truman had at last explicitly refused to provide the United Kingdom with certain specifically requested detailed information, he gave it as his opinion that it was unwise for Britain to build her own atomic energy plants. This was a view no British government, or indeed any government, could possibly accept, but neither Mr Truman then, nor his successors for many years, seem to have worked out at all clearly how far they were against the proliferation of nuclear techniques for reasons of

19. Hewlett and Anderson, op. cit., p. 481.

20. See footnote 13, p. 29.

21. The Russians had presumably been racing since 1962. See footnote 3, p. 25.

22. An attitude which later came to seem almost incredible. See for instance a letter from R. H S. Crossman, the *New Statesman*, 17 May 1963. By then, of course, nuclear weapons had been a chief topic of political concern for several years, a situation which we in turn look back on with some amazement.

American national interest, commercial or military, and how far
for reasons of arms control and international security. The
assumption seems to have been that what was good for the
United States was good for the world, and it was probably held
with as little hypocrisy as Defense Secretary Wilson's view that
what was good for his old firm, General Motors, was good for the
United States. This implicit ambiguity in American, and later in
Russian, anti-proliferation policy was clearly discerned by other
governments and contributed in no small way to the horizontal
spread of nuclear weapons.

3

Proliferation and Anti-Proliferation 1945–60

The British and American governments jointly embarked on the production of nuclear weapons in the early 1940s,[1] partly at any rate because there was and could be no certainty that Nazi Germany was not in the process of acquiring them. Then, as now, deterrence by counter-acquisition was the most obvious policy, but three anti-proliferation techniques were also adopted: secrecy ('We made certain that each member of the project thoroughly understood his part in our total effort – that, and nothing more'[2]); the physical destruction of the other side's plant (two assaults were made on the Norsk Hydro heavy water undertaking in German-occupied Norway, which might have contributed to a German nuclear weapons programme); and the pre-emption of raw materials (the world supply of uranium was neatly cornered early in the war).

The first of these techniques was so operated by the United States that, as we have seen, in 1945 the United Kingdom found itself excluded from both information and control, despite the specific agreements reached and signed by President Roosevelt and Mr Churchill. Mr Churchill had made it clear that, in the event of failure in Anglo-American collaboration the United Kingdom would take 'the sombre decision' of going ahead alone and this was indeed the decision Mr Attlee took: as a first step towards acquisition of nuclear weapons Harwell was established

1. In cooperation also with the Canadian Government and eventually with the collaboration of a small number of French scientists, who, however, viewed themselves as French civil servants, rather than as unofficial employees of a foreign government.

2. Leslie R. Groves, *Now it can be told; The Story of the Manhattan Project*, Deutsch, London, 1963, p. xi. General Groves was Director of the Project.

early in October 1945. The French Government, whose claims to cooperation with either British or Americans were minor, and were not pressed, also set up their Atomic Energy Commission in October 1945.[3] The Canadian Government, too, embarked almost at once on a civil programme but it has not so far sought to make nuclear weapons.

At the end of the war a number of further anti-proliferation techniques became available to the United States Government, including political, economic, and academic pressures,[4] and the possibility of bilateral and international agreements. It was hoped anyway that secrecy could go a long way towards maintaining the American monopoly which (if the Russians rejected American proposals for international control) was judged the least objectionable of possible eventualities. That the Russians might already have a nuclear weapons programme does not seem to have occurred to anyone.

The United Nations General Assembly's first resolution, in January 1946, set up a Commission on Atomic Energy with a membership consisting of the Security Council plus Canada; there, in June 1946, the United States put forward the Baruch plan for an International Atomic Development Authority. International control and inspection would be established over all atomic energy plants and material and would precede destruction of stocks of nuclear weapons (only American nuclear weapons were in existence) and there would be no veto over any of the

3. See Chapter IV. For a French view of 'anti-proliferation' at this and subsequent times, see Bertrand Goldschmidt, *Le problème du Controle International de l'Energie Atomique, Revue de Défense Nationale*, August 1968, pp. 1167, et seq. For an American view of them, see George Ball, *The Discipline of Power*, London, 1968.

4. By 'academic pressures', I mean for instance the editorial policy of subsidized periodicals and publishing houses, the hardly fortuitous dearth of published research in the United States on subjects such as the catalytic use of nuclear weapons, the political use of acquisition or ownership of nuclear weapons in intra-alliance bargaining, the effect on deterrence of alliance nuclear polycentrism, the theory of bee-sting deterrence and so on. The virtual absence of such studies by American scholars of course left large areas of nuclear politics uncharted and unfamiliar to the strategic theorists who so influenced the Kennedy administration.

Authority's activities or over such sanctions as might be devised against infringements of its rights. Three days later, in the same forum, the Soviet Union proposed that the destruction of all stocks of weapons should precede international control and inspection, and that there should be just such a veto.

Thus, within a year of the first use of nuclear energy, the elements of the now familiar scene were established: the Soviet–American nuclear arms race had begun; the essential content of subsequent East–West dialogue had been established; a nuclear power's disappointed and exposed ally had taken steps towards the independent acquisition of nuclear weapons; and the United Nations had been given the role of aim-setter and occasional forum.

During the forties and early fifties the proliferation problem was scarcely distinguished from that of eliminating nuclear weapons. Such proposals as the United Nations Atomic Energy Commission considered were unitary and imprecise; the General Assembly Resolution of 14 December 1946 for instance referred simply to 'prohibiting and eliminating from national armaments atomic and all other major weapons adaptable now and in the future to mass destruction, and the control of atomic energy to the extent necessary to ensure its use only for peaceful purposes'.[5]

General Eisenhower made his Atoms for Peace proposal in December 1953, which eventually led to the creation of the International Atomic Energy Authority, now established in Vienna, and this, coupled with his belief that a threat to use nuclear weapons in Korea had finally brought about the armistice there, perhaps provides the base-line for the distinction between control over nuclear weapons technology and control over peaceful nuclear technology which is today enshrined not too tidily in the Non-Proliferation Treaty.[6] What with the end of the Korean war and the death of Stalin, and Khrushchev presumably preparing his denunciation of Stalin, the new Russian government's near-

5. *United Nations and Disarmament 1945–65*, United Nations, 1967, pp. 26–7.
6. See below, Chapter 6.

acceptance of a compromise Franco-British disarmament plan in the autumn of 1954 suggests that comprehensive agreement migh· then have been reached. But Dulles and Eisenhower were not, when it came to the point, disarmers, there was no agreement and the cold war continued.

'Collateral' and 'partial' measures now began to be ventilated. During the next few years most of the elements of the Non-Proliferation 'Package' discussions of the 1960s emerged, several of them in a major speech by Krishna Menon of India to the United Nations Disarmament Commission on 12 July 1956. There were now three nuclear powers, H bombs had been tested, and missiles and intercontinental-range bombers deployed. Radioactive fall-out had been identified as harmful.

Mr Menon repeated Mr Nehru's two-year-old proposal for a nuclear test ban; he referred to 'what used to be "the third country" problem. Now it is "the fourth country" problem. Next time we meet it may be the "fifth country" problem.' He spoke of the importance of an actual first step in nuclear disarmament. He asked for no trade in nuclear weapons and a freeze on their manufacture, and for no transfer of either nuclear weapons or fissile material. He suggested direct negotiations between the United States and the Soviet Union and that the Disarmament Commission should be more representative. He said 'control is the [expression] of the determination of nations for the securement of agreements that have been reached.'[7] There was also a suggestion in a contemporary British–French working paper that nuclear explosions for peaceful purposes should be placed 'under controls, subject to the approval of an international committee'.[8]

All this was too near the bone: there followed a definite shift away from the United Nations as the disarmament forum, towards a highly select Sub-Committee of the Disarmament Commission, which consisted of Canada, France, the United Kingdom, the United States and the Soviet Union, and various ad hoc committees of experts ('detection of test ban violations', 'surprise

7. Third Report, Disarmament Commission 1956, PV p. 58 et seq.
8. Third Report, Disarmament Commission 1956, Annex 2 (DC SC1/38)

attack') set up in effect by the United States and the Soviet Union. In 1959 the Sub-Committee was enlarged from five to ten, and became more accurately bipolar by adding Bulgaria, Czechoslovakia, Poland, Romania and Italy. Then in 1961 Russian–American agreement added a further eight non-aligned powers, Brazil, Burma, Ethiopia, India, Mexico, Nigeria, Sweden and the UAR, and the Committee became the Eighteen Nation Disarmament Committee (ENDC). In 1969 it was further enlarged, again by bilateral United States/Soviet Union agreement, and became known as the Conference of the Committee on Disarmament (CCD). It is still under United Nations auspices, and serviced by UN staff, but at some remove; which is how the Russian and American permanent joint chairmen like it.

During the next few years non-proliferation appeared annually on the General Assembly's agenda. But by now entropy was taking its toll of what may at one point have been a fairly simple situation: several governments had felt the hot breath of a positive requirement for nuclear weapons under independent control; with the appearance of Inter-Continental Ballistic Missiles (ICBMs) technology was making inevitable a revolution in strategic thinking and in the theory and practice of international relations. It was clear that proliferation, in the sense of the emergence of new centres of independent control over nuclear weapons, was most likely to occur within the two great alliance systems.

In November 1957 Mr Dulles, asked at a press conference whether European governments might have a veto over the use of NATO's nuclear weapons, had answered: 'No, I don't think this involves a veto on their part, any more than an individual citizen has a veto over the action of the policeman on the beat.'[9]

Such a view – though it survived right through into the Johnson years – was fast becoming anachronistic. The Suez affair and the Quemoy and Matsu crisis[10] traumatically brought home to the British, French, and Chinese governments the limits of alliance

9. Quoted in T. C. Weigele, 'The Origins of the MLF Concept 1957–60' *Orbs*, vol. XII, no. 2, summer 1968, p. 468.
10. See Chapter 5.

solidarity:[11] the two latter now began to take up the weapons option their nuclear programmes had till then kept open. The Sandys *Defence White Paper* of 1957 emphasized British reliance on nuclear weapons and British determination to retain national control of them. *Sputnik* went up, making American vulnerability to Russian nuclear weapons clear to all the world. General de Gaulle's suggestion for Anglo-French-American 'joint strategic war planning by combined chiefs of staff on a world-wide scale' was brushed off, making it equally clear to the principal doubter that the Americans liked the alliance how it was.

The Americans contributed most to the nuclearization of the concept of war: the McMahon Act had been amended to permit nuclear cooperation with such allies as were capable of using it (it was hoped that this would mean only the United Kingdom – France's large communist party made it seem unreliable).[12] An American scheme was announced in July 1957 to stockpile tactical nuclear warheads in Europe, for releasing to NATO allies in the event of Soviet attack. American *Thors* and *Jupiters* – medium-range missiles able to reach the Soviet Union – were emplaced in the United Kingdom, and in Greece and Turkey, under a double-key system. There was an offer of American information to such allies as might wish to build a nuclear submarine. First thoughts were being given to the idea of a multilateral alliance nuclear force (MLF).

Within the Communist Alliance there were surprisingly similar developments. A *New York Times* writer, Evert Clark, after China's second nuclear test in 1965, mentioned that 'Soviet officials had indicated to Western diplomats before 1960 that one faction in Russia sought to build up China as a second nuclear power, to off-set British nuclear ability in the West'[13] – as good an

11. British nuclear policy of course was founded on an earlier trauma.

12. General Eisenhower is understood to have offered to sell four atomic bombs to the French Air Force in the spring of 1954 for use at Dien Bien Phu. The local commander is said to have recommended against accepting. See p. 46, fn. 1.

13. *New York Times* (international edition), 21 May 1965. The same sort of motive led the Soviet Union to wish to seat its allies on the Disarmament Sub-Committee – see p. 39.

explanation as any of a period of Russian policy usually considered puzzling. Certainly, in January 1955, a Russian version of Eisenhower's Atoms for Peace programme had begun in earnest, and China received help in the form of a chemical separation plant,[14] an experimental reactor for the newly established Atomic Energy Institute, and many other convenient items. An agreement seems to have been signed on 15 October 1957, concerning 'new technology for national defence' – the equivalent perhaps to the provisions of the contemporary amendment of the McMahon Act. Russian missile and electronics engineers were helping the Chinese in the production of shortish range means of delivery, the Russian SS4, just as the United States were providing their NATO allies with '*Corporal*' and '*Long John*' missiles. In April 1958 the Russians even proposed a joint Sino-Soviet fleet, as well as a long-range radar station on the Chinese mainland – corresponding to the MLF, and to Fylingdales. (The Chinese, unlike the Europeans, refused these last two suggestions point blank.)

Thus in the late fifties there coincided on the one hand a new awareness on the part of the then Nth powers both that they and their senior nuclear allies could differ substantially on matters vital to their national interests and, moreover, that they themselves had the technology and economic resources to acquire nuclear weapons of their own; on the other, an increasingly general belief that war could not but be nuclear and that fall-out from nuclear weapon tests was damaging. The first of the great extra-political political compaigns, the Campaign for Nuclear Disarmament, gathered way. The governments of the nuclear powers deemed that 'proliferation' was the immediately emerging problem.

In United States policy, despite the 'nuclearization' it was imposing on NATO, there had been a continuous anti-proliferation strain. The civil nuclear activities proposed for the American-backed European Defence Community in 1953 were to have been closely constrained; the 1956 proposals of the Monnet Committee

14. A compendious and well-documented account of Soviet scientific and military aid to China appears in Walter C. Clemens Jnr's *The Arms Race and Sino-Soviet Relations*, the Hoover Institution Publications, Stanford, 1968.

of Action for a United States of Europe required Euratom participants simply to renounce military nuclear activities; a French, or
a Euratom, separation plant was opposed in 1956 and 1957; in
1956 Canada was prevented by the United States from freely
selling uranium to France; Congress turned out unwilling actually
to allow NATO allies to share in submarine nuclear technology as
President Eisenhower had suggested in December 1957; after
1960 the sale of large computers to France and of radiation-
measuring equipment was embargoed because they would help
the French nuclear programme.[15]

This anti-proliferation strain became increasingly self-
conscious. A report issued in May 1958[16] by the National Planning Association suggested that 1970 might see eight or twelve
independent nuclear weapons states, and concluded that 'most
nations with appreciable military strength will have in their
arsenals nuclear weapons, strategic, tactical, or both.' In an
enormously influential article, 'The Delicate Balance of Terror',[17]
Albert Wohlstetter adumbrated the view (which he analysed
more precisely in 'Nuclear Sharing: NATO and the N plus 1
Problem')[18] that, quite apart from its other undesirable effects,
nuclear proliferation would endanger the central nuclear balance
between the United States and the Soviet Union.

The proliferation which was seen impcn ing within the two
alliances became the concern of two kinds of people: those who
wished to see the elimination of nuclear weapons, and those who
wished to enhance the stability of what they saw as the central
strategic balance. The disagreement was fundamental, but not
always evident: thus the Campaign for Nuclear Disarmament
(CND) in Britain, and Mr George Ball in the American State

15. British nuclear weapons were being deemed not proliferatory, partly
because of the old wartime cooperation, partly because 'cooperation' now
included substantial American control, both on the production side, and
operationally.

16. *1970 Without Arms Control*, the National Planning Association,
Washington DC.

17. *Foreign Affairs*, January 1958.

18. *Foreign Affairs*, April 1961.

Department, came to be in full agreement about the desirability of unilateral nuclear disarmament for the United Kingdom.

The greater part of the new arms control thinking which emerged in such a remarkable florescence in the late fifties was in fact instinct with a philosophy that assumed American responsibilities and interests to be rationally, necessarily, and glamourously pre-eminent. A consequent assumption was that the developing bipolar power system not only could, but should and would, endure; that its two centres, the United States and the Soviet Union, were not vulnerable to internal or external pressures and developments, but only, and then mutually, to each other's strategic nuclear forces; and that it was irrational of their allies to doubt this either then or for the future. President Kennedy's Secretary of Defense, Robert McNamara, translated this thinking into American national security policy. As Mr McNamara came to see it, the grand strategy of the alliance of which the United States was the acknowledged, necessary, and deserving leader, required a capability for inflicting unacceptable retaliation at all levels of threat, from guerrilla to intercontinental warfare, from bows and arrows to I C B M s with multi-megaton warheads. For this capability to be credible, Mr McNamara declared, the strategic nuclear force had to be a 'single integrated ... force, responsive to a single chain of command, to be employed in a fully integrated manner against what is truly an indivisible target system'.[19] The ultimate decision in the Alliance could not but be American; British and French nuclear forces should be either integrated or, preferably, given up and the consequent savings devoted to rectifying deficiencies on the conventional side. The idea of a nuclear-armed, European-manned, but American controlled, multilateral force was 'conceived as an educational instrument and a healing ointment to relieve the pressures for proliferation'[20] which were regretfully (and rather

19. 30 January 1963. It was the word 'truly' which held the germ of dissolution. This period in American defense thinking is examined more fully below, in Chapter 10.
20. George Ball, *The Discipline of Power*, Bodley Head, 1968, p. 206.

unbelievingly) observed to exist within the Western Alliance.

A more cynical interpretation of this doctrine was that arms control was to be applied to the NATO allies of the United States and to no one else. It was of course its political implications which rendered the doctrine so very impractical; in hindsight it seems astonishing that it should ever have been put forward. For the United States, ultimate military decisions would continue to be taken by the elected government; for the other allies, they would not – a state of affairs unprecedented in peacetime, and cutting right across any government's chief responsibility, the security of its people.

To a limited extent these doctrines were loyally echoed within NATO and in some of the British press. Elsewhere the bloc system was seen to raise at least as many security problems as it solved. Today the doctrine has completely disappeared in the United States – it was very much an expression of that Kennedy *gendarmisme* which Kennedy Democrats now prefer to forget or to disown. The McNamara doctrine has been succeeded for all to see by President Nixon's Guam Doctrine of Help for Self-Help.

More or less parallel views grew up after a certain interval in the Soviet Union, where the ideological primacy of the Soviet Communist Party in the communist world provided fertile theoretical soil, and the McNamara doctrine now survives most purely in the arrangements of the Warsaw Pact. There was an awkward moment for the Russian Government in the spring of 1968, when what tended to be called 'the objectively necessary higher degree of socialist integration in the military sphere' (the words are those of an East German colonel) came to be questioned in both Czechoslovakia and Romania. In February, as the Prague spring was breaking out, one Prague radio programme mentioned the possibility of Warsaw Pact allies being tempted into emulating France because of the lack of nuclear consultation. The Russians themselves later disclosed that 'non-aligned' strategies were being widely discussed in the Czech and Slovak military academies by mature colonels and majors, who rejected the proper 'class approach'; (they were later purged). Although at the time Moscow Radio strongly denied 'Western' suggestions that Warsaw Pact exercises were 'intended to force the Soviet strategic concept on the allies', and referred to the 'uniformity of opinion of the allied armies on fundamental military questions', Czechoslovak generals had in fact been pointing out that the Czech High Command was 'fully capable of developing its military technique independently'. When they proposed a more equal voice for the Pact allies they received notable support from Romania, a country which anyway permitted no Pact manoeuvres on her territory. While it was officially denied in Bucharest that Romania had actually suggested nuclear sharing. It was not denied that the subject was being raised.

The alarmed Russians, who in February had been blandly advocating 'a Europe with blocs, a Europe from the Atlantic to the Urals', and 'a collective system of European security to replace the blocs',[21] by September were telling the world that 'the aim of Soviet troops is to prevent change in the status quo' in Europe.[22] The Czech military had taken that idea of 'Europe without blocs' too literally. When the time came, all the members of the Warsaw Pact dutifully signed the Non-Proliferation Treaty on the first day it was open for signature, and all of them have ratified it. Indeed, that treaty, which finally entered into force on 5 March 1970, and the 'guarantees' which accompanied it, bear many marks of the bipolarism of the early sixties which the Warsaw Pact's entry into Czechoslovakia sought to re-establish. The commander of the Soviet troops in East Germany recently seemed to be echoing the McNamara of those days.[23]

21. e.g. Moscow Radio in English, 7 February 1968.
22. *Soviet News*, 10 September 1968.
23. Further military integration is of first-class importance, he said; 'the fighting union of our armies rests on the firm basis of the uniform interest of the member states of the Warsaw Treaty.' (ADN [East German] 4 November 1971). That 'uniform' is as dubious as Mr McNamara's 'truly' (see footnote 19, p. 43).

4

Proliferation and France

The moment of British 'proliferation' occurred, as we have seen, in October 1945, when Mr Attlee realized that 'we couldn't allow ourselves to be wholly in [American] hands, and [that] their position wasn't awfully clear always', and set up the Atomic Energy Authority at Harwell. The decision to make nuclear weapons was quite soon explicit – the United Kingdom Atomic Energy Authority (UKAEA) was under the Ministry of Supply, whose business was military equipment. The First British Atomic Bomb was tested in 1952. In France the Atomic Energy Commission was set up in October 1945 but the decision that weapons were to be made was explicitly announced by the government only in 1958, and the first tests were not conducted until 1960. Effectively, the decision took itself after France's experience of American lack of solidarity, coupled with Russia's nuclear threats, in 1956, at the time of Suez. The weapons option was open and experience at Dien Bien Phu two years earlier, when the American Government was, reportedly, prepared to provide the French Air Force with four nuclear bombs,[1] had already sensitized official and military opinion.

What follows is a brief account of French nuclear policy, showing it as far as possible in the light in which it makes sense – an exercise not so much difficult as unusual in this country and in the United States, where it is generally assumed to have been

1. See *Aviation Week and Space Technology*, 30 August 1971. According to this story, from 'an informed source', the French Premier accepted the offer 'with reservations'; the Commander-in-Chief in Indochina 'strongly recommended' against using the atomic weapons because of the unknown side effects they could have on French troops in the battle area. The usual tradition is that the British Government successfully dissuaded the Americans from offering atomic weapons.

either unnecessary and ill-conceived or mainly anti-German:[2] proliferation, I believe, is likely to be unnecessarily perpetuated as long as the motives which prompt it go misdescribed.

When the British found themselves excluded from control and information about nuclear energy, Mr Attlee had a generally favourable attitude towards international control if it could be arranged, and he did not believe Anglo-American cooperation would preclude this. However, neither he nor Mr Churchill before him had ever considered that France might be included in this cooperation. British attitudes to French nuclear weapons have not been unlike American attitudes to British weapons, viewing them always as at best supererogatory, at worst perilous to the alliance and to France itself; to be discouraged, even stymied, when opportunity offered. Until Mr Healey's arrival at the Ministry of Defence in 1964, the British have perhaps been even more persistently oblivious of the political and military problems to which the French programme has been an answer than the American Government has been of the equivalent British problems. The British have at least fluctuatingly received some assistance and political, if not strategic, understanding from the Americans, which until quite recently the French have not, either from us or from the Americans.

The form and the style of the French nuclear weapons programme is largely a by-product of American policy. There can be little doubt that after General de Gaulle's wartime experience at the hands of President Roosevelt – and the rights and wrongs of that relationship are irrelevant – liberated France was bound eventually to have a nuclear weapons programme. It is perhaps even fair to suggest that in his presidential dealings with de Gaulle, Eisenhower still behaved in the character of President Roosevelt's general. If American attitudes were the mother of French nuclear weapons, Russian nuclear threats at the time of Suez were their father.[3]

2. See for instance Wolf Mendl, *Deterrence and Persuasion*, Faber & Faber, London, 1970.
3. Nehru is reported to have discerned at Suez the 'end of the Cold War ... and the beginning of Soviet/American joint efforts to preserve international peace'. Bhabani Sen Gupta, *The Fulcrum of Asia*, New York, 1970, p. 83.

The French Atomic Energy Commission (CEA) was established in October 1945, under Frédéric Joliot-Curie, who had stayed in France in 1940 when some of his colleagues left for England, and had taken part in the Resistance. Several French scientists worked in 'Tube Alloys', with a Montreal team, and their official relationship – they regarded themselves throughout as French civil servants – was with the British, not the Americans (there were various agreements about post-war patents). The Americans generally eyed them with suspicion, particularly when they wished to visit France in 1944 after the Liberation: Joliot-Curie was a communist and the French scientists would want to see him. The Anglo-American decision, early in 1945, was that the French Government should not be admitted to any degree of participation or information in Tube Alloys; other, of course, than what the French scientists had picked up in Montreal, and *that* they were under oath not to divulge to their own government. Churchill at that time no doubt still believed the Quebec and Hyde Park agreements would prevail, and that it was plausible to try to exclude the French.

During the first few years of its being, the French Atomic Energy Commission was largely under scientific leadership and control; next it turned to satisfying the requirements of industrial development. There was very little top-level political interference, and the nuclear programme was run mainly by the technocrats of the CEA itself. However, at all points the military option was assiduously kept open and self-sufficiency was studied as General Ailleret's memoirs make clear.[4] In 1954 – the year of the Dien Bien Phu disaster – the Mendès-France government authorized a secret study project for nuclear weapons and submarines, and subsequent French governments, of all political colours, kept up appropriations. One American historian[5] of the French Atomic Programme has suggested that French officials did not give 'much serious consideration to the effectiveness or credibility of a

4. See *Le Monde*, 31 October 1968, for extracts from *L'Aventure Atomique Française*, Paris, 1968.
5. L. Scheinman, *Atomic Energy Policy in France*, Princeton University Press, 1965, p. 219.

French nuclear force' and that they were 'blinded to the inconveniences and problems associated with building a viable one'. Certainly French and American officials were not likely to agree on an interpretation of such words as 'effective' or 'credible' or 'viable', but serious is a serious word: the French were perfectly serious, and Mr Scheinman is ready to admit that their decisions 'may prove to have been correct'.

During this time they had learned the inconveniences and problems of colonial war[6] and it was to these that General de Gaulle put a final stop in 1958. However, a firm admirer of General de Gaulle's, General Ailleret, was in command of that part of the army which would oversee French nuclear tests, should any be made, and since early December 1956 a whole administrative system had been set up. Even though there was still no public decision for such a thing, General Ailleret published, a month after Suez, an outline of a French atomic weapons programme. NATO had already settled for a nuclear defence in 1954 and spring 1957 saw British defence based almost exclusively on 'the nuclear deterrent'. During that summer – 1957 – the French Government made it quite clear that in the absence of a disarmament agreement between the United States and the Soviet Union France would indeed go ahead with its weapons programme. The disarmament agreement was made unthinkable in October by *Sputnik*, and by the subsequent American decision to place Intermediate Range Ballistic Missiles (IRBMs) – '*Thors*' and '*Jupiters*' – In Europe. The French decision to test an atomic bomb by 1960 was publicly announced on 11 April 1958 shortly *before* General de Gaulle's return, and it made very little difference: no major changes were needed either in the programme or in its personnel; General Ailleret continued as Commandant des Armes Spéciales. When Mr Dulles offered de Gaulle nuclear weapons that year under a two-key system, de Gaulle refused.

As M. Debré, the then French Prime Minister, put it, 'to avoid being crushed by agreements between two very big powers, a

6. As a Guadeloupian 'rebel' later put it, people in the French colonies had realized that 'Asterix was not our ancestor.' *Le Monde*, 22 February 1968.

nation like France must have the power to make herself heard and understood.'[7] This was something generally felt by many people in France: nuclear weapons were necessary to maintain national identity and independence. To General de Gaulle it had also become clear that 'since eventually it will be possible for us to be destroyed from any point on earth, our [nuclear] force must be able to act anywhere on earth.'[8] When General Ailleret published in December 1967[9] an article elaborating just this doctrine: *défence à tous azimuths*, there were cries of great surprise in NATO circles.

The French response to Suez had been to set up a time-table for a separation plant and for eventual nuclear weapon tests. The British reaction was to settle back into the 'special relationship' with the United States. 'Nuclear relations' were restored,[10] and the British received a considerable amount of American information – receipt of which barred several kinds of cooperation with European neighbours. By ordering *Skybolt*[11] in 1960, the British Government had attached Britain's future as a nuclear power to a particular and unproved American weapon which, although essential to Britain's whole defence policy, was only of marginal importance to one of the American services. '*Les Anglo-Saxons*' were taking shape, and at Nassau in 1962, where an arrangement was reached for a British purchase of *Polaris* missiles, *Skybolt* having been cancelled, Mr Macmillan was seen to take a perfectly definite step away from France, the European Economic Com-

7. *The Times*, 19 August 1959. M. Debré is at present Minister of Defence (January 1972) and that his views on this issue remain the same is clear from the address he made to the Institut des Hautes Etudes de Défence Nationale on 19 October 1971. (Printed in the January 1972 issue of the *Revue de Défence Nationale*.)

8. August 1959.

9. In the *Revue de Défence Nationale*.

10. Mr Macmillan ended a bread and butter letter to President Eisenhower in 1957: 'I am grateful for the theme which you developed that our two countries are working together not to rule or to impose our will, but to serve.' (Extract from the Macmillan Memoirs, *Riding the Storm*, *The Times*, 4 November 1970.)

11. A strategic missile with a nuclear warhead to be air-launched from a bomber.

munity, and Europe. In the vital matter of defence, M. Pompidou pointed out, 'Britain has shown that she is tied to the United States, which is not Europe.'[12] Early in 1963, and because of this, General de Gaulle halted the negotiations in Brussels over British entry to the European Economic Community. Great surprise was registered in Britain.

Between 1958 and 1960 de Gaulle had made a series of attempts to get discussions going for some serious coordination of Western global policies. Specifically, he suggested 'joint strategic war planning by combined Chiefs of Staff on a world-wide scale'.[13] His view was that, functioning as it then was, the Western Alliance gave no assurance that if war broke out, the proper decisions would have been taken in advance. The most cordial Anglo-American counter-proposal was for low-level 'exploratory' talks on Africa – a suggestion which de Gaulle, not surprisingly, interpreted as a brush off. 'If there is no agreement among the principal members of the Atlantic Alliance on matters other than Europe, how can the Alliance be indefinitely maintained in Europe? This must be remedied,' he wrote.[14] President Kennedy's unilateral attempt at negotiations with Khrushchev over Berlin confirmed General de Gaulle's fears: the original problem was not remedied. On the contrary, it was aggravated, on one level by President Kennedy's Grand Design and its strategic concomitant, the McNamara Doctrine, and on another by the growing vulnerability of the United States to 'direct destruction' by Russian nuclear attack.[15]

The doctrine elaborated by Robert McNamara, President Kennedy's Secretary for Defense, viewed from Europe could be interpreted as a plan for arms control within the Western Alliance. It issued from profound study and a realization of the ever-growing technical complexity of nuclear weapons, of their deadliness, of the speed with which decisions regarding their use

12. 5 February 1963.

13. He first made the proposal to President Eisenhower in a memorandum of 17 September 1958, and repeated it in his press conferences of 25 March 1959 and 5 September 1960.

14. Press conference, 5 September 1960.

15. Press conference, 15 January 1963.

had to be taken, and the content of Albert Wohlstetter's famous 1958 article 'The Delicate Balance of Terror', coloured the minds of almost the whole Kennedy administration.[16] All options had to be kept open for the supreme decision-maker, in whose hands of course all nuclear decisions should be concentrated. Mr Walt Rostow, a close adviser to the president, added as a gloss that 'independent command' of the British and French nuclear capabilities would 'deny the possibility of collective security arrangements' and that anyway they 'would be inefficiently produced, unsystematically targeted, and quite unpersuasive in Moscow'.[17] The validity of the doctrine was seen to be self-evident to all men of intelligence, goodwill, and an adequate grasp of fact.

General de Gaulle's view of the matter was different:

> With the Soviet achievement of long-range nuclear weapons, the Americans find themselves facing the possibility of direct destruction [*d'une destruction directe*] and, naturally, they intend above all to organize their direct defence. . . . In these conditions no one in the world, let alone anyone in America, can say whether, where, when, how, or in what measure, American nuclear weapons would be used to defend Europe. In politics and in strategy, as in economics, a monopoly naturally enough appears to those who have it to be the best system possible.[18]

He was not interested in the kind of independent deterrent on a lead that Mr Macmillan was proud to ask for at Nassau when *Skybolt* was suddenly cancelled.

In fact, neither he, nor anyone else in continental Europe, was prepared to accept that logic dictated the American doctrine – after all, other governments wished to keep their options open too. It was seen to accord very well with American national interests, and only more or less well with the national interests of the various NATO allies. NATO governments supported it with public words and its intellectual elegance captivated a number of people within them, but not sufficiently for it to be success-

16. See above, p. 42.
17. Speech at an Anglo-American meeting of opinion formers at Ditchley Park, England, May 1963.
18. 15 January 1963.

fully transformed from American doctrine into NATO practice, formally accepted and supported with troops and hardware.

Some kind of split in NATO had become inevitable: on one side because an American-defined strategy of 'flexible response' could not make sense in an alliance made up of geographically dispersed and politically sovereign nations. There could be no 'truly indivisible target system' such as Mr McNamara believed in, quite simply because what is 'strategic' to Paris and Warsaw and London might well be 'tactical' to Washington and Moscow. On another side a split was coming because the European members of NATO–particularly, but not only, France and Germany– were beginning to realize that a Washington-led, Washington-dominated, military system could do nothing very much about the reunification of Germany or about the restoration of normal relations with the perfectly European countries beyond the Iron Curtain.

This line down the middle of Europe in the early sixties had several characters: one set for the European powers on either side of it; another for the super-powers. It divided a country which would not indefinitely put up with division. It divided a country whose neighbours were apprehensive of its reunification. It was a frontier between the American and Russian spheres of interest as established nearly a quarter of a century ago, and the only considerable land interface of their military systems. It was the focus of an unprecedentedly enormous agglomeration of military hardware and personnel. At it, and particularly in West Berlin, the Soviet Union was able to apply pressure at once symbolic and effective on the United States. It was because of it that West Europeans desired a forward strategy and instant deterrence, and in spite of it that the United States preferred a defence in depth and flexible response.

France's withdrawals from NATO and NATO exercises[19]

19. General de Gaulle was perfectly explicit that France was withdrawing only from the military organization and not from the North Atlantic Treaty itself. Moreover, he told President Johnson, excepting fundamental changes in the bases of East-West relations, France would remain a party to the North Atlantic Treaty after 1969, when its first period would run out. See *Le Monde*, 3 March 1971.

were part of this running argument about strategy. When France withdrew from the 'integrated' NATO organization in spring 1966[20] it was partly, as de Gaulle explained, that France did not wish to have her territory, her communications, her forces, her ports and bases 'automatically implicated', by the fact of 'integration', in American conflicts and engagements over which France had no control. It was also, as M. Pompidou added, that it had been

enough that Mr McNamara should renounce Mr Dulles's conceptions, for a strategy never approved by the NATO Council to be adopted by the Supreme Command. Certainly we protested; we refused to take part in exercises which rested too evidently on this new theory; we have discussed and negotiated; our military chiefs and diplomatic representatives have lengthily put forward our views, which *do* conform to NATO's official doctrine. The whole machine has nonetheless obeyed the directives of the American Government. And I can affirm, without violating any secrets, that a large number, perhaps even the majority of allied military chiefs, share our point of view. But as soon as the discussion becomes public not one among our allies will oppose the sovereign argument of the United States. This is 'integration'.

Specifically, in case of attack, 'flexible response' was seen to involve initial withdrawals, the battle being fought on West German or French soil, and the whole conducted with conventional weapons. After an initial withdrawal, the opportunity to use (or to threaten to use) 'tactical' nuclear weapons would be lost. Parts of Western Europe would be totally and permanently destroyed, despite the possibility of eventual reconquest. The French Government's view was that 'the Americans may not evaluate an attack on Europe as seriously as the Europeans themselves . . . the difficulty lies in settling on the authority who will judge whether an attack is a major or minor one. We want to retain this power of judgement for ourselves, as do the British.'[21]

In fact 'flexible response' never won the day because European

20. Announced by President de Gaulle at his 22 February 1966 press conference.
21. M. Habib Deloncle, then Sécretaire d'Etat for Foreign Affairs in M. Pompidou's government, quoted in the *Sunday Times*, 20 October 1963.

governments chose neither to increase their defence budgets to the levels the new strategy required, nor to provide the number of troops deemed necessary. Nor indeed to be much impressed by the proposal for a multilateral force with which the American Government hoped to allay European anxieties and win back the Germans from de Gaulle's blandishments. (There had been news stories in 1963 that he was actually inviting them to participate in the 'force de frappe'.)[22] Rows from time to time broke through the surface, as when it was rumoured that a ninety-day conventional war was being planned for, by the Americans, before the 'use' of tactical nuclear weapons. Then they were reported stalling on supplies of enriched uranium for France's nuclear submarine programme,[23] which they were treaty-bound to supply. Frequently there was an hysterical note in official American comment on de Gaulle.[24]

General Lemnitzer, the American Commander-in-Chief of NATO, later admitted that by *not* providing the requisite troops the European NATO allies had assured the French requirement that the escalation ladder should visibly be steeply tilted in central Europe; and that the withdrawal of French territory and air space had ensured that NATO defence could not be 'in depth'. Denis Healey, the British Minister of Defence, made clear again and again in Parliament that there was no country on the continent which did not believe that a prolonged conventional war would inflict damage on it quite as difficult to bear as the damage resulting from a strategic nuclear exchange. He realized full well that that was not an option which any of the European allies had any intention of accepting, and that this was not a French idiosyncrasy. He seems also to have persuaded Washington that prolonged 'tactical' nuclear war in Europe was no less unacceptable than prolonged conventional war. It was finally agreed that

22. See, for example, stories in the *Daily Express*, September 1963.
23. *New York Times*, 17 April 1965.
24. Even as late as 1968, Paul-Henri Spaak, former Secretary General of NATO, could describe General de Gaulle as the 'grave-digger' of the Atlantic Alliance and of European Unity, 'destroying the system which has given peace to Europe for the last twenty years, and . . . not proposing anything valid in its place'. *International Herald Tribune*, 28 March 1968.

the main role of tactical nuclear weapons must be to demonstrate NATO's willingness to escalate rather than accept defeat.

In 1967, the French being absent, NATO's official strategy was finally changed from 'Massive Retaliation' to 'Flexible Response', but the option of major war limited to the continent of Europe had been, as far as possible, excluded. At last, real consultation on nuclear affairs had begun to take place in the new Nuclear Defence Affairs Committee and the Nuclear Planning Group. France's stand had borne fruit, NATO-French military relations eased up. M. Messmer, French Defence Minister, in October 1968 confirmed the existence of agreements between General Lemnitzer and General Ailleret on 'collaboration in the use of forces'. 'It is normal,' he was reported as saying, 'that general staffs should prepare for the hypothetical use of our forces alongside those of our allies.'[25] In the spring of 1971, it was announced that a small French naval squadron was to take part in a NATO exercise and the occasion was taken to reveal the extent – which continued to expand – of NATO/French cooperation. A rapprochement had even occurred in the traumatic zone of strategic doctrine, and just as NATO's flexible response in 1971 was a different animal from the old McNamara beast, so had France's *défence à tous azimuths* become a lot less shaggy than it used to be.

Having been refused consultation as an equal, General de Gaulle had been forced to carry on with deeds the discussion with the United States that he felt was necessary for France's and Europe's security. He was right, we can now see, to expect that sooner or later an American administration would find itself under domestic pressure to withdraw from foreign parts; he was right to advise President Kennedy against involvement in Indochina. He was right in his European policy both towards Germany and towards the countries of Eastern Europe. He was quite

---

25. *Le Monde*, 7 October 1968. In December 1968 there were even reports in the American press that the French were 'dropping feelers [sic]' about the possibility of the French armed forces being equipped with American tactical nuclear weapons: *International Herald Tribune*, 25 December 1968. The French Government denied the story.

candid in his anti-hegemonism; as he said to Mr Brezhnev, 'We are not displeased that the existence of the Soviet Union counterbalances American hegemonic tendencies; but equally we are not displeased that the existence of the United States counterbalances Soviet hegemonic tendencies.' M. Debré, as Minister of Defence, welcomed the admission of the People's Republic of China to the United Nations as signifying the end of the period when the two super-powers felt entitled to settle world affairs between themselves.[26]

The Atlantic being the width it is, there is much in the French position we in Britain can sympathize with. Particularly, with the demonstrably non-offensive character of French defence arrangements. These, like those of Switzerland and Sweden over the centuries, have made France into a thoroughly unattractive target for conventional attack, more especially because they are reinforced with a small nuclear force which, while vulnerable, and useless for any offensive purpose, can turn war in Europe nuclear. Czechoslovakia-type conventional walkovers are demonstrably precluded; so are Vietnam-type slow deaths.[27] If Europe, if even only Western Europe, is to have a common defence, there is a lot to be said for choosing this kind of hedgehog-cum-inkfish deterrence, until a proper security system can be set up, with real arms control and real disarmament stretching indeed from the Atlantic to the Urals.[28]

26. *The Times*, 27 October 1971.
27. It is commonly supposed (see, for example, the quotation from Albert Wohlstetter, referred to below, p. 159) that France with her land-based missiles has sought, and failed, to acquire a second-strike force, that is to say, one which would be used in retaliation against a nuclear attack from elsewhere. This type of bee-sting deterrence could indeed be the function of France's submarine-borne missiles when they are deployed. However, the extreme vulnerability of France's land-based missiles and Mirage-borne bombs suggests that their function is to disabuse any potential aggressor of the idea that an attack on France would not become nuclear. French nuclear weapons have been deployed in the realm of politics, not of war-making. M. Debré's address (see footnote 7, p. 50) conveniently sets out the French Government's current views.
28. Or to the Don, the traditional Eastern limits of 'Europe' from the dark ages. See Denys Hay, *Europe: the Emergence of an Idea*, Edinburgh

But is not, the reader may say, the French attitude to the international disarmament conferences deplorable? The empty chair at Geneva? The unsigned arms control treaties? Well, no. The French view has consistently been that disarmament is indeed a necessity for the world if disasters are to be avoided, but that unless the purpose of disarmament negotiations is disarmament, they are not worth having. Disarmament involves the destruction of existing nuclear weapons, and their vectors, effective provisions for international control, verification, and Chinese cooperation. The purpose of recent negotiations has been, to quote one French minister, to 'castrate the impotent'.

M. Couve de Murville, when he was foreign minister, put it more expansively: the purpose of a non-proliferation treaty is 'not to disarm those who are armed, but to prevent those who are not armed from arming themselves'.

The Moscow Agreement [the partial test ban] has in no way contributed to disarmament: the nuclear powers continued to test. . . . Proliferation is assuredly a problem. . . . But there is something much more important, which is that those who possess nuclear weapons should make no more and destroy those that they have. . . . One should not lead the world to believe there is disarmament where there is in fact only the consolidation of the super-powers' monopoly. . . . I do not wish to believe that it is *less* dangerous for a great power like the United States, Soviet Russia, and later China, to have the power to destroy the world than to see some small countries possess nuclear weapons which would scarcely be capable of reaching their immediate neighbours.[29]

All of which is true. If the super-powers wish to discourage proliferation, they will first of all cease to utter nuclear threats. Unlike those of the treaty-signing nuclear powers, France's governments have told no lies about disarmament.

University Press, 1957, pp. 123–5, essential reading for Europhiles and Europhobes alike. The evident similarity between disputes about the Papacy and the keys of St Peter, and disputes about whose finger should be on the nuclear trigger, is at once chastening and reassuring.

29. *Le Monde*, 8–9 January 1967.

5

Proliferation and China

China has been the object of nuclear threats on three notable occasions: from the United States at the end of the Korean war; again from the United States during the Quemoy and Matsu crisis of 1958; and from the Soviet Union on and off during the Sino-Soviet border dispute which broke out in March 1969.

The first Chinese nuclear weapon test took place in October 1964, and immediately after that (and also after each subsequent weapon test) the Chinese Government declared that it would never be the first to use nuclear weapons, that 'By developing nuclear weapons, China aims only at self-defence.'[1] It also proposed, then and since, not only a universal ban on the use of nuclear weapons, but also a conference to achieve their total abolition, by way of the 'cessation of all kinds of tests, the prohibition of the export, import, proliferation, manufacture and stock-piling of nuclear weapons, and their destruction. . . . Nuclear weapons are not created by God. If man can manufacture them, man can certainly eliminate them.'[2]

That China, with its experience of nuclear threats and nuclear encirclement, should seek to develop nuclear weapons is not astonishing. China's disarmament proposals are neither unreasonable nor unfamiliar – they closely resemble Krishna Menon's list of July 1956 and the 'package' proposals of the 1960s. Yet China's reputation for folly, rashness, and irresponsibility in nuclear matters far exceeds that even of Gaullist France.

As in the case of France, we shall follow the course of this nuclear sinner's policy with, I hope, sympathetic objectivity and frequent quotations. Two things should be kept in mind in considering Communist China. The first is that since 1949, when the

1. Peking Home Service, 21 October 1964.
2. Ibid.

Communist Government achieved control of all mainland China, most of our news of China has reached us through various propaganda media: those of the Soviet Union, of Chiang Kai-shek's Taiwan and of the China lobby in the United States and, for a shorter period, of highly chauvinistic India. The second thing is that when we hear Mao Tse-tung's 1938 phrase about political power growing out of the barrel of a gun, we should remember that Henry VII felt that way too, exercised arms control, and nationalized the armed forces of this country – something we have never had cause to regret. Mao has also framed the proposition: 'Whoever wants to seize and retain state power must have a strong army.' China's hundred years from 1850 to 1950 were at least as debilitating as England's Wars of the Roses. Indeed internal chaos was accompanied by foreign corruption, invasion and dismemberment, Tsarist Russia performing in the North and East, Britain and France in the South.

Although in 1949 President Truman's first instinct had been to recognize the Communist Government in Peking, the outbreak of the Korean war put paid to any such idea. There is no reason to suppose that the Chinese had any hand whatsoever in the commencement of that war; it was a Russian-powered exercise, and the Chinese were dragged into it, at great expense to them, only when their own borders were directly threatened. However, it was they who found themselves facing American nuclear weapons at the end of it in 1953. Chiang Kai-shek continued to hold Taiwan, and also to keep a garrison on the two small islands of Quemoy and Matsu, a couple of miles from the mainland in the Formosa Strait, and to enjoy the rather wary protection of the United States.[3] By the summer of 1958 a number of things had happened to make the world look different. Not only had the United States' virtual monopoly of nuclear weapons been broken, but the Soviet Union had tested an ICBM, and had sent *Sputnik* into orbit. Was not the East Wind prevailing over the West Wind?

3. The United States continued to recognize him as head of state of the Republic of China, but not of Taiwan, which he has been held merely to be occupying.

Sino-Soviet relations had wavered very considerably during the fifties: there was the purported deep ideological common interest, which the West chose to see as the monolith of International Communism, but which was already showing polycentric to its component members. Not only Tito's Yugoslavia in the West, but also Mao's China in the East were quite ready to dispute the pre-eminence of the Soviet Union's communist party and its experience of revolution. The Chinese had no doubt, specifically, that China's experience was more informative and provided the better model for colonial liberationists to follow. As Mao's own influence wavered within China, Russian approval tended to increase with the decrease of his power, and to decrease with its increase. By 1956, the Soviet view was that the course of socialism in China had at last been given a sound foundation, and the 8th Congress of the Chinese Communist Party of that year is recalled as the occasion when 'Sino-Marxism' seemed to be discarded and Marxism-Leninism was properly recognized as alone providing correct explanations of the laws of social development.

A 1954 textbook with a map showing most of the Soviet lands east of Lake Baikal as 'state territory of China' was generously overlooked as the result of laxity or the provocative activities of nationalistic elements; in fact, 1956 saw the rise of 'petty bourgeois nationalists' to prevail again in the party leadership. Their Great Leap Forward and the preponderance of peasants they permitted in the party were deeply incorrect, and the destruction of large-scale industry during the leap showed particularly heinous disregard for Lenin's judgement. Mao's cavalier attitude to the party, the Great Helmsman navigating the waters of time and multitudes with idiosyncratic virtuosity, has never ceased to incense those who believe in a Leninist 'party of iron' and have no desire to 'become Buddhas'.[4] In 1950, Nehru was already publicly animadverting on the differences that were developing between Russians and Chinese, both ideologically as communists,

4. That they will 'not become Buddhas till their doom' is a prognosis of the fate of imperialists and the new Tsars quite frequently come upon in Chinese broadcasts.

and politically as nation states.[5] In 1958 the differences emerged from previously shrouding privacy. What ought to have been more than an alliance was publicly put to the test.

As we saw in Chapter 3, in Khrushchev's early days Russia had been spreading nuclear and other technology, with much the same verve as Eisenhower's America. No doubt the same kind of deferentially grateful cooperation was expected in return, that was providing the United States with such strategic conveniences as SHAPE, Fylingdales, Holy Loch, and so on. Suggestions for a joint fleet and a radar station on the Chinese mainland were made by the Russians in early summer 1958, and refused by the Chinese out of hand: Russians might be communists and allies and useful suppliers, but they were nonetheless foreigners, and nothing in China now would be owned or run or part-owned by foreigners.[6]

Certainly the Chinese bombardment of the islands of Quemoy and Matsu which began on 23 August 1958 was a probing of the current quality of American support for Chiang Kai-shek. It may well also have been a probing of the quality of support that the Sino-Soviet Treaty of 1950[7] provided China – Khrushchev had visited Mao in Peking three weeks before and the joint communiqué omitted any mention of Taiwan. In the event,[8] the Russians hardly passed the test: they behaved very cautiously indeed, and were evidently more interested in events in Berlin, where crisis was also developing. On 27 August the Chinese announced imminent invasion to the Quemoy garrison. On 31 August the newspaper *Pravda* declared that the Soviet Union would render 'moral and material aid' in the event of an attack on the Chinese People's

5. See Bhabani Sen Gupta, *The Fulcrum of Asia*, Relations among China India, Pakistan and the USSR, New York, 1970, p. 34.

6. There were not even joint training exercises and manoeuvres between these allies. During 1965 the Russians again sought bases and transit rights, the better to assist North Vietnam; again the Chinese refused.

7. In fact this only guaranteed immediate military assistance in the event of one of the High Contracting Parties being attacked by Japan or any state allied with her.

8. For a careful and most useful account of the crisis, see John M. Thomas, 'The Quemoy Crisis of 1958' in R. I. Garthoff (ed.), *Sino-Soviet Military Relations*, Praeger, New York, 1966, pp. 114 ff.

Republic (CPR). There was still no official statement. Russian concern no doubt rose when Mr Dulles declared on 4 September that the United States was prepared itself to defend the islands. Also on 4 September, the Chinese declared twelve-mile territorial waters, and spoke, but now vaguely, about the right to liberate the islands; on 6 September they stopped the shelling and offered, in unyielding language, to negotiate with the United States. Had the Russians put pressure on them? Perhaps. The following day, 7 September, Mr Khrushchev sent President Eisenhower what Radio Moscow described as 'an energetic warning' against nuclear blackmail of the CPR. He stated – and it looked un-ambiguous – that 'an attack on the People's Republic of China . . . is an attack on the Soviet Union' but Moscow Radio re-marked that the islands were not considered part of China. However, over the next few weeks Mr Khrushchev whittled away at this defensive commitment, which had only been issued after the Chinese had already climbed down. He brandished Russia's nuclear capability but as soon as the United States brandished back, he stopped. Above all, he made it perfectly – and publicly – clear that the Chinese Government could expect no Russian help in voiding even these dim little islands of their counter-revolutionary garrisons.[9] The Americans had made it equally clear that they would defend these garrisons with nuclear weapons, and the Chinese Government drew its own conclusions.[10]

The Russians still occasionally remind the Chinese of these events. Thus, in June 1970, Moscow Radio was jeering at the Peking Government for its failure to liberate 'even the two tiny

9. The Chinese, who appear to enjoy public counting games, later started shelling the islands again, but only on alternate days. Not dissimilar activi-ties are the issuing of 'the 487th serious warning' to the United States con-cerning overflying of Chinese territory; accusing the Russians of provoking 4,189 border incidents within a certain period, and, oddest of all, repeatedly playing the tapes backwards for an hour or so in their Russian language broadcasts.

10. Mr John R. Thomas, to whose paper the reader has already been referred, points out interestingly enough that although the Russian political press reported Khrushchev's various post-crisis expressions of support, nuclear and other, the military press and the military leadership remained pointedly reticent.

islands of Quemoy and Matsu, which are very close to the mainland'.[11] And in November Moscow suggested that the Chinese 'please recall the period in 1958 when there was trouble in the Taiwan Strait. The Soviet Union warned the United States president that we would regard an invasion of China as an invasion of our country, the Soviet Union. The Soviet Government's firm stand crushed the aggressive scheme of United States imperialism.'[12]

Something else the Russians remember of this time is that 'regrettably, the end of the 1950s witnessed the complete triumph in the CPR leadership of the nationalist forces, which pushed the country on the road of social and political gambles.'[13] This had led to a 'great social and political tragedy', in which those who suffered most were 'the industrial workers, and intellectuals, i.e. the social groups born of social progress and of the development of the productive forces' (a point of Marxist doctrine which opposed them to 'poor peasants and other bankrupt strata in urban and rural areas'[14] with whom the Chinese communists were improperly concerned). There was 'a new military political organization called upon to be an obedient tool in Mao's hands, a blind executor of his will'; and 'concealed behind ... the ideology of anti-sovietism ... is the desire to fence off Chinese society from the ideas of scientific socialism.'

There was in fact no concealment – the methods and motives of Mao's China were merely differentiating themselves from those of Khrushchev's Russia – and the 'new military political organization' grew out of very exactly calculating apprehensions

11. 26 June 1970: S U 3417 A3 6.

12. 8 November 1970: S U 3531 A3. An alternative Russian version of events:'the noisy demonstrations staged by the Mao leadership in the Strait of Taiwan in the fall of 1958. The main thing was to aggravate the international situation. Everyone knows the result. Taiwan remains occupied. The American brass [consolidated] its positions. . . . Nothing but the firm stand of the Soviet Government prevented a serious armed conflict.' *Moscow in English* (etc.) 8 August 1971.

13. Quoted from a review reprinted by *Soviet News*, 18 August 1970, of a recent Soviet History of China, *China Today*.

14. Moscow Radio in standard Chinese, 7 July 1971.

of nuclear war – apprehensions which the Russians declare the Chinese not really to have. The purpose of this 'new military political organization' was not so much to be 'an obedient tool in Mao's hands, a blind executor of his will', but rather to enable post-revolutionary China to survive nuclear war if this were inflicted on her, either by the Americans, as seemed possible to Peking in 1958, and likely in 1965, or by the Russians, which seemed likely from 1969 on.

In 1958 China was in no position actually to denounce its alliance with the Soviet Union, or even publicly to display the ever-growing differences of opinion. Cooperation of a sort continued, the Russians not delivering 'the samples of nuclear weapons which Peking had been insisting on receiving',[15] the Chinese merely disappointed at the meagreness of the nuclear weapons technology vouchsafed but making do with their own bootstraps. Still, Chinese scientists remained working at Dubna[16] until 1965, by which time the Chinese had already carried out their first nuclear weapon tests, and the public dispute was already two years under way. That same year, 1965, there was even a fifteenth anniversary celebration of the Sino-Soviet Pact in Peking, at which Chen Yi proposed toasts.

The Partial Test Ban, which was signed by the United States, the United Kingdom and the Soviet Union in July 1963, was the occasion of the public split. Precisely what the Soviet Union had in mind in the late fifties, when it was both contributing technology and plant to what China certainly considered a nuclear weapons programme, and at the same time negotiating a test ban, is not quite clear – it was likely to have been simply beefing-up the Communist posture – but the day when governments pursue only consistent and coherent policy aims is yet to come: the Russian Government was probably not alone in believing that the United States at that time was trying to provide Germany with actual nuclear arms, and a test ban certainly was no certainty. It is perfectly possible, moreover, that the Chinese themselves would

15. Alexandr Yevstafayev, Radio Moscow, 16 August 1961.

16. The Joint Nuclear Research Institute of the Communist Countries, set up in the Soviet Union in 1956.

have been prepared to sign a comprehensive test ban if it was clearly to be a first step towards a programme of general and complete disarmament, such as both the United States and the Soviet Union had tabled at Geneva in 1962. The Chinese may have been alerted to the unlikelihood of this by the opinion Russians and Americans were publicly airing that a simple NPT – rather than any curb on existing weapons – should be the next partial measure to be negotiated after the test ban. Alerted or not, the Chinese were horrified when the Russians accepted the exemption of underground testing from the general ban.[17]

... In signing the tripartite treaty [i.e. the Partial Test Ban] the Soviet leaders betrayed their original stand, betrayed the interests of the Soviet people, betrayed the interests of the people throughout the world ... as late as 15 June 1963 the Soviet leaders were still saying that the position of the West was unacceptable. .... The essence of the matter is that the United States is in the lead in the field of underground nuclear testing. Without the tripartite treaty, the United States would have been condemned when it engaged in underground testing, which precisely helps the United States maintain and improve on its lead.

In the short period since the conclusion of the tripartite treaty the United States has already conducted three underground nuclear tests. On 24 August, the US Defence Department submitted a programme to the Senate, proposing a great increase in underground nuclear tests. Deputy Defense Secretary Gilpatric said: 'The underground testing programme [of the United States] will be comprehensive. Therefore, it will be revised to include as many as feasible of the objectives of the tests which we would otherwise do under conditions of unrestricted testing, so as to ensure the highest practicable rate of progress in technology.'

All this is shocking to people who are truly concerned about peace. How can the Soviet leaders pretend blindness? ... The Soviet Union is not giving nuclear weapons to China, but has the United States under-taken an obligation not to arm West Germany with nuclear weapons?

17. Wayland Young, writing in the *Guardian* ('From one cold war to the next', 31 July 1963) identified the end of one – between the United States and the Soviet Union – and the beginning of another, between China and the proponents of the Partial Test Ban; also the risk that this would enable the Chinese to 'claim the leadership of the yellow, brown and black world by saying nuclear weapons are the white man's toy'.

... The real point is that the Soviet leaders hold that China should not, and must not, manufacture nuclear weapons, and that only the few nuclear powers, and particularly US imperialism, the enemy of the people of the whole world, are entitled to the continued production of nuclear weapons.

The Soviet statement asserts that China can rely on the nuclear weapons of the Soviet Union and need not manufacture them herself; that if it tries to manufacture them it will result in a great strain on China's economy.

Should or should not China itself master the means of resisting US nuclear blackmail? True, if the Soviet leaders really practised proletarian internationalism, it might not be necessary for China to manufacture its own nuclear weapons ...

These quotations all come from the 'Statement by the Spokesman of the Chinese Government' of 1 September 1963. The reference to Roswell Gilpatric's remarks on 24 August shows considerable alertness on the part of the Foreign Office in Peking.

The Soviet Union had already begun to accuse Mao Tse-tung and the Chinese Government of a mad and bloodthirsty yearning for thermonuclear war, after which the remaining few million Chinese would build a new world society in their own image. The 1 September spokesman's statement included the text of Mao's 'bloodthirsty' remarks:

'It is my opinion that the international situation has now reached a new turning point. There are two winds today, the east wind and the west wind. There is a Chinese saying, "either the east wind prevails over the west wind or the west wind prevails over the east wind." It is characteristic of the situation today, I believe, that the east wind is prevailing over the west wind. That is to say, the forces of socialism are overwhelmingly superior to the forces of imperialism.'

Proceeding from that estimate, Comrade Mao Tse-tung pointed to the steadily growing possibility of preventing imperialism from launching a new world war. Comrade Mao Tse-tung then added:

'At present another situation has to be taken into account, namely, that the war-maniacs may drop atomic and hydrogen bombs everywhere. They drop them and we act after their fashion; thus there will be chaos and people will be lost. The question has to be considered for the worst. The political bureau of our party has held several sessions to

67

discuss this question. If fighting breaks out now, China has got only hand grenades and not atomic bombs – which the Soviet Union has, though. Let us imagine, how many people will die if war should break out? Out of the world's population of 2,700,000,000 one-third – or if more, half, may be lost. It is they and not we who want to fight; when a fight starts, atomic and hydrogen bombs may be dropped. I debated this question with a foreign statesman [Nehru]. He believed that if an atomic war was fought, the whole of mankind would be annihilated. I said that if the worst came to the worst and half of mankind died, the other half would remain while imperialism would be razed to the ground and the whole world would become socialist; in a number of years there would be again 2,700,000,000 people and definitely more. We Chinese have not yet completed our construction and we desire peace. However, if imperialism insists on fighting a war, we will have no alternative but to make up our minds and fight to the finish before going ahead with our construction. If every day you are afraid of war and war eventually comes, what will you do then? First, I have said that the east wind prevails over the west wind and that war will not break out, and now I have added these explanations about the situation in case war should break out. In this way, both possibilities have been taken into account . . .'

The meaning of these words is very clear:

(1) China wants peace, and not war.

(2) It is the imperialists, and not we, who want to fight a war.

(3) A world war can be prevented.

(4) Even in the eventuality that imperialism should impose a war on the peoples of the world and inflict tragic losses on them, it is the imperialist system, and not mankind, that would perish and the future of mankind would still be bright.[18]

On slightly different ground, Russians and Chinese disagreed about wars of national liberation. The Russians were at this time alarmed at the possibility of escalation from small violence to

18. Just how traumatic reports of this text have been is exemplified in this concluding statement in a book review in *International Affairs*, the Chatham House quarterly: '. . . Mao, like Hitler, believes his truth will prevail and is persisting towards a similar end, a more ghastly incineration in a larger but more wretched bunker.' E. Stuart Kirby, *International Affairs*, April 1971, p. 416. The Soviet Radio is currently attributing similar views on nuclear war to Ukrainian nationalists. Kiev Ukrainian service, 16 November 1971, S U 3868 B/2.

nuclear war; the Chinese believed that nuclear weapons were irrelevant to the kind of fighting national liberation wars involve. The discussion on this issue – or rather, dispute; the language used was often venomous – certainly demonstrates that the Chinese perfectly well understood the dangers and limitations of nuclear weapons; but that they believed, just as the nuclear powers themselves did, that they could best avoid nuclear attack by having nuclear weapons of their own.[19]

A very long article, 'Two different lines on the question of war and peace – comment on the open letter of the Central Committee of the CPSU', published on 19 November 1963 made the Chinese position quite clear.

... the leaders of the Communist Party of the Soviet Union assert that, by advocating support for the peoples' wars of national liberation and revolutionary civil wars, the Chinese Communist Party wants to provoke a nuclear world war. This is a curious lie.

The CCP has always held that the socialist countries should actively support the peoples' revolutionary struggles, including wars of national liberation and revolutionary civil wars. To fail to do so would be to renounce their proletarian internationalist duty. At the same time, we hold that the oppressed peoples and nations can achieve liberation only by their own resolute revolutionary struggle and that no one else can do it for them.

We have always maintained that socialist countries must not use nuclear weapons to support the peoples' wars of national liberation and revolutionary civil wars and have no need to do so.

We have always maintained that the socialist countries must achieve and maintain nuclear superiority. Only this can prevent the imperialists

19. In 1963 an influential, and subsequently just and acute, commentator on Chinese nuclear affairs, Alice Langley Hsieh, then of the Rand Corporation, discerned three major objectives in China's expressed intention to acquire nuclear weapons ('Communist China and Nuclear Force', R.N. Rosecrance (ed.), *The Dispersion of Nuclear Weapons*, Columbia U.P., 1964): 1) the achievement of great power status and the ouster of Taiwan from world councils; 2) hegemony in Asia, including the eroding of local American power; and 3) the acceleration of the world Communist revolution and China's role therein. The deterrence of nuclear attack, or of nuclear threats, or even the reduction of local nuclear imbalance was nowhere mentioned in her paper. Nor did she evaluate the effect of the local American presence as other than calming and legitimate.

from launching a nuclear war and help bring about the complete prohibition of nuclear weapons.

We consistently hold that, in the hands of a socialist country, nuclear weapons must always be defensive weapons for resisting imperialist nuclear threats. A socialist country absolutely must not be the first to use nuclear weapons, nor should it in any circumstances play with them or engage in nuclear blackmail and nuclear gambling.... The CCP is firmly opposed to a 'head-on' clash, between the Soviet Union and the USA, and not in words only. In deeds, too, it has worked hard to avert direct armed conflict between them. Examples of this are the Korean war against US aggression in which we fought side by side with the Korean comrades and our struggle against the USA in the Taiwan Straits. We ourselves preferred to shoulder the heavy sacrifices necessary and stood in the first line of defence of the socialist camp so that the Soviet Union might stay in the second line.... How would a socialist country use nuclear weapons to support the revolutionary struggle of an oppressed people or nation? Would it use nuclear weapons on an area where a war of national liberation or a revolutionary civil war was in progress, thereby subjecting both the revolutionary people and the imperialists to a nuclear strike? Or would it be the first to use nuclear weapons against an imperialist country which was waging a conventional war of aggression elsewhere? Obviously, in either case it is absolutely impermissible for a socialist country to use nuclear weapons.

The fact is that when the leaders of the Soviet Communist Party brandish their nuclear weapons, it is not really to support the people's anti-imperialist struggle. Sometimes, in order to gain cheap prestige, they just publish empty statements which they never intend to honour. At other times, during the Caribbean crisis, for instance, they engage in speculative, opportunistic and irresponsible nuclear gambling for ulterior motives. As soon as their nuclear blackmail is seen through and is countered in kind, they retreat one step after another, switch from adventurism to neo-colonialism and lose all by their nuclear gambling.[20]

20. Peking Home Service and NCNA, 18 November 1963, PE 1409/C/ 10–1. Chinese policy at this time was recently summed up in an article by Kirichenko in *New Times*. 'The Chinese leaders were dead set against any steps to relax international tension. They boosted the arms race and tried to provoke international conflicts whenever possible. They underscored that a war would accelerate the world-wide revolutionary process and that power comes from a gun barrel.' (28 July 1971, SU 3748/A3/3.) China is particularly accused of always having thought of 'China as a super-power, capable

There is no evidence that Chinese views have changed.

During 1965 the Chinese Government, watching developments in the Vietnam war, began to fear that the Johnson strategy of 'escalation' was going to result in the Americans using nuclear weapons against North Vietnam, or in the invasion of China, or both. They had evidently read their Herman Kahn.

For months the Johnson administration has been repeating the lie that military moves in the aggression in Vietnam are 'appropriate, measured and carefully limited'. But the actual facts are that the US 'advisers' from serving as 'advisers' in South Vietnam have become direct participants in the war; from aggression in the South, the USA has gone onto attacks on the North, from bombing raids south of the 18th parallel to bombing raids north of the 20th parallel; from day raids to night raids; from bombing of military targets to bombing of peaceful inhabitants. All these prove that Johnson's 'appropriate', 'measured' and 'carefully limited' military moves are actually calculated steps for a gradual expansion of the war.[21]

China's nuclear weapons programme was progressing, but still insignificant. There was no hope, and probably no desire by now, for help from Russia. On 24 January 1966 excerpts began to go out on Peking Radio[22] from a report made by Hsiao Hua, director of the army's political department, entitled 'Hold high the great red banner of Mao Tse-tung's thought and resolutely adhere to the five-point principle of putting politics first'.[23] The

---

of imposing its will on others and of steering the development of international relations', virtually the language used by Mr Gromyko to the 24th Congress of the CPSU in March 1971 to describe the Soviet Union's satisfactory situation in the world.

21. Peking Home Service, 24 April 1965. General Curtis LeMay, Chief of Staff of the American Air Force in President Kennedy's days and later on Governor Wallace's ticket as candidate for Vice President, recommended a tougher military style: 'We need only,' he said in October 1966, 'go after the economic jugular vein, instead of yapping at the logistical leg.' ((US News and World Report, 10 October 1966.)

22. FE 2071/B/1.

23. A Soviet view is that 'before politics, the people must be given food and clothing', Moscow Radio in Standard Chinese, 26 June 1971, SU 3723 A3 1.

report was interpreted in the West as indicating an imminent purge of the Army, or at least crisis between Army and Party. In fact it was the beginning of the Cultural Revolution, of an unprecedented and hectic attempt to prepare for war by spreading a spirit of small-scale self-reliance and devotion throughout the whole great country.

U S imperialism is frenziedly enlarging its war of aggression in Vietnam, and directing the spearhead of its aggression against China. . . . It has always wanted to impose war on the Chinese people and to have a contest of strength with us. . . . We resolutely support and help the people of other countries in their struggle against U S imperialism. This is our bounden internationalist duty. We must make full preparations against the war of aggression which U S imperialism may launch at an early date, on a large scale, with nuclear or other weapons, and on several fronts. All our work must be put on a footing of readiness to fight . . .

The outcome of war is decided by man, and by politics. . . . In fighting, the most important thing is whether or not one fears death. . . . Our revolutionary wars in the previous decades were contests of politics, contests of human valour. . . . War is politics, with bloodshed. . . . Victory is impossible if the theory that 'weapons decide everything' is followed. We always rely for our victories on the factor of man, the factor of politics. This is the moral atom bomb that our side alone possesses.

. . . Our army should act with the utmost warmth towards the masses of civilians and really identify itself with them. As for the soldiers, crude, harsh attitudes or repressive means must never be used, only the democratic method of persuasion and education. The only way to generate immense material strength is to put politics first . . .

. . . The cadres should always be solicitous of the masses and be at one with them. Our cadres must behave like ordinary labourers and ordinary soldiers, refrain from putting on airs or making themselves special . . .

Ideological work must go right home and must penetrate the very heart and mind of every fighter. Certain laws govern the mental activities of our fighters, and there are both common, universal problems and particular, concrete ones. . . . The concrete problems must be faced and remedies applied to each case . . .

. . . It is therefore our greatest duty to the people of our motherland

and the people of the whole world conscientiously to prepare well for war against aggression. . . . We can definitely drown the American aggressors in an ocean of people's war. Armed with the thinking of Mao Tse-tung, closely linked with the people throughout the world, we shall be more than a match for such a thing as US imperialism and final victory will certainly be ours.

President Johnson's escalation stopped short. The Cultural Revolution did not, and what Hsiao Hua had recommended for the army it was now the turn of the students and the intelligentsia to enact: just as politics was to be 'in command' in the army, so it was to be in schools, universities and factories. The Cultural Revolution did not particularly impede the nuclear weapon programme, and China's first thermonuclear tests took place while it was going on.[24]

In August 1968 the Warsaw Pact marched into Czechoslovakia and the ideological split opened wider and wider. Not only China, but Yugoslavia and Albania and Romania began to wonder if they might not be next on the list for forcible reintegration into the socialist community under the principle of proletarian internationalism. The Yugoslavs inaugurated a system of 'people's defence' such as the Albanians already had; the Romanians set up machine-gun nests along the runways of their civil airports. . . . On 2 March 1969, fighting broke out on the island of Chen Pao, in the Ussuri River, on the Sino-Soviet border. Both sides issued statements alleging the other side started whatever it was that actually happened.[25]

Over the years the Chinese, with reasonable give and take, had discussed and settled precise frontiers with all their neighbours

24. May and December 1966; June and December 1967.
25. It may be worth pointing out that the Russian Government, usually very slow to public reaction about unexpected events (e.g. a whole week before responding to the news of Mr Nixon's visit to China), issued a rather full statement in the afternoon of the day the 'events' occurred; a few days later as part of a massive propaganda campaign, Russian ambassadors called on foreign ministries the world over, just as they had in August 1968 when the invasion of Czechoslovakia was in process, to explain their view of events. The second battle of Chen Pao, on 15 March, is generally thought to have been started by the Russians.

except, and not through China's fault, with India[26] and the Soviet Union. Khrushchev had at one time in the early sixties twitted Mao for doing nothing about those products of 'unequal treaties', unliberated Macao and Hong Kong. The Chinese smartly recalled the Chinese territories now part of the Soviet Union which had been appropriated by Czarist Russia, also by way of 'unequal treaties', and that the time for rectification would come. Worse, in July 1964 Mao mentioned as questionable, to visiting Japanese journalists,[27] the whole gamut of Russian territorial gains after the Second World War. The issue is dynamite. The Brezhnev doctrine of proletarian internationalism – the ideological tightening up in the Soviet Union, the stiffening of CMEA and the Warsaw Pact after the Czech invasion, the propaganda battery against American militarism at a time of maximum Russian military deployment – all these suggest[28] that it was probably the Russians who initiated the border fighting in March 1969, or decided to play it up, if it was a 'normal' border incident. Moscow had been seriously concerned to prove that the Prague Spring was the result, not of native discontent and desire for 'socialism with a human face', but of President Johnson's sinister 'bridge-building' – or 'creeping counter-revolution',[29] a strategy stage-managed by the CIA and international Zionism, and designed by Herman Kahn and Zbigniew Brzezinski. This scenario of the imperialists seeking to 'tear Czechoslovakia from our ranks' was offered to

26. For a fascinating and cool account of the Chinese 'attack' on India see Neville Maxwell, *India's China War*, Cape, 1970.

27. The Soviet Union's relations with Japan are persistingly soured by the Russians' till now absolute refusal to discuss the return of the Kurile islands to Japan, which F.D.R. had agreed at Yalta should go to the Soviet Union if it entered the war against Japan. For the Soviet Union to accept discussion of the return of these islands to Japan would release an unbearable load of other territorial gains to discuss the return of: to Finland, Poland, Romania, Mongolia and Czechoslovakia, as well as China and Japan; the status of the Baltic States would be in the same melting pot. The Soviet Union's attitude to territories which it itself has acquired by military victory (or, in the case of the Kuriles, plain carve-up) is notably different from its attitude to Israeli gains in the Six Day War.

28. To me: this is not the commonly held view.

29. Moscow Radio in Polish, 14 July 1971.

disapproving communist parties as a finally conclusive argument for the invasion.

Mr Brezhnev may have been tempted to circumvent the political threat represented by Chairman Mao's highly successful 'philosophy' by transmuting it, as had already been done with the 'bridge-building', into a military threat, indeed a visible attack, with real blood, on the still undoubted citadel of World Communism: the facts of war may be counted on to elicit loyalty of a more reliable kind than do threats of heterodoxy. Sure enough, Mr Ulbricht claimed at a Warsaw Pact summit conference conveniently held in mid-March, 'We were unanimous . . . in our assessment of those aggressive acts, all the more since *the Chinese actions were provocations of a clear-cut aggressive and military nature*'[30] (emphasis added). And, in April 1969, the super-loyal Bulgarian foreign minister was reported as envisaging the possibility of the Warsaw Pact itself intervening militarily on the Soviet side, as they had had to in Czechoslovakia, the last time the socialist camp was menaced.[31] It was also no doubt absolutely necessary to prevent the Chinese Communist Party from turning up at the great International Conference in May 1969,[32] to preach its sinister doctrine of putting politics first, and to document the czarishness of the Brezhnev doctrine.[33]

During the years of the Sino-Soviet dispute, Soviet propaganda had frequently been directed towards the Chinese army, reminding them how inadequate their weapons were, how it was advanced Soviet weapons alone that permitted the North Viet-

30. *International Herald Tribune*, 24 March 1969.

31. *Le Monde*, 11 April 1969. The Czechoslovaks and Romanians seem strongly to have disagreed.

32. An interesting little line-up of communist government allegiances took place at the Albanian Embassy in Peking in November 1970. The Albanian Ambassador referred, undiplomatically, to Soviet revisionism: the Chinese in the audience applauded; the Czechoslovaks, East Germans, Hungarians, Poles, Bulgarians and Mongolians left the room. The Yugoslavs, Romanians, Cubans, Koreans and Vietnamese remained seated. There were no Russians present. *Le Monde*, 1 December 1970.

33. In March 1971 'the Kremlin' reportedly specifically denied having invited the P R C to the 24th Congress of the Communist Party of the Soviet Union. (A. Shub. *International Herald Tribune*, 17 July 1971.)

namese to stand up to the Americans, how stupid and deceitful was Mao Tse-tung's talk of 'paper tigers' and 'China's moral atom bomb'. This question of weapons from the Soviet Union had been hotly disputed within the Chinese hierarchy from 1958 on, and it was only finally settled in Mao's favour in the mid-sixties, when the sombre decision to go it alone with bootstraps was confirmed, and Lo Jui-ch'ing, the Chief of Staff of the Army, who favoured reconciliation with the Russians, was sacked. By 1969 China was prepared, after the great fright of winter 1965–6, to face nuclear war, whether from the North or from the South West, and the Russians do not seem to have found as much anti-Mao support in the army as perhaps they expected. They continued to describe their own strength and China's weakness in special radio programmes for the Chinese Army:

. . . We consider it our duty to remind you of and to call to your attention certain facts about the Soviet armed forces and their equipment. Rockets form the backbone of the Soviet armed forces; nothing can stand in the way of the rocket and there is no defence against it. It hits its target with great accuracy and its devastating power is unprecedented in the history of war; it can be launched not only from special ground sites but also from submarines. At present, the Soviet Union has a full arsenal of these rockets. What do Mao Tse-tung and his lackeys have to counter them? Nothing.

However, if they dare to kindle the flame of war on our borders, they themselves will be the first to perish. The Soviet Government has solemnly warned them of this and the whole Soviet people and the might of the Soviet armed forces stand solidly behind this statement. Dear listeners, it is still not too late. We beg you to ask yourselves whether you should throw in your lot with the handful of adventurists who have treated their people with savagery.[34]

The Chinese had already noticed that Marshal Grechko had arrived in Delhi the same day as the fighting broke out on Chen Pao, that he was accompanied by the commander of the Turkestan Military District, which borders on China further West, and that he made a tour to inspect the use India was making of Soviet military aid. 'Obviously, the aim . . . is to turn Indian nationals

34. Radio Peace and Progress in Chinese, 17 March 1969. S U 3030/A3/1.

into cannon fodder for military adventure against China.'[35]

After usurping the Party and Government power in Soviet Russia and degenerating into social-imperialism, the Soviet revisionist renegade clique has enthusiastically acted in harmony with ... US imperialism, and has regarded the formation of the anti-China encirclement as an important element in the Soviet-US counter-revolutionary holy alliance ... the Soviet revisionist renegade clique has turned Mongolia into a huge military base, dispatched numerous troops to Mongolia and deployed them along the China-Mongolia border.... Prodded by Soviet revisionism, the Japanese reactionaries have gradually shifted their major troop deployments from Hokkaido, near the Soviet Union, to Kyushu, near China.... The Soviet revisionist renegade clique has joined US imperialism in placing large stakes on the Indian reactionaries, and regards India as an important link in this encirclement ... the Soviet revisionist renegade clique has ... plunged into political deals with the reactionary ruling cliques of such countries and areas as Indonesia, Burma, 'Malaysia', Singapore, Thailand and the Philippines whose hands are covered with the blood of communist and revolutionary peoples.[36]

The Soviet Union was even 'stepping up its counter-revolutionary collusion with the Chiang Kai-shek bandit gang,' by sending one Victor Louis[37] to Taiwan for an 'exchange of views' with Chiang's defence minister.

By July, Radio Moscow was telling the world:

It is reported that Chinese towns and villages are in the grip of a veritable anti-Soviet hysteria.... They want to convince the Chinese population that the Soviet Union is preparing to attack China. This absurd fabrication is readily being echoed, commented upon and given world-wide publicity by the press of the imperialist state. It is hardly necessary to point out how ridiculous these assertions are.[38]

Local authorities in China had been instructed to lay in supplies of grain in order to weaken the masses' resistance, the Maoists, taking advantage of their ignorance regarding international affairs, were putting it about that a military attack by the USSR was to be expected ...[39]

35. *New China News Agency* (NCNA) in English, 11 March 1969.
36. NCNA in Chinese, 11 March 1969.
37. 3 March 1969: FE 3019/A2/5. For V. Louis, see p. 78.
38. 9 July 1969: SU 3122/A3/1.
39. 14 July 1969: SU 3126/A3/1.

Within the country the Maoists are noisily advocating war against the Soviet Union, India, Mongolia and other countries.... This is causing a new wave of anti-Maoist activities and dissatisfaction among the people...[40]

Why should the officers and men of the Chinese army suffer hardships and make sacrifices if there is no one who threatens their fatherland, their families and themselves? Who is so hostile to them that they must suffer and make sacrifices?... Mao Tse-tung is advocating war against the Soviet Union. But why should you fight the Soviet Union? You must know that the Soviet Union is willing to coexist with China in peace and friendship.... The Chinese patriots... have long realized that Mao Tse-tung has been shamelessly deceiving the people and putting out lies about Soviet aggression.... The Soviet Union cannot exercise forbearance for ever. It has sufficient power to wipe out for ever at one blow the possibility of raids by provocateurs, no matter where such raids come from.[41]

On 16 September 1969 Victor Louis, the London *Evening News*'s well connected Russian correspondent in Moscow, who had 'exchanged views' in Taiwan earlier in the year, adumbrated the possibility of the Russians 'taking out', as the phrase is, China's nuclear installations. Events in the previous year, he recalled, had confirmed the right of the Soviet Union to intervene in the internal affairs of other socialist countries, viz. in Czechoslovakia. 'Well-informed circles in Moscow were surprised at Western surprise at such an idea...'[42] *Newsweek*'s Stewart Alsop, who seemed to have been talking to the American intelligence community, revealed on 22 September that 'President Kennedy had secretly ordered a study of the feasibility of a "surgical operation" to

40. 6 July 1969: S U 3122/A3/3.

41. 12 July 1969: S U 3126/A3/2.

42. A Russian source for such a pre-emptive counterforce strike theorizing is to be found in *Methodological Problems of Military Theory and Practice*, edited by N. Yashushko and T. R. Kondratkov, which was published after the 23rd Party Congress: 'Since nuclear strikes will be of primary importance for the outcome of any battle or operation, each warring side must, first of all, discover and destroy the enemy's means of nuclear attack.' Quoted by A. H. S. Candlin, 'Nuclear Aspects of the Sino/Soviet Confrontation', *Journal of the R U S I*, March 1971, p. 45. It had been reported earlier that Russian diplomats were sounding out Western capitals on their reactions to a resort to nuclear weapons by either side.

accomplish the "nuclear sterilization" of Communist China.'
The Russians, he added, 'are not the only people with reason to
fear a nuclear armed China. Fear of nuclear weapons in irrational
hands is not an irrational fear' – a view of the Chinese Government fortunately not shared by the White House.

Crisis subsided. Set up at Ho Chi Minh's funeral, brief talks
were held in Peking between Kosygin and Chou En-lai and
'negotiations' were to follow. After all, Moscow Radio told the
Albanians, 'even when Soviet-Chinese relations were at their
worst, the Soviet Union remained calm and composed, stating
honestly that she was ready to negotiate with the CPR on all
problems still outstanding.'[43] Chinese comment was inscrutable:
'Chairman Mao teaches us: "How to give tit for tat depends on
the situation. Sometimes, not going to negotiations is tit for tat;
and sometimes, going to negotiations is tit for tat." '[44] Talks in
fact opened on 20 October and have lasted ever since. However,
in the October Revolution Anniversary slogans, broadcast on
19 October, Soviet troops who the previous year had been urged
merely to repulse 'imperialist aggression' were this year urged to
repulse '*any* aggression'[45] (emphasis added).

And so it went on. The Soviet Union continued its appeals to
the military intelligentsia, and to the Revolutionary students who
were by now far from home learning practical things from the
masses, presumably in some discomfort. 'A resolute blitzkrieg,
making every use of the latest combat technology and equipment'[46] continued to be opposed to the people's war in which
'even primitive weapons, such as spears and swords, can play an
effective role . . .'[47] The Russians practised war games, with simulated mushroom clouds, in which the 'Northern Command'
launched a nuclear strike against the 'Southern' enemy.[48] The
Chinese too prepared:

43. 29 October 1969.
44. Nanking service, 17 October 1969.
45. S U 3208/i.
46. Moscow, 10 January 1970.
47. Peking, 30 January 1970.
48. *International Herald Tribune*, 14 March 1970.

At present, US imperialism and social-imperialism are rapidly engaged in arms expansion and preparations for war. While developing our local industry, we must increase our awareness of the presence of the enemy, strengthen our concept of preparedness for war and adhere to the principle of paying attention to producing industrial goods needed in both peacetime and wartime and for civilian and military use. In peacetime, our industry must serve agricultural production, serve the livelihood of the people and serve our socialist revolution and socialist construction. If US imperialism and social-imperialism dare to impose a war of aggression on us, the local industries distributed in various areas throughout the country will be able immediately to serve revolutionary war by producing quarter-master goods and to ensure the needs of revolutionary war. In this way, all parts of the country can fight the war on their own and, while we remain invincible, the enemy will be drowned in the vast ocean of people's war.[49]

In July the *New York Times* published an apparently authoritative account[50] by William Beecher of the armed forces then facing each other along the Sino-Soviet border. On the Russian side these included 'many hundreds' of 'tactical' nuclear weapons, including a new mobile solid fuel missile, tank-mounted, with an estimated range of 500 miles and a warhead of over a megaton. There were said to be thirty-five combat-ready divisions, with twenty-five more available for rapid reinforcement. Mr Beecher's sources told him that the Russian military build-up 'provides a clear offensive option, either conventional or nuclear'; and that it 'shows no sign of stopping'. New air bases and landing strips would permit a massive airlift.

Moscow Radio continued to complain that 'the enemies of Soviet-Chinese friendship are disseminating various provocative slanders, particularly about the situation on the Soviet–Chinese border.'[51] 'The Peking press and radio constantly speak of a so-called "threat from the north" as if the Soviet Union . . . intends to overthrow socialist China, annex or divide up the Chinese, or attack China and so on and so forth. . . . The fact that the Soviet

49. Peking Home Service, 28 May 1970.

50. William Beecher, 'Russia versus China along their 4,500 mile border', *International Herald Tribune*, 22 July 1970.

51. Moscow in Chinese, 30 September 1970: SU 3498/A3/1.

Union has never posed a threat to China needs no verification.'[52] It was the West which was rash, selling strategic material to China: 'the history of 1933 is being repeated. At that time these imperialists [France, Britain and Sweden] provided economic aid to Hitler, encouraging him to set out on his military adventure against the Soviet Union.'[53] Instead of doubting China's animosity, the West was perhaps making a deal: after all, 'the US Senate rejected the proposal to build an anti-ballistic missile system against the Chinese threat, but at the same time . . . doubled the appropriation for . . . a similar system against a possible threat from the Soviet Union . . .'[54] By October the American administration believed that the Soviet Union had more troops facing China than facing Europe, and deployed further forward.[55] A few months later, the Russians were reporting that China had transferred to the Soviet border 'most of their troops and all their heavy artillery' from the coastal area facing Quemoy and Matsu,[56] and in autumn 1971 Mr Chou En-lai told an Italian visitor that there were 1,200,000 Russian soldiers along the border.[57] He added that they had asked the Russian representative why, but that he did not answer. The IISS Strategic Survey of 1971 reports 21 Russian divisions here in 1969, 30 in 1970, 44 in 1971. The Chinese may now have some 20 MRBMs deployed.

This account of Chinese experience with the nuclear superpowers covers the period during which Russians and Americans were putting forward and securing international agreement on a number of 'partial' or 'collateral' measures of arms control, mainly of an anti-proliferation kind. China accepted none of them, and it is easy to see why. That there has been another strand in the world's thinking about the nature of proliferation and how it might be controlled is the subject matter of the next chapters in this book.

52. Moscow in Chinese, 8 August 1970: SU 3448/A3/1.
53. Moscow in Chinese, 8 August 1970.
54. Radio Peace and Progress, 9 August 1971.
55. *International Herald Tribune*, 14 October 1970.
56. Radio Peace and Progress, 10 March 1971: SU 3632/A3/1.
57. *Le Monde*, 11 November 1971.

6

Achieving the Non-Proliferation Treaty

(i) 1961–6

The first Russian–American agreed text in the whole field of arms control was the September 1961 Zorin–McCloy Joint Statement of Agreed Principles on the Basis of which Disarmament might be Negotiated. Beyond the fact that it was drawn up in private by the two super-powers, it was non-discriminatory. Only one principle (no. 6, about the maintenance of a balance throughout the disarmament process) made any kind of reference (and that oblique) to the confrontation of the two nuclear alliances. The relationship between a 'total programme' and 'partial measures' was precisely and usefully accepted. However, an appended exchange of letters between Mr McCloy and Mr Zorin showed that their governments continued to disagree entirely about the nature of verification: one believing it 'necessary to ensure that [agreed] levels are not exceeded', the other remaining 'resolutely opposed to the establishment of control over armaments', in contrast, that is, to 'control over the destruction of armaments'. The problem of verification was not only unsolved, but insoluble; and so it it likely to remain as long as American and Russian convictions about its nature and its purpose are what they are. This is probably a matter of basic philosophy, of the theory of knowledge which actually prevails among the people who make (or omit to make) political decisions in Washington and Moscow. As long as they do not agree about a method whereby facts can be ascertained and verified, there is unlikely to be any arms control between them. None of the so called 'collateral measures' of the sixties, the Partial Test Ban, the Space Treaty, the Non-Proliferation Treaty, the Seabed Treaty, have had any effect at all on the central arms race between the Soviet Union and the United States. In any agreement reached in the Strategic Arms Limitation Talks, the verification problem is likely initially to be by-passed rather than solved. It will soon arise again.

That this was bound to be so was not as evident in 1961 as it is now. Indeed, hopes were rather high then, particularly because American and Russian scientists had, in the Pugwash meetings, found ground which was not only common, but important, in that the whole technological arms race was erected on it. If the arms race was built on common ground, was there not also common ground from which it could be dismantled?

The Zorin–McCloy statement was unanimously welcomed by the governments of the world; and the enlargement, by United States and Soviet Union agreement, of the bilateral Ten Nation Disarmament Committee[1] with eight neutrals was also unanimously approved by the General Assembly. The Eighteen Nation Disarmament Committee (ENDC) met in Geneva on 14 March 1962 at foreign minister level (though without the French) under procedures jointly devised by the United States and the Soviet Union and under their permanent joint chairmanship, and set to work, concurrently, on General and Comprehensive Disarmament, on 'collateral measures', and on the discontinuance of nuclear tests. A sub-committee, consisting of the United States, the United Kingdom and the Soviet Union, was swiftly hived off to continue the discussions which they had previously carried on in the Conference on the Discontinuance of Nuclear Weapon Tests. The Soviet Union and the United States each produced general and comprehensive disarmament drafts, on 15 March and 18 April respectively. Both texts – though otherwise discrepant – laid a 'no transfer' obligation on nuclear powers in the first stage of the proposed disarmament process. About non-proliferation, and only about non-proliferation, the super-powers were in almost complete agreement.

Ireland was now in the habit of annually submitting draft Resolutions to the General Assembly of the United Nations on the subject of non-proliferation. The draft resolution of 1959 went into considerably greater detail than the previous year's, and was acceptable to Ireland's Western neighbours, except France, but

1. See p. 39.

not to the Soviet bloc. It suggested that the Ten Nation Disarmament Committee which had just been set up should study how to prevent both the dissemination and the horizontal proliferation of nuclear weapons. The Soviet Union did not support it because it failed to mention the dispersal of nuclear weapons onto the territory of allies. The resolution was carried 68 to 0, with 12 abstentions.

Ireland's 1960 resolution directly called on the nuclear powers voluntarily to refrain from disseminating control over or information about nuclear weapons, and on the non-nuclear powers to refrain from acquiring them, pending a permanent agreement. This time the Soviet bloc supported the resolution, but the NATO powers, evidently eyeing the possible desirability of American dissemination within NATO, abstained. The United States objected uncharacteristically that it was the continuing vertical proliferation that encouraged horizontal proliferation, and, characteristically, that the restraint called for would be unverified. The resolution was carried by a different 68 to 0. with 26 abstentions.

In 1961, the Irish draft called for an agreement under which the nuclear states would undertake to refrain from relinquishing control of nuclear weapons and from transmitting the information necessary for their manufacture to states not possessing such weapons, and under which states not possessing nuclear weapons would undertake not to manufacture or otherwise acquire control of such weapons. The Irish spokesman suggested that the nuclear powers work out an agreement in private and that, when they had agreed, they should submit it to the international community – a suggestion taken up in the second half of 1966, which eventually resulted in the 1968 Non-Proliferation Treaty.

For the first time the resolution was unanimously adopted. An additional Swedish proposal for curbing the dispersal of nuclear weapons by way of a 'non-nuclear club' recalled that the 'countries not possessing nuclear weapons have a grave interest, and an important part to fulfil, in the preparation and implementation of such measures' as could halt further nuclear weapons tests and prevent the further spread of nuclear weapons.

This resolution also required the secretary general to inquire into 'the conditions under which countries not possessing nuclear weapons might be willing to enter into specific undertakings to refrain from manufacturing or otherwise acquiring such weapons and to refuse to receive, in the future, nuclear weapons in their territories on behalf of any other country'.[2] Sixty-two answers were elicited, and they ranged from the vague (Afghanistan was against proliferation and favoured an international convention to prevent it) to the precisely dubious (Australia was concerned at the emergence of possibly aggressive military power in East Asia and the Western Pacific, doubted the effectiveness of regional arrangements for de- or non-nuclearization, and would not be satisfied with declaratory statements). But the consensus was clear: although it was those countries closest to nuclear status who were the most certain that they would be likely to adhere to such an undertaking only if it was universal and comprehensive and involved the nuclear powers too, this was also unmistakeably the general opinion.

Non-proliferation was not resolved on by the General Assembly in 1962, but in discussion it was mentioned as the next 'collateral' measure to be sought after the Test Ban then ripening in the afterglow of the Cuba crisis.

The Partial Test Ban[3] was the first of the series of Russian–American agreed treaties that dot the 1960s. It was in process of negotiation for five years, and there is no doubt that the 'shifting technological base' (as the American historians[4] of the negotiations called it) presented complicated and interesting problems, not only of actual negotiating technique, but also for policy itself. Nuclear tests were themselves providing not only straight weapons information, but information about the possibility of control and about the possibility of avoiding control. The eventual political agreement was a compromise between the three strands: above-ground tests could be controlled; underground

2. Doc. DC 201.
3. 5 August 1963.
4. H. K. Jacobson and E. Stein, *Diplomats, Scientists and Politicians*, Ann Arbor, 1966, p. 145.

85

tests could not be controlled without verification of a kind unacceptable to the Russians; weapons research could be satisfactorily carried on with underground tests, by a technologically advanced country, though not by others. Moreover, aboveground tests were, in the democracies, becoming a political liability because of the damage from radioactive fall-out. Public pressure was mounting, and it was backed by a mounting scientific consensus.

A complete test ban, whether adequately verified or not, would, as we have seen, have been an arms control measure: the Partial Test Ban was a clean air bill, a victory for the environmentalists rather than the arms controllers. It did not slow down the superpowers' arms race, it did not inhibit any other power from becoming a nuclear power, although both super-powers used it to revile France and China for conducting nuclear tests in the atmosphere. Its anti-proliferation function was only to be in the field of propaganda.

However, at the time it seemed to be a promising first step for curbing the arms race; the Hot Line,[5] a desirable innovation; the resolution (and eventual treaty) on the banning of weapons of mass destruction in outer space,[6] useful; the declarations about cut-back in the production of plutonium and enriched uranium,[7] by the Soviet Union, the United States and the United Kingdom, again promising. Next would be a Non-Proliferation Treaty; and then. . . . But alongside the Test Ban there had also been ripening the project for the NATO Multilateral Nuclear Force, and for the next few years this chimera remained in the centre of the stage: chimera, because to its Western proponents it was an intra-alliance anti-proliferation measure; to its Western opponents it was either a eunuch's fig-leaf, or a red herring; and to the Soviet Union it was proliferation under another name. The Non-Proliferation Treaty could not move until it was seen off. This gave the non-nuclear powers plenty of time to examine the concept of such a treaty very carefully, the ENDC nuclear powers main-

5. 20 June 1963.
6. Resolution of 17 October 1963; Treaty, 27 January 1967.
7. 20 April 1964.

taining high obliviousness to the non-nuclears' patient, meticulous, and increasingly disenchanted expositions of the problems.

The secretary general's inquiry of 1962 had shown just how comprehensive any non-proliferation exercise would have to be. The small significance of the various super-power agreements to date was gradually becoming apparent: the Kennedy administration, in recommending the Partial Test Ban Treaty to the Senate for ratification, had even given assurances that underground test programmes would continue 'to add to our knowledge and improve our weapons in all areas of significance to our military posture for the future'.[8] This had been said in spite of the paragraph in the preamble to the treaty which declared the signatories to be 'seeking to achieve the discontinuance of all test explosions of nuclear weapons for all time . . .'.

In Geneva, the eight non-aligned governments, and no doubt some of the aligned governments as well, were becoming dissatisfied with the procedure of the committee but their complaints went unheard, and so did their proposals for improvement: working parties and *ad hoc* informal meetings, if necessary with technical experts present; an orderly agenda; the recall of the three-power sub-committee on the discontinuance of nuclear weapons tests to negotiate the completion of the Partial Test Ban, as promised also in its preamble.[9] None of these happened.[10] Time passed.

The Brazilian delegate's remark in September 1964 that 'the separate study of proposals which in practice should be complementary has hampered our work'[11] was repeated more vigorously

8. Quoted from the 'Nuclear Test Ban Treaty; Hearings before the Committee on Foreign Relations of the US Senate August 12th–27th, 1963', in R. R. Neild, *What has happened to Disarmament?* David Davies Annual Memorial Lecture, 1968, p. 6. See also p. 66, for the Chinese Government's statement on the treaty.

9. See ENDC/144 (17 September 1964).

10. Very much later informal meetings, some with experts, were allowed. U Thant in his 1971 Report on the Work of the UN actually proposed the addition of a non-aligned chairman to liven things up and for the UN to be 'officially informed about the progress of the arms limitation discussions'. (Paras. 52 and 148.)

11. DC/PV 75 (4 May 1965) p. 11.

by the Indian delegate, Mr Chakravarty, in the United Nations Disarmament Commission in New York: 'We have ... now reached a stage when isolated collateral measures are no longer easy to undertake or to implement,'[12] he said. Moreover, 'it is unrealistic to ask countries to forswear for ever a programme of nuclear weapons production, when the existing nuclear powers continue to hold on to their awesome arsenals and when, we may add, new countries embark on nuclear programmes.' However, 'an integrated programme of purposeful measures can still bring us back on the road leading to a disarmed world.'[13] His 'package', reminiscent of Krishna Menon's of 1956, included:

(1) An undertaking by the nuclear Powers not to transfer nuclear weapons or nuclear weapons technology to others;

(2) An undertaking not to use nuclear weapons against countries which do not possess them;

(3) An undertaking through the United Nations to safeguard the security of countries which may be threatened by powers having a nuclear weapons capability or embarking on a nuclear weapons capability;

(4) Tangible progress towards disarmament, including a comprehensive test ban treaty, a complete freeze on production of nuclear weapons and means of delivery as well as a substantial reduction in the existing stocks;

(5) An undertaking by non-nuclear Powers not to acquire or manufacture nuclear weapons.

He went on:

It is an integrated proposal of this nature which alone could solve the problem of the spread of nuclear weapons. . . . For example, it is no use telling countries, some of which may be even more advanced in nuclear technology than China, that they should enter into a treaty which would only stipulate that they must not acquire or produce these weapons. Again, it is no use telling them that their security will be safeguarded by one or other of the existing nuclear powers. Such an assurance has to be really dependable. . . . Unless the nuclear powers and would-be nuclear

12. ENDC/144.
13. DC/PV 75, p. 16.

powers undertake from now on not to produce any nuclear weapons or weapons delivery vehicles and, in addition, agree to reduce their existing stockpile of nuclear weapons, there is no way of doing away with the proliferation that has already taken place or of preventing further proliferation.

This desire for a package-deal was not shared by the ENDC nuclear powers, the highest common multiple of whose views had been snugly put by the British delegate, Lord Chalfont, the week before: 'We should all concentrate our efforts on securing a firm agreement which would bind the nuclear Powers not to transfer control of nuclear weapons or to assist non-nuclear Powers in making them and which would bind the non-nuclear Powers neither to manufacture nor to seek control of nuclear weapons.'[14] He went on indeed to recommend a comprehensive test ban which he saw as 'closely involved in the problem of nuclear spread', bu only because 'underground tests could help other countries, non-nuclear countries, to produce nuclear weapons'. In fact the ENDC nuclear powers were still held apart in their basic agreement about a non-proliferation treaty by the continuing, if increasingly desultory, discussion within NATO of the Multilateral Force, which itself was a symptom of suspicions and disagreements within the Western Alliance.

What seems particularly to have been lacking at this time among the three ENDC nuclear powers was any real understanding, or perhaps rather acceptance, of the actual gait of proliferation, and of its relationship to what their still prevailingly bipolarist philosophy saw as the 'central strategic balance'. Thus Russian statements about the Chinese nuclear programme have always used terms like 'nationalist ambitions' and 'political adventurism', but even careful American evaluations of it[15] managed to avoid seeing it as a natural reaction to the massive

14. DC/PV 74, 4 April 1965, p. 17.
15. See, e.g., Alice Langley Hsieh (of Rand Corporation), 'Communist China and Nuclear Weapons', in R. N. Rosencrance (ed.), *The Dispersion of Nuclear Weapons*, Columbia University Press, 1964, p. 157 et seq. See footnote 19, p. 69.

American nuclear presence in the Far East, or to Chinese experience of the actual quality of Russian support in the Quemoy–Matsu crisis of 1958.

Equally, the French programme was interpreted by Washington in general (and dismissive) terms of prestige and frustration, rather than as the decision taken responsibly by a particular elected government in a particular political-military-historical setting, to keep open its options, alliance and prophecy being not too certainly dependable. General Eisenhower's answer to General de Gaulle's proposal in 1958 for tripartite joint strategic war-planning had included the phrase '. . . we cannot afford to adopt any system which would give to our other allies . . . the impression that basic decisions affecting their own vital interests are being made without their participation.'[16] It was precisely because he feared that basic decisions affecting France's own vital interests were being taken without her participation that General de Gaulle had made his proposal.

This Trobriand Islander-type sentiment continued active in American official thinking to inform the Multilateral Force discussion. It was echoed in a much reproduced paper by the Rand scholar Malcolm Hoag:[17] 'If we appeared to agree with the French claim that a national deterrent is needed for first-class status in the alliance, we would stigmatize the others. In an alliance where all members are proud, could anything be more divisive?' Equally, George Ball of the State Department believed that in Western Europe, 'in spite of Gaullist efforts to undermine confidence in American intentions, a widespread belief exists that the deterrent provided by our nuclear umbrella is fully effective so that the security issue is not one of priority. What does concern several of the Western European nations, however, is the problem of prestige, of world status implied by the possession of nuclear weap-

16. 20 October 1958, quoted in T. C. Weigele, 'The Origins of the MLF Concept 1957–60', *Orbis*, vol. XII, no. 2, summer 1968, p. 467.

17. *Nuclear Strategic Options and European Force Participation*, Rand, pp. 2,594–2,601, 2,733, and 2,743); *Foreign Affairs*, January 1963; Rosecrance (ed.), *The Dispersion of Nuclear Weapons* (Columbia, 1964); and Kissinger (ed.), *Problems of National Security: A book of readings*, Praeger, 1965.

ons.'[18] And yet no more than anyone else could he bind the future to leave the American guarantee unscathed, or convince an old world that had looked on the works of Ozymandias, King of Kings . . .

Mr Pardo of Malta, not a nation to harbour great-power ambitions, put the historically better founded view to the Disarmament Commission in May 1965:

We do not believe that States deliberately decide to expend immense sums on nuclear weapons' development exclusively, or even mainly, for reasons of prestige or as some sort of status symbol. . . . This is or may be one factor. Another and probably more important consideration is that while it is all very well to rely on friends for the protection of one's vital rights or interests, it can never be entirely certain that friends will respond as and when needed. The vital rights and interests of a state may not be considered in the same light by those on whom it relies for nuclear protection.[19]

The arguments used in favour of non-proliferation have always been rather general: that a world of many nuclear powers would be dangerous; that the alliance would be badly run. On the other hand, the arguments individual governments face when deciding whether or not to keep open particular nuclear options are always specific. The Russian and American governments for instance have always claimed to find an underground test-ban desirable in theory, but it has been 'not negotiable' because each side has publicly deemed that its security would be unacceptably threatened either by a one-figure number of on-site inspections or by a two-figure number of unidentified explosions.[20] Other governments are no less fastidious about their country's security.

18. George Ball, *The Discipline of Power*, Bodley Head, 1968, p. 203. How this attitude survived can be seen from Robert C. Rothstein's *Alliances and Small Powers*, Columbia University Press, 1968. Professor Rothstein could even then still declare that 'The rationale [for British and French nuclear forces] rested primarily on the "Great Power syndrome" and its behavioural imperatives. But' he went on 'the Indians . . . must make their decision in a context dominated by the existence of a real enemy armed with nuclear weapons. Their case, in this sense, differs radically from the British and French cases.' (p. 311.)

19. 75th Meeting Disarmament Commission, May 1965, p. 15.

20. In a statement in the General Assembly, Committee I, 5 December 1968, Mr Foster, Director of the US Arms Control and Disarmament

A package approach to non-proliferation, like the one suggested by the Indian delegate in the spring of 1965, would have attempted to satisfy as many of the specific apprehensions of specific could-be nuclear powers as possible. But the two draft non-proliferation treaties submitted respectively by the United States in August 1965 and the Soviet Union in September 1965 were both, to use the Swedish delegate to the ENDC, Mrs Myrdal's, word, 'naked'; that is, they still sought to deal exclusively with the horizontal proliferation of nuclear weapons to new centres of control. Caustically, the UAR delegate pointed out that the function of a non-proliferation treaty must not be 'to bless and perpetuate the nuclear monopoly and supremacy of the five powers which possess the bomb'.[21] The chief distinction between the two drafts was that the American draft would have permitted alliance arrangements like the Multilateral Force, where a nuclear power committed itself to retain control over the nuclear weapons involved, and the Soviet draft would not have.

The non-aligned ENDC members made various patient suggestions towards clothing a non-proliferation treaty, first at ENDC itself and then at the XXth General Assembly – that of 1965. There they submitted a resolution which stated specifically that a non-proliferation treaty should 'embody an acceptable balance of mutual responsibilities and obligations of the nuclear and non-nuclear Powers', and that it should 'be a step towards the achievement of general and complete disarmament and, more particularly, nuclear disarmament'. It made no reference to the Multilateral Force problem, and was approved by 93 to 0, with 5 abstentions.

By 1966 the Vietnam war made agreement between the United

Agency, spoke of seismically unidentifiable explosions 'which are of great military significance'. See also Russian spokesmen, passim, on the security risks inherent in an international verification system for a comprehensive test ban. Equally, the Soviet Union, while advocating nuclear-free zones in general, has not signed the relevant annexe to the treaty of Tlatelolco which makes Latin America a nuclear-free zone, on account of 'a number of vague and ambiguous clauses'. See, e.g., A. Shevchenko, 'Disarmament, a problem that can be solved', *International Affairs* (Moscow), May 1971, p. 68.

21. ENDC/PV 245, 3 March 1966, p. 6.

States and the Soviet Union difficult in principle, but when ENDC reconvened in Geneva in January 1966 it was still the Multilateral Force option (rather than the project itself, which was now moribund) which continued to hold them apart. Each draft continued 'naked', though President Johnson's 'Message' to the reopening of ENDC mentioned the need to 'strengthen the United Nations, and other international security arrangements. Meanwhile, the nations that do not seek the nuclear path can be sure that they will have our strong support against threats of nuclear blackmail.'[22] He also referred, but tantalizingly, to the possibility of 'a freeze on offensive and defensive strategic bombers and missiles designed to carry nuclear weapons', i.e. to an agreement on Strategic Arms Limitation.

The first neutral to speak in the new session, after the Russian and American spokesmen, was Mr Obi of Nigeria, and he made again the perennial points that 'A universal approach . . . is not only essential but . . . inescapable.'[23] He repeated that 'the thesis that the desire of hitherto non-nuclear States to acquire nuclear weapons is only a matter of prestige', and the top table, and so on, was glib, and that they have legitimate and genuine fears which 'any realistic approach to the problem of proliferation' must take account of.

He was, of course, supported by his fellow non-aligned spokesmen, whose contributions to the discussion were constantly increasing in insight and in informedness. Mrs Myrdal's speech of 24 February was perhaps intellectually the most powerful, and raised the most difficult questions for the super-powers. Doubting the 'simple division of countries into nuclear and non-nuclear', she broke the 'spectrum of positions' into categories: 'the nuclear super-powers, other powers with at present certain nuclear-weapon capabilities, states with potential nuclear-weapon capabilities, and definitely non-nuclear-weapon countries. Can we really hope.' she asked, 'to encompass these highly different situations with one treaty?'[24]

22. ENDC/165, p. 2.
23. ENDC/PV, 27 January 1966. p. 31.
24. ENDC/PV 243, 24 February 1966, p. 8.

Mr Fisher, Deputy Director of the US Arms Control and Disarmament Agency, argued that it would be a mistake to 'link the entry into force of one measure with that of another for fear we might not get either', and that it was a misapprehension that a 'non-proliferation treaty is advantageous to nuclear-weapon States and disadvantageous to non-nuclear-weapon States'.[25] Mr Tsarapkin of the Soviet Union argued that 'it would hardly be conducive to our purpose to tie up a series of measures in a single package or to make agreement on any one of these measures dependent on the implementation of other measures. . . . In our opinion this would complicate negotiations which are difficult enough already.'[26] That neither the Americans nor the Russians took the argument beyond statement on this or any other occasion was conspicuous. The United Kingdom, the third nuclear power at ENDC, in general took the attitude that although it was necessary to negotiate the Non-Proliferation Treaty naked, a naked Non-Proliferation Treaty not swiftly succeeded by other measures would not stick; and this was also the line taken by the other NATO ENDC powers, Canada and Italy. The Soviet bloc's line was homogeneous except for the Romanians whose view came very close to that of the eight non-aligned powers.

At the end of the 1966 session the non-aligned eight tried again, this time presenting a 'joint memorandum on Non-Proliferation of Nuclear Weapons'[27] which recalled the General Assembly Resolution they had sponsored the year before:[28]

(a) The treaty should be void of any loopholes which might permit nuclear or non-nuclear Powers to proliferate, directly or indirectly, nuclear weapons in any form;

(b) The treaty should embody an acceptable balance of mutual responsibilities and obligations of the nuclear and non-nuclear Powers;

(c) The treaty should be a step towards the achievement of general and complete disarmament and, more particularly, nuclear disarmament;

25. ENDC/PV 245, 3 March 1966, p. 26.
26. ENDC/PV 245, 3 March 1966, p. 35.
27. ENDC/178, 19 August 1966.
28. 2028 (XX) see p. 92 above.

(d) There should be acceptable and workable provisions to ensure the effectiveness of the treaty and

(e) Nothing in the treaty should adversely affect the right of any group of states to conclude regional treaties in order to ensure the total absence of nuclear weapons in their respective territories.

In fact the log-jam was about to shift; if only to re-form a little further downstream. Apprehensions about a great sudden burst of proliferation had subsided during the early sixties: in part calmed by the doctrinal self-confidence of the bipolarists, who felt that the very magnitude of the American and Russian nuclear missile forces put them beyond the reach of competition. But as many people were now pointing out[29] the rapid spread of civil nuclear technology was placing ever more sizeable – and weaponable[30] – quantities of plutonium into the hands of ever more governments, which in turn were becoming ever less certain about the ability of the existing powers to maintain the world's peace or even its stability. Slowly, too, weaknesses in the military doctrines established in the early sixties were emerging: the unwillingness of events to coincide with even the best funded and best calculated American expectations; the lapse of time since that misleadingly formative, most ideal, pattern-like, and unrepeatable event, the Cuba crisis of October 1962; the China phenomenon; the world wide decline of alliance solidarity; the evident sea-change in the applicability of military power instanced particularly in Vietnam – nothing seemed to fit the conventional wisdom of the early sixties, only combined to make an atmosphere of gloom and pessimism.

On 26 August 1966 President Johnson leapt into the breach: 'Our common task', he declared, unequivocally addressing the Russian Government, 'is this: to search for every possible area of agreement that might enlarge the prospect for cooperation between the United States and the Soviet Union. . . . [The Vietnam]

29. e.g. Leonard Beaton, *Must the Bomb Spread?*, Penguin, 1966; Alastair Buchan (ed.), *A World of Nuclear Powers?*, Prentice Hall, 1966; etc. See also Adelphi Paper no. 29, *The Control of Proliferation; Three Views*, October 1966; Sir Solly Zuckerman, Alva Myrdal, and Lester Pearson.

30. 'Each reactor makes enough plutonium in a year for thirty atom bombs.' Richard Wilson, 'Politics of Nuclear Power in the United States', *Nature*, 15 October 1971, p. 453.

conflict does not have to stop us from finding new ways of dealing with one another.'[31] It was the beginning of the American policy of bridge-building, and among the earliest and least unacceptable of bridges offered was the possibility of Russian–American agreement on a non-proliferation treaty.

(ii) 1966–8

In spite of their clearly perceived shared interest in stopping proliferation, actual Russian–American agreement about a non-proliferation treaty required a substantial revolution in Washington thought. That super-powers as such had interests in common was by now received doctrine, but the State Department had little enthusiasm for any non-proliferation treaty which discriminated against West Germany and which would banish for ever any kind of Multilateral Force, and these were conditions on which the Soviet Union was likely to insist. However, to the extent that non-proliferation was at once a recognized arms control measure and an essential element in the prevailing strategic doctrine, both the Arms Control and Disarmament Agency and the Department of Defense favoured even such a non-proliferation treaty: the Multilateral Force was the darling of neither.

British enthusiasm for a non-proliferation treaty – to which the new Labour Foreign Secretary, Michael Stewart, had lent authority during his Washington visit in October 1965 – had been deemed somewhat uncritical. It irritated the State Department, whose concern for West German status and loyalty had been sharpened by divisive French blandishments, particularly because there was no accompanying sign of British willingness to give up independent control of its own nuclear weapons, which, it was thought, would have simplified non-discrimination within NATO.

Mr McNamara in a statement in March 1966 said, rather surprisingly, that 'the decisions on this matter [of a non-proliferation treaty] will not be made only in Washington, Moscow, London, Paris and Peking, they will be made in the capitals of [the] "threshold countries".'[32] He went on to point out that the

31. Speech at Idaho Falls, 26 August 1966.
32. 7 March 1966; USIS text, p. 2.

achievement of an atmosphere in which such countries could decide that the acquision of nuclear weapons was not in their national interest depended 'upon the development of a comprehensive programme'. 'Since the Non-Proliferation Treaty is essentially an act of self-denial on the part of potential nuclear states, we cannot expect potential nuclear powers to accept these restraints upon themselves unless we take steps in a third area: we too must be willing to accept both restraints and obligations.'

This percipient and catholic view was not shared by his State Department colleagues[33] and, when the President's 'bridge-building' speech at Idaho Falls was followed up, it was the 'naked' line that Mr Fisher and Mr Tsarapkin had backed in ENDC that prevailed.

A Joint Communiqué, issued at the end of a visit by West German Chancellor Erhard to Washington in late September 1966, mentioned simply but firmly the necessity of putting an end to the proliferation of nuclear weapons under national control and of subordinating alliance nuclear arrangements to this criterion. Dr Erhard resigned soon after, victim perhaps of his own role as over-obedient ally. It was surmised in Western Germany that secret Soviet–American talks had in fact already taken place, and this was effectively confirmed a few days later when the State Department announced that President Johnson and Mr Gromyko had recently spent 'almost two hours' discussing disarmament matters, including non-proliferation. The spokesman added that a non-proliferation treaty was a matter for the Atlantic Alliance 'at large, and no agreement should be reached without consultation'.[34] But confidential Soviet–American discussions continued, and both parties declared on 20 October, to the Political Committee of the United Nations General Assembly, that agreement would soon be possible. Together with the British and others they co-sponsored a Resolution calling on all parties meanwhile to refrain from actions which might hamper agreement on a non-

33. See Mr Fisher's remarks at ENDC four days before; quoted on p. 94 above.
34. 12 October 1966; USIS text.

proliferation treaty.[35] This General Assembly also accepted, although rather half-heartedly, a Pakistani proposal for a conference of non-nuclear-weapons states to consider the security of non-nuclear states and the peaceful applications of nuclear energy.[36]

Through the autumn and winter Soviet–American talks continued still privately, though with occasional British participation and agreement. In February 1967 the storm broke. Dr Kiesinger's new West German coalition government, whose attitude to the United States was rather more open-minded (or equivocal) than that of Dr Erhard's had been, viewed the sudden snuggling up between the United States and the Soviet Union on the subject of non-proliferation with considerable alarm. As the Soviet Union continued to address the Federal Republic with persistent venom,[37] this was hardly surprising. Dr Kiesinger referred to the 'atomic complicity' which was being erected above the Atlantic Alliance.[38] Particularly objectionable to the West German Government, it appeared that a text had been more or less agreed by the United States, the United Kingdom, and the Soviet Union, and that in it the 'European option' (i.e. the option a united Western Europe might have of becoming a nuclear power) had been barred; non-nuclear powers, but not nuclear powers, would be required to accept IAEA safeguards and inspection over all their nuclear activities; to them the explosion of nuclear devices for peaceful purposes would be forbidden.

The British Labour Government had now come to find its simple-hearted zeal for a non-proliferation treaty something of

35. The Russian spokesman said this was to 'forestall' West German moves to secure access to nuclear weapons.

36. Resolution 21538 (XXI). After being postponed the conference met in Geneva, 29 August–28 September 1968. See below, p. 118.

37. The State Department is said to have recommended some mitigation of this campaign to the Russians, and to have stated that it was putting obstacles in the way of a treaty that Dr Kiesinger in principle accepted. See Theo Loch: *Estrangement between America and Europe*, Europa–Archiv. 2/1968. This intervention was not effective.

38. Statement made in Bonn, 27 February 1967.

an embarrassment to the country's second application to join the EEC: the first application had come to grief after that other Anglo-American huddle, the Nassau Agreement. A speech in which Lord Chalfont (the British Minister for Disarmament) remarked that those who opposed the Non-Proliferation Treaty would be condemning the world to twenty or thirty years' precarious and dangerous existence was noticed in France,[39] and elsewhere, and considered not merely anti-German but anti-European. Mr Wilson did some swift fence-mending on a visit to Bonn and a few weeks later Lord Chalfont was describing the NPT as 'a quite small step towards other measures of arms control' and declaring that 'it is less important that the Treaty should be signed immediately and perhaps too precipitately than that the international community should continue to engage itself in a dynamic strategy of non-proliferation.'[40] A little later still he was taking up the cause of Euratom in arguments about inspection and safeguards.

During the spring of 1967 the negotiations within NATO which had previously been neglected began. Just what had allowed the State Department and the Foreign Office to suppose that negotiations within NATO might be omitted is not clear, unless it was still the belief, expressed by a highly respected State Department Adviser during the campaign for the Multilateral Force, that 'the secret of leadership is the *fait accompli.*' First reactions in Washington to Bonn's alarm were unsympathetic – it was dismissed as hard-line right-wing nationalism – which scarcely improved the atmosphere; nor did a remark Mr Kosygin was now reported to have made in London to the effect that Western Germany would have to sign the non-proliferation treaty, whether she liked it or no.[41] At the same press conference, Mr Kosygin was also ambiguous about whether the Soviet Union might be willing to discuss with the United States a curb on the deployment of Anti-Ballistic Missile Defence, and on this, the next growth point for

39. *Le Monde*, 16 February 1967.
40. House of Lords Hansard, vol. 280, no. 121, 8 March 1967, col. 1533.
41. 10 February 1967. He may perhaps have been mistranslated.

the central nuclear arms race, several beady non-nuclear eyes were already fixing.

Consultations within NATO did now start in earnest, and it was becoming clear that the treaty, as it reputedly stood, would not satisfy either the security or the technological requirements of the 'threshold' powers, or of many others. The relevant European members of NATO – particularly the Federal Republic and Italy – were also members of Euratom, and the Euratom Commission announced in April that it was not prepared to accept any discriminatory system of inspection and safeguards such as was being proposed.[42] France took no part in the discussion. Various American reassurances were given to the Federal Republic, particularly about the 'European option',[43] and these, of course, were denounced by the Russian press which, together with Russia's allies at ENDC, kept up an anti-German chorus. Soviet–American discussion began again late in April after what American officials described as a green light from the NATO allies; a West German official commented, 'it looks more like a yellow light to us'.[44] It was announced that the Japanese Foreign Office was getting in touch with non-nuclear members of ENDC 'in an effort to prevent the committee from drafting a treaty which will only serve the interests of the nuclear powers'.[45]

Another kind of negotiation was going on at the same time in ENDC, where objections were equally strong, particularly to the proposed treaty's lack of guarantees and to the prohibition of peaceful explosions. The 'acceptable balance of mutual responsibilities and obligations' of the 1965 Resolution was mentioned again and again for its absence in what was presumed to be being proposed.[46] Lord Chalfont opined that the 'great powers ... are understandably very unlikely to begin to dismantle their own armouries while the possibility of what has been called "horizontal" proliferation still exists' – an example of the kettle calling

42. *Le Monde*, 10 April 1967.
43. *New York Times*, 30 March 1967.
44. *New York Times*, 21 April 1967.
45. *Kyodo*, 23 February 1967.
46. ENDC quotations on what follows are all from ENDC/PVs of 1967 and 1968.

the milk jug black. Mrs Myrdal emphasized again the package: the 'logical interdependence' of the non-proliferation treaty, the banning of underground tests, and the cut-off. 'An increase in confidence would be gained ... if we were informed that an agreement between the super-powers to halt the anti-ballistic missile race was nearing completion.' The Romanian delegate gave vigorous and rallying pep talks to all and sundry.... At some meetings there was no speaker at all.

On 24 August 1967, despite the Vietnam war, the United States and the Soviet Union each submitted identical texts[47] of a non-proliferation treaty; in their sponsoring statements Mr Foster and Mr Roshchin each mentioned that they were discussing security guarantees. Negotiations changed gear yet again.

The proposed treaty was indeed perfectly 'naked'; it consisted of a preamble in which a number of desirable eventualities were referred to; an article forbidding dissemination from nuclear to non-nuclear powers; an article forbidding non-nuclear powers to proliferate by reception or manufacture; an article on the right to peaceful uses; articles dealing with ratification, amendment, review after five years; 'unlimited duration'; and grounds for withdrawal. The inspection article was left blank, and some of the language (particularly about prohibited recipients of nuclear weapons or weapons technology) was decidedly more porous than in the 1965 American and Russian drafts. It was possible to interpret Article I as allowing 'the European option'.

If the super-powers expected unanimous applause they did not get it: *parturient montes, nascetur ovum curati*. Mr Caracciolo of Italy noted drily that 'some of our suggestions have not yet found a place in the text of the treaty', mentioning particularly: non-discrimination as between the two categories of signatories, the problem of security, and the 'means to be adopted in order to avoid discouraging the development of European unity'. Mr Mulley (who had by then succeeded Lord Chalfont) warned against insisting on concurrent measures, for fear of making 'the best enemy of the good'; but he also reminded the super-powers of their responsibilities, particularly in relation to 'the develop-

47. ENDC/192.

ment of anti-ballistic missiles [which] threatens an increased impetus to the nuclear arms race and not its cessation'. The Brazilian delegate said that the drafts 'contained practically only obligations for the non-nuclear nations'. There was a 'manifest imbalance'. He went on to mention guarantees, the need for a 'universal application of safeguards concerning fissionable material and the undesirability of banning peaceful nuclear explosions if they were conducted under international control'.

Mrs Myrdal spoke of the need for 'more binding obligations on the main powers' to follow up this particular treaty with an underground test-ban and a cut-off agreement. She also presented a draft text for Article III, the article on international controls left blank in the Soviet Union–United States text. The Czechoslovak delegate mentioned security guarantees. The Nigerian 'sincerely [hoped] that no one here will take the view that the draft texts . . . are near what can be considered'. The Bulgarian praised the preamble. Mr Trivedi of India, with typical vigour, spoke of

attempts to confuse the issue by vivisecting the corporate body of non-proliferation as it were, and then lumping part of that amputated portion of non-proliferation with other aspects of disarmament, such as the reduction of nuclear delivery vehicles or the reduction of stocks of nuclear weapons, and saying that it is difficult to have all these things done together, that the best is the enemy of the good, that we must not be over-ambitious, and so on, do not help matters. What is pertinent is that proliferation has to be prevented; and, as General Assembly Resolution 20 28 [XX] points out, proliferation by both nuclear-weapon and non-nuclear-weapon powers has to be prevented. . . . What I want to emphasize is that it is not desirable, profitable, effective, appropriate, or adequate, to vivisect the integral problem of the proliferation of nuclear weapons.

After this bubblingly lukewarm reception, Mr Foster sought to persuade the conference that 'the treaty would put heavy burdens on nuclear powers'; among them that, mentioned only in the non-binding preamble, of 'achieving the cessation of the nuclear arms race at the earliest possible date'. Another 'significant obligation' Mr Foster mentioned was the nuclear powers' giving up the right of 'selling last year's sophisticated weapons to other countries'. He concluded by assuring 'all delegations that the co-chairmen have done their utmost, within the inescapable limits of what is realistic and feasible, to comply with all the basic principles and requirements in the joint memoranda and in Resolution 20/28 [XX]. In our view the draft does comply with these principles and requirements.' Mr Roshchin did not at this time seek to answer objections. Four days after Mr Foster's speech, Mr McNamara announced his government's decision[48] to embark on an anti-ballistic missile programme ...

During the following months various improvements to the 24 August drafts were proposed in ENDC. The United States having announced its ABM programme, Mr Foster's deputy at ENDC declared that the 'decision did not lessen the desirability of a non-proliferation treaty to other nations', and indeed that American ABM would improve the quality of American guarantees to its Asian friends. 'I believe [our anti-ballistic missile deployment] will favour non-proliferation.'

Discussions were now initiated in NATO about the possibility of ABM defences for Europe which might reasonably be expected to involve devolution of control over nuclear warheads. The Soviet Union put on an unprecedentedly massive display of military hardware, which included a nuclear Orbital Bombardment System. This apparently was not considered by the United States administration to be incompatible with the Space Treaty, because it had not, they thought, been tested with a nuclear weapon *in situ*. Mr McNamara optimistically named it a Fractional Orbital Bombardment System.[49] It was less than a year since the two super-powers had joined in sponsoring a United Nations resolution calling on all parties to refrain from actions which might hamper agreement on a non-proliferation treaty.

In ENDC there was no procedure for decision-taking by the whole committee, or even for the detailed discussion and amendment of the drafts before it. It became clear that the Co-chairmen's intention was to 'consider' amendments in private, and eventually

48. 17 September 1967.
49. Russian descriptions of this system do not qualify it as 'fractional'.

come up with an 'amended' text. As Mr Foster euphemistically put it after one procedural tussle, 'for several years it has been the practice of the Committee to utilize the Co-chairmen as its agent with regard to procedures.' Because it had been set up not by the General Assembly, but by agreement between the United States and the Soviet Union at the time of the Zorin-McCloy talks, and then 'approved' by the General Assembly, the Committee had become as difficult to reform as the House of Lords.

During the winter of 1967–8 the procedural inadequacies became more and more evident. Tempers in ENDC were roughened by the fact that negotiations had been carried on elsewhere and with little regard, if any, to the opinions expressed in ENDC year in, year out, since its formation. Mr Trivedi particularly objected to the negative use of the argument that

one has to be realistic. Surely realism should be a criterion to be applied to all States. If it is unrealistic to believe that the nuclear-weapon powers will agree to a treaty which prevents the proliferation of their own weapons, it is equally unrealistic to assume that the non-nuclear nations, and particularly the non-aligned nations which are facing the threat of nuclear weapons, will be enthusiastic about a discriminatory and ineffective treaty, a treaty which not only does not add to their security but in fact increases their insecurity.

He quoted Zorin-McCloy on the need for balance; and, on the question of security, stated that 'the threat to the security of non-nuclear-weapon countries comes from the arsenal of nuclear-weapon countries.'

Throughout the next three months the non-aligned countries, and others, advanced suggestions for improving both the text and the scope of the August draft. Mr Castaneda, of Mexico, noticed that the wording in the non-binding preamble of the declaration of intent about actual measures of disarmament was such as to 'make agreement on each of the measures listed entirely conditional upon its inclusion within the framework of a treaty on general and complete disarmament'. The UAR delegate, Mr Khallaf, noticed that the draft would not forbid a non-nuclear signatory from assisting a non-nuclear non-signatory state towards the acquisition of nuclear weapons; he presumably had

Israel in mind, or South Africa, both of which Russian propaganda insisted were helping and being helped by West Germany towards nuclear weapons.

The various formal amendments and more general suggestions for improvement submitted by Sweden, Mexico, the UAR, Romania, Italy, Brazil, Nigeria and the United Kingdom's Mr Mulley were punctuated with assurances from the co-chairmen that they had 'met many times to discuss all the suggestions which have been made' and that, all things considered, the treaty should not be encumbered with other issues. Neither co-chairmen otherwise took much part in the discussion; to some extent the American view was at this time being put by the Canadian delegation and the Russian view by the Polish, Bulgarian or Czech.

On 5 December the American and British spokesmen declared that their governments would accept such international safe-guards as the treaty might specify in their own territories, 'subject to exclusions for national security reasons only'. This was to demonstrate that a safeguards system would not impose 'industrial or economic burdens on treaty signatories'. Mr Caracciolo of Italy agreed that if 'other nuclear Powers' followed with similar declarations 'it will prove to be a great step towards the conclusion of our work.' The Russian delegate remained silent, then and thereafter.

The Committee wound up for Christmas, and when it reassembled on 18 January the Co-chairmen presented a revised draft, complete with an Article III.

Pravda now declared that the 'obstacles standing in the road of conclusion of a treaty on the Non-Proliferation of nuclear weapons, resistance to it, is nothing but a manifestation of the imperialist course . . .'[50] – or, alternatively, of German revanchism. The *New York Times*, which a year before had been urging the United States to 'do a better job of education among its friends and allies' on the merits of the treaty,[51] was now declaring it 'hard to believe that any of the nuclear-capable nations . . . will

50. Quoted by *Tass*, 23 January 1968.
51. 23 February 1967.

be able to resist Soviet, American, and world pressure to go along with completion of the treaty this spring'.[52] *The Times*, more awake to the realities of the situation, headlined its leading article 'Last Thrilling Episode?' and warned the super-powers that if they wanted a treaty they would have to take account of 'the more valid objections' of the non-nuclear countries.[53]

The principal amendments the co-chairmen had made to the draft of 24 August 1967 were the following: the gist of paragraph 8 of the preamble, which dealt with 'the potential benefits from nuclear explosions', now appeared in the text as Article V: these were to be available to non-nuclear-weapon powers not only through 'appropriate international procedures' but, also, (new language), 'on a bilateral basis'. The declaration of intent about further disarmament measures remained in the preamble; but a new Article VI required signatories to 'undertake to pursue negotiations in good faith regarding cessation of the nuclear arms race and disarmament'. The preambular paragraph about nuclear free zones now became Article VII. There were useful alterations to the procedures for ratification and amendment. The review conference after five years reappeared, but without the British-suggested amendment that it consider the preamble as well as the text. Article X(2) now allowed for a conference after twenty-five years to consider the continuation of the treaty. The major infilling lay in the new control article, Article III, and in the expansion in Article IV of rights of participation in peaceful uses of nuclear energy. The successful compromise between the United States and the Soviet Union in Article III lay in a phrase allowing States, 'either individually or together with other States', to negotiate an inspection arrangement with IAEA: Euratom would thus be able to do so on behalf of its members. Mr Fisher, of the United States, moreover made clear that 'in order to avoid duplication, the IAEA should make appropriate use of existing records and safeguards;'[54] also that everything not prohibited in the treaty was permitted.

52. *International Herald Tribune*, 23 January 1968.
53. 15 January 1968.
54. ENDC/PV 357, p. 17; 18 January 1968.

Once again, the super-powers tried to persuade the non-nuclear-weapon powers that this was indeed the treaty they desired; and once again they failed.

When the ENDC met again, on 18 January, the Italian delegate, Mr Caracciolo, suggested 'that it would be desirable to review the various proposals that have been made by delegations so as to determine to what extent they have been taken into account, or the reasons which have prevented their acceptance'. Mr Mulley, who was much less super-power oriented than his predecessor, Lord Chalfont, suggested that the Committee meet more often. General Burns of Canada raised a query about international controls over 'explosive services arranged bilaterally' and enquired after security assurances: he suggested 'action parallel to but separate from the Treaty'.

Outside the ENDC the West German Government took up a wait-and-see attitude; so did the Japanese. The Chinese, who had all along attacked the non-proliferation treaty negotiations as designed to legitimize a Russian–American nuclear monopoly, said of the new draft:

Whatever changes there may be, the aim of the treaty remains the same, that is, to deprive the non-nuclear nations which are under US–Soviet nuclear threat of their right to develop nuclear weapons and to place some countries under the US imperialist and Soviet revisionist nuclear umbrella so that US imperialism and Soviet revisionism may maintain their status as nuclear overlords.[55]

Mr Messmer, the French Defence Minister, said simply: 'Ce traité est un mauvais traité.'[56] He is also said to have said that it aimed merely to castrate the impotent.

A vigorous, indeed breathless, critique of the new draft came from Mr Ecobesco, of Romania, on 6 February, when he asked twelve awkward questions about, among other things, the discrimination involved in applying controls only to the activities of the non-nuclear-weapons countries and not, for instance, to the nuclear powers' undertaking not to transfer nuclear weapons. And what about the rest of the package? Once again Mr Fisher

55. *Jenmin Jih Pao*, 24 January 1968, reported by New China News Agency.
56. *Le Monde*, 26 January 1968.

deplored the 'tendency to view a commitment to nuclear disarmament by the nuclear-weapons states as *quid pro quo* for the renunciation of nuclear weapons by other states' – for most of whom, after all, the nuclear weapons option was not open. Mr Roshchin avoided that line of argument. He simply referred to the autumn's crop of amendments and declared that 'it now seems legally inadmissable to consider additions and amendments to a text which has in fact been withdrawn.' Mr Caracciolo rightly disagreed: they were discussing not a new text, but a revised draft. Mrs Myrdal and Mr de Arauju Castrol of Brazil continued the attack, particularly on the absence of nuclear-weapon states obligations.

ENDC itself, working to a deadline of 15 March so as to be ready for a specially-to-be-convened General Assembly, began to meet more frequently. Romania's questions went unanswered, and a new emphasis on the benefits of peaceful uses emerged; also, from Mr Roshchin, the implication that non-signatories would not be allowed to enjoy those benefits. . . . The autumn's amendments were re-tabled.

What appeared to be a first contribution from the nuclear powers to the non-proliferation package desired by the non-aligned powers came on 7 March 1968 when a Draft Resolution for the Security Council on Security Assurances was presented to ENDC by the Soviet Union, the United Kingdom, and the United States, which each of these countries proposed to back with a unilateral declaration of intention.[57] These 'intentions' did not unfortunately go beyond existing obligations under the UN Charter, if indeed as far. The problem of 'guarantees', which had been haunting advocates of a non-proliferation treaty for years, had proved insoluble, and outside some far more general system of arms control and disarmament it looked like so remaining.

After they had gone into some detail about what little they had found acceptable and what a lot not in the various amendments that had been suggested, the co-chairmen on 14 March produced a yet further amended draft.[58] The preamble now mentioned the

57. See pp. 111 and 126 below.
58. ENDC/225, Amendment A.

desirability of completing the Partial Test Ban; Article VI on 'negotiations relating to the cessation of the nuclear arms race' was more strongly worded; the 'purposes of the preamble' became subject to the review conference after five years, and to similar conferences subsequently convenable at five-year intervals. The alterations were minor; and dissatisfaction remained, to be next ventilated at the United Nations, where the Political Committee of the General Assembly started to discuss the latest draft at the end of April 1968. A massive American underground test on 26 April attracted some comment. The draft was strongly recommended by the United States and the Soviet Union, and received enthusiastic support from Byelorussia and the Ukraine – UN members not, perhaps, too likely to sign the treaty or implement its inspection provisions.[59] It was clear that the ENDC had been an accurate microcosm: the 'security assurances' were widely judged inadequate and, because action in the Security Council is subject to the veto of its permanent members, they were interpreted as directed against China rather than against nuclear threats and aggression as such.

It was several times mentioned that this was a treaty to stop the proliferation of nuclear powers, and that there should now be one to stop the proliferation of nuclear weapons. African states expressed anxiety about South Africa acquiring nuclear weapons. Some countries – including South Africa – made it clear that, though they might sign, they would not ratify the treaty until they knew precisely what the safeguards arrangements might be – which would in turn put off the date of ratification of several African states. The Pakistani delegate said: 'Even if almost all the non-nuclear states signed and ratified the treaty, and the near-nuclear-weapon states did not, the main purpose of the treaty would be defeated.'[60] The delegate of Ireland, decennial protagonist of a non-proliferation treaty, recommended signature and ratification now, amendment later; and that the Conference

59. Neither has, so far, signed the treaty. As parts of the Soviet Union, it is difficult to know if they count as nuclear or non-nuclear-weapon powers.
60. One of Mr Bhutto's first actions on taking office in December 1971 was to take personal charge of the Pakistan Atomic Energy Commission;

of Non-Nuclear-Weapon States, now due to meet in August, should formulate further agreements. Mr Rusk spoke optimistically about talks with the Soviet Union on a strategic missile freeze. Other American officials hinted again that non-signatories would probably find themselves out in the cold as far as assistance in peaceful uses was concerned – as Mr Roshchin had already made clear in Geneva.

The draft was further revised. The preamble acquired a new paragraph 'recalling that ... States must refrain ... from the threat or use of force ...'; and Articles IV and V were altered to emphasize and extend the rights of non-nuclear powers to benefit from the peaceful applications of nuclear power. It was then 'commended' by the Political Committee, by 92 votes to 4, with 22 abstentions; and subsequently by the General Assembly on 10 June by 95 to 4, with 21 abstentions. The treaty's four opponents were Algeria, Cuba, Tanzania, and Zambia, all of whom objected to its inequalities: Mr Nyerere said of it, in Peking, 'This is the first time that a tremendous and far-reaching human discovery is made the monopoly of the few.'[61]

Among the abstainers was France, whose delegate, M. Bérard, announced that while 'France ... will behave in the future exactly as the States adhering to the treaty',[62] the real question was not the treaty. 'Nor can it be the mere confirmation by the international community of the monopoly of the Powers which at this time happen to possess this capability. The real question

---

Pakistan Home Service in English, 30 December 1971, FE 3877, C1 3. Pakistan has not signed the NPT. Quotations in the following passages are from verbatim reports of the First Committee and the General Assembly of the United Nations.

61. NCNA, 21 June 1968.

62. That France had not always followed an anti-proliferation policy can be seen from General de Gaulle's *Le Renouveau* (Paris, 1970). On his return to power in 1958 he had, he said, put an end to the 'abusive pratique de collaboration' established between Paris and Tel Aviv after the Suez expedition. 'Ainsi cesse en particulier le concours prêté par nous à un début, près de Bersheba, d'une usine de transformation d'uranium en plutonium d'où un beau jour, pourraient sortir des bombes atomiques.' p. 279.

is ... the complete disappearance of nuclear weapons.'[63] Referring to the 'security assurances' he went on: 'France believes that the nations of the world will receive the guarantees of security to which they have the right to aspire only when the world has embarked on the road towards nuclear disarmament and on condition that such disarmament is carried out to the full.' President Johnson declared that 'What we have achieved here today, few men would have dared to even hope for a decade ago'; and Mr Kuznetsov, for the Soviet Union, described the treaty as 'a great step towards eliminating the threat of a destructive nuclear war'. Lord Caradon, for Britain, referred more equivocally to a 'feeling of achievement'.

A few days later the Security Council considered the formal declarations made by the three nuclear Powers active in ENDC, and on 19 June voted on a resolution which welcomed them. The three Powers were affirming their intention, as permanent members of the Council, 'to seek immediate Security Council action to provide assistance, in accordance with the Charter, to any non-nuclear-weapon State party to the Treaty on the Non-Proliferation of Nuclear Weapons that is a victim of an act of aggression or an object of a threat of aggression in which nuclear weapons are used'. They re-affirmed the right of individual and collective self-defence under Article 51 of the Charter, if an armed attack occurs, 'until the Security Council has taken measures necessary to maintain international peace and security'.

The vote was 10 in favour, none against. Algeria, Brazil, France, India and Pakistan abstained. The Paraguayan delegate optimistically read into the declarations a great deal more than was there. The Brazilian, the Ethiopian, and the Indian all contrasted the announced intentions for the benefit of NPT signatories with the more embracing juridical obligations the three States already had under the Charter towards all members of the United Nations without discrimination. The delegate of Pakistan suggested the vote be put off till after the Conference of Non-Nuclear-Weapon States which was specifically going to discuss guarantees. The Chinese comment on the 'security assurances'

63. A/PV 1672, 12 June 1968.

when they had been proposed back in March had been that here was 'a malicious conspiracy [by US imperialism and Soviet revisionism] for the control and enslavement of the non-nuclear nations . . . to turn these people into their nuclear slaves'.[64] Within the existing military alliances there was some feeling that the neutrals were trying to muscle in on the benefits of alliance without the responsibilities.

64. Article by 'Commentator', *Jenmin Jih Pao*, 3 March 1968.

7

The Non-Proliferation Treaty: Text, Peaceful Uses, Safeguards and Guarantees

The world thus found itself on 1 July 1968 with a Non-Proliferation Treaty commended by the General Assembly of the United Nations and open for signature.

But commendation is not signature, signatures are not ratification, less than forty-three ratifications are not operation, and operation does not mean much unless the operating parties are the right ones. The Soviet Union improved the shining hour by publishing a long memorandum of disarmament and arms control proposals, after insisting for many months, along with the United States, that it was 'unrealistic' to consider more than one measure, i.e. the Non-Proliferation Treaty, at a time.

In practice the NPT is today still in process of negotiation. As governments of the defeated powers of the Second World War, the West German and Japanese could hardly refrain from signing, but otherwise no independent government can be forced into it; and unless the relevant governments – those in Mrs Myrdal's third category of countries with a real nuclear weapons capability[1] – receive some further satisfaction, the NPT will remain a dead letter.

Effectively there are three issues still unsettled: the peaceful applications of nuclear explosives, guarantees and 'security assurances', and the safeguards to be administered by the International Atomic Energy Authority in accordance with Article III. But before turning to them it is worth looking at the treaty itself, the text of which remains unenticingly porous in spite of all the international attention it received between 1966 and 1968.

1. See p. 93.

The Text

Article I reads as follows:

Each nuclear-weapon state party to the treaty undertakes not to transfer to any recipient whatsoever nuclear weapons or other nuclear explosive devices or control over such weapons or explosive devices directly, or indirectly; and not in any way to assist, encourage, or induce any non-nuclear-weapon state to manufacture or otherwise acquire nuclear weapons or other nuclear explosive devices, or control over such weapons or explosive devices.

Thus signatory nuclear-weapon states are not forbidden from 'assisting, encouraging or inducing' parties other than non-nuclear-weapon states 'to manufacture or otherwise acquire nuclear weapons and nuclear explosives', although they may not 'transfer to any recipient whatsover nuclear weapons or nuclear devices or control' over them. It has always been known that this article was very carefully drafted[2] so as to preclude a nuclear-armed UN force but not to preclude a nuclear force put together from the British and French forces, in the event of Western European political unification. However, there appears to be a second loop-hole. It is not only their fellow nuclear-weapon powers that nuclear-weapon powers may 'assist, encourage and induce', but apparently any recipient whatsoever who is not a 'non-nuclear-weapon state'. There is an unfilled gap, carrying the implication that units other than states may be assisted. The UN force in fact might get in here; and who else? The Vietcong? The Mafia? Individuals like Dr No? American firms? International companies? Probably not the first three, which *de jure* must be under the control of some state or other, though *de facto* in a civil war for instance, they may not be.[3] In 1968 there were reports that the American firm El Paso National Gas Company was financing more or less entirely some of the American Atomic Energy Commission's non-weapons underground *Ploughshare*

2. NPT drafts earlier than the joint one of September 1967, both Russian and American, were not porous.

3. Don Brennan has located a chilling little incident: see *Arms Control and Disarmament*, 1968, p. 59, for an account of how in 1961 the rebel French generals in Algeria were able to eye the taking over of a test nuclear device.

tests.[4] This firm's activities both as a consultant on peaceful uses of nuclear explosions and as a service company were paralleled in the international field by the firm Nobel Paso Geonuclear in which it had a 50% interest, Nobel Bozel and Poudreries Réunies de Belgique holding the other 50%. Indeed, Article V, which treats of making available through an international body the benefits of peaceful nuclear explosions to non-weapon states, mentions that these may also be obtained 'pursuant to bilateral agreements' with the nuclear-weapons powers. This possibility of bilateral arrangements, which would bypass the international control body, considered together with the permitted non-state, assistable units of Article I, would allow commercial undertakings associated with the United States and the Soviet Union to enjoy substantial advantages, if peaceful explosions become economically interesting: it was quite widely thought they would when the treaty was drafted. After a rather bad press for a few years, *Ploughshare* is now trying to stage an acceptability comeback.[5]

There were reports in late 1968 that the American Government was raising difficulties with the British Government over the planned Anglo/German/Dutch gas centrifuge enrichment plants on the grounds of possible infringement of the NPT. Mr Foster was saying in November 1968 that American enrichment facilities (the sale of which to private enterprise by the Atomic Energy Commission was that year under discussion)[6] 'should be capable

4. *Le Monde*, 12 December 1968; *New Scientist*, 10 December 1968.
5. A prototype device called 'Miniata', 'wholly fabricated for a commercial task' was exploded by the American Atomic Energy Commission in Nevada on 8 July 1971; the aim of the test was to show the 'cleanness, safety and economic soundness of nuclear explosives for freeing rock-bound gas' – United States Information Service statement, 12 July 1971. Exactly similar activities have been announced recently in the Soviet Union. Bilateral Soviet/United States talks on the Peaceful Uses of Nuclear Explosives opened in Washington on 13 July 1971. The AEC during the summer of 1971 was urging the administration that a further research and development programme be funded, and after the Amchitka test explosion, its officials were mentioning a gas-releasing test nuclear explosion in 1972 as 'conceivable'. (*International Herald Tribune*, 8 November 1971.)
6. *New Scientist*, 22 August 1968, p. 380.

of handling all foreseeable demands . . . through the late 1970s',[7] but whether that 'should' derived from arms control criteria or from commercial criteria was not at all obvious, and raised questions about how in practice the treaty was going to be interpreted. In June 1971, the AEC announced a plan to share its secrets, with ten firms at most,[8] but by then industry's enthusiasm had shrunk, partly in alarm at the scale of investment required – $25 billion to build the right amount of plant is one industrialist's guess[9] – and partly at the possible obsolescence of current American techniques. The gas centrifuge plans are going ahead but now the Russian Government is offering enriched uranium to Western Germany, at a competitive price and, rather oddly, without requiring anything more than a minister's personal guarantee that the material will not be diverted to non-peaceful uses;[10] it is also being offered to Japan. The Australian and Japanese governments have expressed interest in joint enrichment operations to the United States and to France, and the South African Government claims to have come upon a new process. The NPT is no longer being mentioned as an impediment, partly no doubt because it is clearly the intention of the British, Dutch and German governments virtually to build inspectability into their plant and to have their agents and customers observe the treaty's provisions; and partly because of the scale of the world's energy requirements.

The first two articles of the NPT had been the earliest to be agreed between the United States and the Soviet Union and consequently, in the words of one English official, were 'as if engraved on stone', and untouchable. So, although the United Arab Republic delegate in Geneva had pointed it out in October 1967,[11] an asymmetry remains uncorrected in Article II: a signatory non-nuclear-weapon state is not barred by the Treaty from giving assistance towards the acquisition of nuclear weapons or of explosive nuclear devices, etc. to a non-signatory state (or to a

7. UN First Committee, 19 November 1968.

8. And a number of other governments, including Britain and the Six – see *Financial Times*, 9 November 1971.

9. *International Herald Tribune*, 10 November 1971.

10. *Le Monde*, 29 April 1971.

11. See p. 69 above.

firm or individual) but only from acquiring them itself. Mr Foster's assurance[12] that no government would have any reason for helping others except to acquire nuclear weapons for itself in violation of the treaty seemed a little unworldly. If a government decided to go nuclear, would it not seek to hire help, and denounce the Treaty only at the last moment? Moreover, Mr Fisher had stated in ENDC while the treaty was being negotiated that what it did not specifically prohibit was permitted.[13]

Throughout Article III, when the word 'peaceful' occurs, it is a limiting qualification: a government may escape the safeguards machinery by describing the purposes for which it requires fissile material as 'military but non-explosive', in which case no safeguard or inspection is proposed. This loophole was intended to allow non-nuclear-weapon states to acquire and use fissile material in submarine nuclear reactors without it being subject to IAEA examination or control. The loophole appears to offer a state a way of defeating the treaty without actually denouncing it, until it has an actual weapons capability and is ready to test – or use – nuclear weapons.

Paragraph 2 of Article III reads:

Each State Party to the Treaty undertakes not to provide: (a) source or special fissionable material, or (b) equipment or material especially designed or prepared for the processing, use or production of special fissionable material, to any non-nuclear-weapon State for peaceful purposes, unless the source or special fissionable material shall be subject to the safeguards required by this article.

However, it is not impossible that triggers to fusion weapons (H-bombs) will be devised using some other process than fission. Lasers may not just yet be in the running, but the treaty is intended to last, and its wording limits its control system to one contemporary technology.

Moreover, there is no indication of what is to happen if a 'peaceful' nuclear explosive technology becomes distinguishable

12. ENDC/PV 371, 28 February 1968.
13. See p. 106.

from the definitely military. Japanese scientists are said to foresee the achievement by means of nuclear explosive technology of transuranian elements; elsewhere work has been done on very small fusion bursts and some time it may succeed. If this kind of thing is to be banned as the use of 'nuclear explosive devices' under Article II – and presumably it is – the propriety of reserving *all* explosive technology to the nuclear weapon powers becomes questionable.

Peaceful Uses

The organization of 'benefits' from nuclear technology, including explosives, which the Treaty anticipates, to developing areas of the world was considered by the Non-Nuclear-Weapons States Conference of September 1968 at some length.

The Conference derived from a rather half-heartedly supported General Assembly Resolution, which Pakistan had sponsored (and which India had been alone in voting against). It met in Geneva from 29 August to 28 September 1968, the invasion of Czechoslovakia very present in all minds. Ninety-six countries were represented, including four nuclear-weapon powers (France, the Soviet Union, the United Kingdom and the United States) whose delegates had no vote, in fact did not speak, but were very active in the corridors. The Federal Republic of Germany was present; the German Democratic Republic was not.

The conference discussed two main topics: the security of the non-nuclear-weapons powers, and the business of cooperation in the field of peaceful uses of nuclear energy. It adopted a Declaration[14] and forwarded a number of recommendations to the UN General Assembly.

The 'peaceful uses' recommendations showed the Conference divided up into three groups of states: the nuclear-weapons powers (who were silent), the non-weapons nuclear powers, and the non-nuclear powers for whom there is no weapons option at all. The super-powers, in omitting to make this second distinction during the non-proliferation treaty negotiations, despite Mrs

14. A/7277, pp. 17 ff.

Myrdal's warnings, had allowed themselves to use the prospect of untold nuclear goodies as an inducement to the third, non-nuclear, non-weapons group to support the Treaty. ('The potential benefits from the carrying out of such explosions will be available on extremely advantageous and favourable terms to the parties to the Treaty,' had said Mr Roshchin.[15] 'We believe that usable, though not optimum, nuclear explosive designs for certain applications will be available in the near future ... to domestic users and to non-nuclear parties to the Treaty,' had said Mr Foster.[16])

A conference paper which claimed explicitly to be 'based on American sources' concluded: 'The development of nuclear explosives ... works for mankind as an answer to the increasing demand for energy, water, minerals, transportation links and food supply.'[17] Consequently most of the 'peaceful uses' recommendations of the conference displayed the uncritical, even greedy, enthusiasm with which the non-nuclears were responding to an apparent promise of economic miracle. They pointed out that they would require financial along with the technical assistance, suggested that special funds be set up for the purpose, and that representation on I A E A be reconstituted, wider and poorer.

The non-weapons nuclear powers included such highly aligned countries as Australia, West Germany, Italy, Japan and Spain, as well as neutrals like Sweden, Switzerland and India. These, with whom arguably it would have been more realistic for the nuclear weapons powers to have negotiated the non-proliferation treaty and with whom negotiation may still be necessary,[18] had two

15. ENDC/PV 366, 16 February 1968, p. 8.
16. ENDC/PV 384, pp. 6 and 7.
17. Theo Ginsburg (of the École Polytechnique Fédérale, Zurich), *The Question of peaceful explosions for the benefit of non-nuclear weapons States*, A/Cont. 35/Doc. 2, p. 20.
18. When Japan signed the Treaty (3 February 1970), a lengthy statement was issued giving a very clear idea of the conditions under which Japan would ratify. Several other countries have issued similar statements. See Cmnd. 4474, *Treaty on the Non-Proliferation of Nuclear Weapons*, H M S O. See also p. 125.

major concerns: the reduction of the monopolistic advantages that the nuclear-weapons powers might derive from the prohibitions and loopholes of the non-proliferation treaty and the need to relate the provision and control of peaceful nuclear explosions to a comprehensive test-ban. The hope was 'most earnestly' expressed that 'the other nuclear-weapon states' would join the United Kingdom and the United States in submitting their peaceful nuclear activities to IAEA safeguards. Delegates of some states with a potential commercial interest were suspected of being active on behalf of what may euphemistically be called free trade. Mrs Myrdal had earlier remarked that 'the profit motive is evidently not excluded . . . we might even fear that vested interests, in the world of international commerce, could come to act as a pressure against [an underground] test ban'.

A recommendation sponsored by Sweden and Nigeria specifically endorsed the views of the non-aligned ENDC members on the necessity of linking the international body and the procedures to be devised for regulating and controlling peaceful nuclear explosions (and referred to in Article V of the NPT) with a comprehensive test ban. Mr de Palma of the United States had 'emphasized' at the ENDC that these international procedures 'would apply to both bilateral and multilateral projects',[19] but this was not unambiguously written into the Treaty. Moreover, he had said nothing at all (nor had his Russian colleague) about the 'unilateral projects' which nuclear-weapon powers (or such non-state units as they might license) might wish to conduct and which ought to be subjected to just as much international agreement and planning as multilateral projects.[20] One conference paper[21] gave some idea of the enormous complexity – political, economic, legal, health, environmental, etc. – of these issues, which enthusiasts, both technical and commercial (and indeed

19. ENDC/PV 369, 22 March 1968.

20. A United States Senate Sub-Committee headed by Senator Edmund Muskie has been reported as calling for IAEA supervision of all peaceful nuclear explosions. *International Herald Tribune*, 2 November 1971.

21. A/Conf. 35/Doc. 3, 3 July 1968, by Dr Ulf Ericsson, of the Stockholm National Defence Research Institute.

political – see Mr Roshchin and Mr Foster above), tended at that time to skate over, and which may well prevent large-scale peaceful nuclear explosions from being usable for many years. Neither the United States nor the Soviet Union have recently shown much enthusiasm for their respective scientists' pet first nuclear earth-shifting schemes, the new sea-level Panama Canal and the re-routing of the North-flowing central Asian rivers.[22] This latter project might well have climatic consequences for Western Europe; the former, by joining the waters of the Atlantic and Pacific Oceans would have substantial ecological effects. Neither scheme would be internationally insignificant, and in fact the British Government, as a depository power, would have a veto over the amendments to the Partial Test Ban which would be required to legitimate such uses of nuclear explosives overground.

The decline in super-power enthusiasm may partly derive from the enthusiasm the non-nuclear conference disclosed among its participants for what they interpreted as promises implicit in the NPT and its theoretically not binding preamble. When the Conference Declaration and Resolutions came up for endorsement at the United Nations later that year, a new climate of opinion and interest was evident: international discussion of the Non-Proliferation Treaty and at the Conference of Non-Nuclear-Weapons States had at least been successful as a course of study in arms control. The level of information and understanding was now high: the members of ENDC no longer had to carry the whole weight of it, and the proposals and intentions of the super-powers were being subjected to a scrutiny ever more beady-eyed, skilful, and up to date: scarcely a 'third world' speaker but spoke of the need for the super-powers to start their talks on the limitation of strategic arms; scarcely one but mentioned the necessary connection between an underground test-ban and international control

22. The re-routing of rivers seems likely to happen, without the use of nuclear explosive devices. The American AEC and their Russian colleagues have recently been sweet-talking about the use of nuclear explosives for freeing subterranean gas from shale. See footnote, p. 115. Governmental enthusiasm remains limited.

over *all* peaceful nuclear explosions (that is, including those conducted by the nuclear-weapons states for their own purposes); almost all mentioned the need to keep the sea-bottom free for peaceful uses and for the benefit of all mankind: these being the three areas where suspicion of super-power intentions was most acute. They proved their new tenacity the following year by refusing to accept a Seabed Non-Nuclearization Treaty that the super-power chairmen of E N D C had determined to present to the General Assembly.

The Soviet Union in particular showed itself thoroughly alarmed by the new atmosphere, and Mr Roshchin's speech in the Political Committee[23] was angry and withdrawn to an unusual degree. To ask for better guarantees than the June 1968 Security Assurances was to undermine the Non-Proliferation Treaty; there would be no peaceful explosions at all for non-signatories; no funds for anyone and no international service for peaceful explosions; certainly no periodic non-nuclear conferences . . . all these proposals were but ignorant and malicious attacks on the Treaty. In solitude, the Soviet bloc[24] voted against the resolution which endorsed the Declaration of the Non-Nuclear-Weapons States and which asked the Secretary General to commission an experts' report on the possible contribution of nuclear technology to the economic and scientific advancement of developing countries. This was because, said the Soviet delegate, the Soviet Union 'decisively opposes any division of States into groups on only one basis, nuclear or non-nuclear'[25] – an argument which came oddly from one of the permanent co-chairmen of E N D C, who owed his position entirely to his country's pre-eminence in nuclear weapons.

Safeguards

The Treaty itself declares that safeguards negotiations with the I A E A shall start for states which have ratified the treaty within

23. A/C1/PV 1624, pp. 11 ff. 1968.
24. This no longer included Romania; it sometimes included Mongolia but not on this occasion.
25. A/PV/1750, p. 22.

180 days of it entering into force, and that the safeguards agreements shall in turn enter into force not more than eighteen months after that. The Treaty does not contemplate that states should ratify only after negotiating a safeguards agreement, but in practice this is what is happening. The Board of Governors of IAEA sensibly enough established a committee in 1970 to devise a basic safeguards agreement that would, *en principe*, suit all types of signatory, from the Vatican and Botswana to Canada and West Germany. This is now done and individual negotiations have started.[26] What is not clear is the point at which the IAEA will expect ratification. The progress of ratification is necessarily geared to the sense governments have about which way world events are moving: by ratifying they can give meaning to the NPT; by not ratifying, the whole network of negotiations can turn out to have been meaningless. The Treaty's moment of consummation is still to come.

The five relevant EEC powers (France is not only a nuclear-weapons power, but also a non-signatory) may not ratify until Euratom – the European 'atomic' community, where a unanimity rule obtains – signifies it is content that they should.[27] The other 'threshold' nuclear powers are not likely to ratify, or to agree, before knowing what bargain Euratom has struck; and even then several of them will wish to be among the last to ratify . . .

Political pressure could be attempted on Japan and West Germany to ratify, but they are unlikely to be successful. Both issued substantial 'statements' on signature, which make it clear that by the time they ratify they expect their security to be at least undiminished, nuclear disarmament between the weapons powers to be in progress, and non-discrimination as between weapons powers and non-weapons powers in the peaceful uses of nuclear energy to obtain. Neither super-power is at all keen to have attention drawn to the relation between Article VI of the Treaty (in which they undertook to negotiate 'in good faith

26. First agreements were reached in 1971 with Finland, Uruguay, Austria, Poland and Hungary.
27. Because of Soviet opposition, Euratom and IAEA had not over the years had any formal relationship.

on effective measures relating to cessation of the nuclear arms race at an early date and to nuclear disarmament, and on a treaty on general and complete disarmament under strict and effect international control') and the Strategic Arms Limitation Talks which are being carried on in almost complete privacy. No non-super-power is likely to forget the connection.

So when the time comes for 'threshold' governments actually to take the plunge into permitting international inspectors into their countries and into their advanced technologies on a quite unprecedented scale, a number of things will in practice be established: (i) they will be satisfied with the prospects for their own security in a world still containing nuclear-weapon states; (ii) they will be satisfied about the intentions of those nuclear-weapons states to implement Article VI; (iii) they will be satisfied that the IAEA's verification procedures are not being used for purposes of industrial spying, or of other commercial advantage; (iv) they will be satisfied that the non-signatory and non-inspected weapons powers, the French and the Chinese, and the Russians, are not benefiting, commercially or politically, from their self-exemption from the system, or parts of it: (v) they will be satisfied that no other states are taking advantage of the loopholes in the NPT.

Before that, the Soviet Union's position of beneficiary from and participant in the administration of the safeguards system without its bearing any balancing obligations, will have become inconveniently outstanding, particularly if the SAL Talks get stuck with an inadequate definition of strategic arms.[28] The United States, in

28. Land-based intercontinental-range and anti-missile missiles are certainly within the currently prevailing definition. So apparently are intermediate and medium-range submarine-launched missiles. The United States is understood to have proposed the inclusion of land-based I- and MRBMs. This was refused by the Russians, who counter-proposed that any vehicle capable of delivering a nuclear weapon onto the soil of the 'European socialist countries' should count, which would include American carrier-based and Europe-based aircraft. (Col. Kharich, writing in *Red Star*, reprinted in *Soviet News*, 20 July 1971). It is of course Soviet IRBMs and MRBMs which pose the chief strategic threat to Japan, China, India, Israel and the countries of Europe, among whom are some of the principal non-signatories and non-ratifiers of the NPT and these would not count:

national psychology, is set for agreed limitations and national withdrawals; whether the Soviet Union is ready to make the world safe for widespread NPT ratification and all that means remain to be seen.

Guarantees and Security Assurances

Guarantees and security assurances continue impossibly difficult for the present international system to provide: on the one hand it is widely believed that one nuclear threat can only be neutralized by another equal and opposite nuclear threat; on the other, it is existing (and developing) nuclear weapons which call other nuclear weapons into existence. This man's guarantee is that other man's threat.

There has certainly been a qualitative reduction recently in alliance guarantees. The emotionally almost total American withdrawal from empire, President Johnson's and his party's retirement from the Vietnam commitment,[29] President Nixon's Guam doctrine and the scale of Senate opinion favouring substantial troop reductions in Europe – all these must make any government which has relied on its American connection think twice before permanently renouncing the nuclear weapons option. Japan, Australia, the Euratom powers, including particularly West Germany and Italy, are all in this boat; all have signed the NPT, none has ratified. In statements made on signature,[30] they make clear their concern not only with a satisfactory safeguards arrangement, and with the super-powers bringing their own arms race under control, but also with the continuation of existing security commitments. It is precisely these security arrangements that they

---

the US's NATO allies are to be evaluated differently from the Soviet Union's Warsaw Pact allies in this Soviet suggestion.

29. I am not praising that commitment (on the contrary): only noticing that the US military has been plunged so deeply and long into South East Asia that its extraction, unlike its insertion, requires political and military surgery of a very high order. Presidents Kennedy and Johnson and their Democratic administrations insouciantly landed the United States with responsibilities that many Americans would like to claim do not exist.

30. See footnote 18, p. 119.

see withering on the American bough as the imperialist instinct ceases to pulse. Not, of course, that a nuclear guarantee within an alliance is enough to prevent a capable country from deciding to acquire nuclear weapons, but it helps: if the American nuclear guarantee were explicitly withdrawn from Japan or West Germany, there can be little doubt that they would immediately withdraw from the NPT and seek to acquire nuclear weapons.

For the non-aligned, the difficulties about guarantees are different. These have no doubt been well enough ventilated in private – for instance, between the Indian Government and the United States and the Soviet Union in early 1967 when the NPT was being devised and India's problems were being specifically studied[31] – but they never really surfaced publicly either at ENDC in Geneva in March 1968 when the three nuclear powers made their security assurances declarations,[32] nor at the General Assembly in New York in May and June, nor at the Non-Nuclear-Weapon States Conference in September of that year.

An assumption that general nuclear guarantees are plausible has all along been the logical linch-pin of the 'naked' Non-Proliferation Treaty. Mr Foster (Director of the US Arms Control and Disarmament Agency) wrote in 1965 that 'the incentives for others to acquire nuclear weapons can undoubtedly be reduced, if not controlled, by adequate security assurances or guarantees; a point of particular importance since the Chinese nuclear test.'[33] This is part of the conventional wisdom. If only for this reason, the difficulties about guarantees are worth rehearsing: they explain not necessarily proliferation itself, but rather the disinclination near-nuclear governments have to permanently renouncing the nuclear weapons option.

31. India has not signed the NPT and now has both a vigorous nuclear programme and a vigorous space programme.
32. When Mr Rusk testified before the Senate Foreign Relations Committee about the 'Security Assurances', he made clear that the United States had undertaken no new commitments.
33. William Foster, 'New Directions in Arms Control and Disarmament' *Foreign Affairs*, July 1965, p. 596. Mr Foster went on to limit the effect of such guarantees and assurances to 'the near or medium term'.

So far all proliferation has taken place within alliances where far stronger guarantees obtained than can possibly be proposed either universally or to specifically vulnerable countries, such as India. There have been half a million American troops, plus their families, plus 'tactical' nuclear weapons and other systems that could not be let fall into enemy hands, in Europe. Between the Soviet Union and China there purported at least until the late 1950s to be ideological unanimity. Respectively these might well have been thought adequate to guarantee the American and Russian guarantees but, as became clear in the late fifties, they did not. The Multilateral Force was an attempt to improve the credibility of the American guarantees to Western Germany, but no solution could be found to the problem of political control. In the case of non-alliance guarantees the problem is even more intractable. National political control over military decisions is a fundamental principle, at least in democracies, and such control is, simply, not applicable to an extraneous guarantee.

In the specific case of Asian countries, the Soviet Union and the United States over the years each established postures of animosity towards China and, as we have seen, each at one time or another has issued nuclear threats to China. Consequently any Asian country, overtly guaranteed either by the United States or the Soviet Union, or by both of them in a joint guarantee, would necessarily find itself inserted into the American or Russian nuclear threat and deterrence system. At any moment of crisis between China and either of those guarantors, it would willy nilly be identifiable with China's opponents, and so, unavoidably, a target for Chinese pressure, even perhaps for Chinese short-range missiles. Certainly at any level lower than the nuclear, a guarantee given by an antagonist of China's would probably reduce rather than enhance the security of the recipient. Ally as hostage is a familiar European nightmare and one of the most comprehensible reasons for British and French national nuclear forces. It is sometimes suggested, as by Mr Fisher at ENDC,[34] that American Anti-Ballistic Missile Defences could improve the quality of American guarantees to countries within range of Chinese nuclear

34. See above, p. 103.

weapons. To the extent that American guarantees (or Russian) cannot be disinfected of animosity towards China, this would not be so; and the hostage situation which has activated proliferation in Europe would do the same in Asia.[35]

Some areas are even more obviously incapable of housing nuclear guarantees. In the Middle East the super-powers can effectively do no more than neutralize each other, as we have seen.[36] There are always the rumours that Israel is on the brink of disclosing nuclear weapons, and in November 1968 the *New York Times* was reporting that Israel was asking as a 'price' for signing the Non-Proliferation Treaty something like a formal guarantee of 'territorial security' from the United States (Senator Fulbright was later proposing something of just this sort); she has not signed yet.[37] Israel could well suppose that only her own nuclear weapons *or* such a specific guarantee internationally declared could adequately safeguard her integrity; without the guarantee the military requirement could come to seem peremptory. If so, it would be the first development of nuclear weapons outside the central nuclear arms race systems arising out of a local military and political situation, and not directly out of alliance problems.

Sometimes the possibility of 'guarantees and security assurances' is advanced as a reason why the United States and the Soviet Union should not begin to dismantle their nuclear forces. Hedley Bull wrote a few years ago that 'it is clear that if the United States and the Soviet Union were to progress indefinitely down this road [i.e. beginning to dismantle their nuclear forces]

35. One of the first intractable problems facing China on its return to international forums will be the matter of the United States' nuclear relationship with Japan. China would like to see the Americans out of Asia, but American withdrawal will strengthen pressures inside Japan for the acquisition of nuclear weapons.

36. See Introduction, p. 12. Super-powers' interlocking nuclear guarantees coupled with cornucopias of conventional weaponry merely ensure that the war is, militarily, interminable.

37. Further stories appeared in October 1971, this time associated with an Israeli-built delivery vehicle called *Jericho*, widely deemed nuclear-capable and 'too expensive' for a mere conventional warhead. *International Herald Tribune*, 6 October 1971.

... [their] ability to protect states ... would then come to be called in question.'[38]

This is to ignore what almost all the near-nuclears have been saying over the years: that the threat to their security which persuades them towards acquiring nuclear weapons derives from the nuclear weapons already in existence. Particularly, it derives from the nuclear weapons in the hands of the nuclear super-powers who alone so far have actually engaged in nuclear threats (the British, French and Chinese have not done that) and thereby have hastened such proliferation as there has already been. The near-nuclears see proliferation as a side effect of the central arms race: hence their conviction that a genuine non-proliferation policy must consist in a package of measures, of which 'guarantees' can only be a small part, and, at that, preferably bolstered with some kind of no-use declaration, or no-first-use declaration, or declaration of no-use against powers not having nuclear weapons on their territories. This is frequently proposed by the Soviet Union, and supported in the United Nations, as a separate measure and indeed the Chinese have already made a No-First-Use Declaration, which they repeat after each nuclear test they make. A plain no-first-use declaration can probably not be accepted by the NATO powers, at least not as far as Europe is concerned, because the mutual deterrence system whose interface is at the Elbe is far too asymmetrical for any single element in it safely to be extracted or declared null: the system must be dismantled as a whole.[39] This local argument does not necessarily apply outside the European theatre, especially in the 'no-use against non-nuclears' version; indeed, the United Kingdom and

38. Hedley Bull, 'The Role of the Nuclear Powers in the Management of Nuclear Proliferation', in *Arms Control for the late Sixties*, ed. Dougherty and Lehman, van Nostrand, 1967, p. 147.

39. The French view is that the asymmetricality is such as to make the Mutual and Balanced Reduction of Forces (MBFR) in Central Europe (an old NATO suggestion which Mr Brezhnev took up again in spring 1971, to Washington's delight) quite unacceptable: the French believe the matter can only plausibly be negotiated within the ambit of a European Security Conference. Since Mr Brezhnev's visit to Paris in October 1971 the Soviet Union has let this matter rest, to the disappointment of the United States.

the United States have implicitly made such declarations for Latin America in accepting[40] the Treaty of Tlatelolco, for the prohibition of nuclear weapons in Latin America.

The non-nuclear conference had been the first opportunity for most of the world's governments to declare themselves, not so much on the NPT itself, as on the context that was going to allow it to operate – or, as the case might be, not. The conference produced the resolutions we have already mentioned on the peaceful uses of nuclear explosions; its Declaration also reverted to the prevailing conviction that only a wide-ranging and well coordinated 'package' of arms control and disarmament measures made sense. The United States and Soviet Union were specifically requested to start their discussions on limiting their offensive and defensive missile systems. And so they planned to do.

But the very day set for announcing the agreement by the United States and the Soviet Union to start the Strategic Arms Limitation Talks, the Soviet Union invaded Czechoslovakia.

40. The Soviet Union has not.

8

The Other Treaties

The other treaties need not detain us very long: they have achieved no disarmament and precious little arms control. The Antarctic Treaty[1] was thoroughly agreeable, sensible, and harmless, and risked no one. The agreement to establish a 'Direct Communications Link' between Moscow and Washington preceded the Partial Test-Ban by a few weeks.[2] Such a hot line may well be useful provided it is not used to convey over-hasty angers and impatiences between one button-pusher and another. This agreement has recently been somewhat expanded by two further little agreements, one on 'Measures to Reduce Risk of War between the United States of America and the Union of Soviet Socialist Republics', and one listing technical improvements to be made in the Direct Link system itself.[3] The former

1. Signed in Washington, 1 December 1959; entered into force, 23 June 1961. The texts are all in *The United Nations and Disarmament, 1945–70.*

2. *Memorandum of Understanding (with Annexe) Regarding the Establishment of a Direct Communications Link*, signed at Geneva, 20 June 1963.

3. Both signed in Washington, 30 September 1971. These two little agreements issued from the corridors of SALT. A bilateral discussion is now going on between Russian and American Navy officials concerning the avoidance of 'incidents' at sea. It is difficult to see why this discussion should be bilateral: 'incidents' do not occur only between Russian and American naval vessels and aircraft. The practice of aircraft 'buzzing' naval vessels particularly needs controlling: the vessel's captain has instantly to decide if this time it is legitimate surveillance, or an irresponsible game of 'silly buggers', or whether it may not be the beginning of a coordinated and world-wide first strike attack. Just how ambiguous the situation is a recently retired American Admiral makes clear: 'We pride ourselves on being very, very circumspect professionals. . . . When their aircraft approach our ship and we intercept them far out from the ships that they might be reconnoitering, there's no

spells out the kind of thing that the Direct Link should be used to communicate: accidental or unauthorized nuclear 'incidents', detection of 'unidentified objects' by missile warning systems, interference with such warning systems, and so on. The most interesting provision is the one whereby 'each party undertakes to notify the other party in advance of any planned missile launches if such launches will extend beyond its national territory in the direction of the other party', but there seems no reason why such notification should not be multilateral, or indeed public. The reference in this text to 'missile warning systems', which are not defined, but which do not in principle differ from other inspection satellites, may be the thin end of a very desirable wedge as far as verification is concerned.[4]

The Partial Test-Ban[5] was certainly environmentally useful, but more nuclear weapon tests have been carried out each year since the treaty was signed than before. The Partial Test-Ban did almost nothing to impede the Russian–American nuclear arms race, or the proliferation of nuclear weapons. It is clear that neither superpower has much interest for the time being in completing it to cover underground tests: an undertaking completely to discontinue testing nuclear weapons is probably too close to an undertaking to discontinue making or stockpiling nuclear weapons for such an agreement to emerge except from the Strategic Arms Limitation Talks. There is also the matter of peaceful nuclear

---

nonsense, no playing around, pointing things at one another – absolutely none. They will open the bomb bays and we go under and look up inside – no bombs.' Vice-Admiral Isaac C. Kidd, until October 1971 Commander of the US VIth Fleet, interviewed in *US News and World Report*, 15 November 1971.

4. At one point during the negotiations that preceded the Partial Test Ban, Mr Khrushchev accepted three on-site inspections per year in principle. There was also considerable discussion about tamper-proof 'black boxes' monitoring seismic events in the Soviet Union. Both possibilities are now water under the bridge.

5. *Treaty Banning Nuclear Weapon Tests in the Atmosphere, in Outer Space, and under Water*, signed at Moscow by the USSR, the UK and the USA on 5 August 1963.

explosions. The complete test ban has been non-negotiable on political not technical grounds.[6]

Neither the UN resolution of 1963 which banned weapons of mass destruction in outer space,[7] nor the eventual Space Treaty[8] anywhere defined space, or prohibited either the deployment on the ground of orbiting nuclear weapons systems or the testing of such weapons without nuclear weapons aboard, or made any provision for verification. As an arms control treaty, it was basically misleading: the Soviet Union is deploying and has tested such weapons.[9]

The Treaty banning nuclear weapons in Latin America[10] does not ban non-military nuclear explosive devices, whose technology is not at present distinguishable from that of nuclear weapons.

The Seabed Treaty[11] prohibits the 'emplacing' or 'emplanting', of nuclear and other weapons of mass destruction on the seabed,

6. For a detailed examination see R. R. Neild, *The Test Ban: SIPRI Research Report*, October 1971. The United States announces some of its own underground tests and some Russian ones. The Russians announce none. The recent American 'Amchitka' test attracted strong objections world-wide, both as environmentally risky and provocative during the SALT. Russian tests of roughly equivalent power have however also been monitored during the SAL Talks. *Moscow Radio* in foreign language broadcasts described the Amchitka test as a 'criminal act' (SU 3837/A1/5, 10 November 1971), and a 'challenge to the whole complex of international efforts and measures, either taken or planned, to reduce the threat of nuclear war'. Novosti Press Agency, quoted in *Soviet News*, 11 November 1971.

7. 17 October 1963: UN Resolution 1884 (XVIII).

8. *Treaty on Principles governing the Activities of States in the Exploration and Use of Outer Space including the Moon and Other Celestial Bodies*, signed at London, Moscow and Washington, 27 January 1967.

9. On 4 June 1971 the Soviet Union published the text of a further draft Treaty Concerning the Moon which it was submitting to the United Nations. Text in *Soviet News*, 15 June 1971. There was some feeling that the sentiments embodied in this draft could more usefully be applied to a regime for the Sea and Seabed – an area of internationalist endeavour where the Soviet Union is noticeably dragging its feet. See also pp. 103 and 212.

10. *Treaty for the Prohibition of Nuclear Weapons in Latin America*, signed at Mexico City on 14 February 1967. Also known as the *Treaty of Tlatelolco*.

11. *Treaty on the Prohibition of the Emplacement of Nuclear Weapons and other Weapons of Mass Destruction on the Sea Bed and Ocean Floor*. Approved by the UN General Assembly, December 1970.

a technique explicitly considered and abandoned by the US Navy in the early sixties, and unlikely ever to appeal to any other navy. Mobility under water is not only militarily preferable, but technically easier, than fixedness, and is likely to remain so. Robert Neild, of the Stockholm International Peace Research Institute (SIPRI) has, quite fairly, described this as a treaty equivalent to one prohibiting the bolting of aeroplanes to the ground. It will have the environmentally useful side effect of banning the dumping of unwanted biological and chemical weapons on the ocean floor.

The General Assembly of 1971 approved a convention banning biological warfare[12] (with a vote of 110 to 0, France abstaining[13] and China absent) but, just as the Seabed Non-Nuclearization Treaty banned a kind of nuclear emplacement that lacks all military desirability, so this convention will outlaw a form of warfare which is not only repulsive, but too incalculable and dangerous for military use. Several months before the draft convention was agreed between the Russians and Americans and presented to the CCD, President Nixon had announced the discontinuance of the American Biological Warfare programme (except for research on defences against it) and the destruction of stocks. Fort Detrick is now housing cancer research. What biological warfare capability the Soviet Union has or has had is not known. The draft convention makes no provision for verification; it is assumed that it will be self-policing and signatories are to report within a period of the treaty entering into force that they have destroyed their germ warfare stocks. There is to be a right of appeal to the Security Council to investigate violations which are 'found' – several governments would have preferred appeal to the Secretary General. The Italian Government at one point suggested that WHO be entrusted with this job.

The Geneva Protocol of 17 June 1925 for the Prohibition of the

12. *Draft Convention on the Prohibition of the Production, Development and Stockpiling of Bacteriological (Biological) Weapons and Toxins and on their Destruction.* CCD/353, 28 September 1971.

13. The French Government has introduced a project of law making the manufacture etc. of biological weapons illegal, despite its abstention.

Use in War of Asphyxiating, Poisonous or Other Gases, and of Bacteriological Methods of Warfare still obtains, badly dented by the (non-adhering) Americans' use of tear gases and defoliants in Vietnam and by the British Government's curious attempts to re-write history and to legitimate the use of tear gases and defoliants in war.[14] It had been widely hoped in the CCD that biological and chemical warfare would be banned together, but in fact there has never been much chance in the short term of a treaty banning chemical weapons. Armies, including the Soviet Army,[15] *are* equipped to conduct chemical warfare; a treaty banning chemical weapons would not convincingly be self-policing; and it would not be verifiable (as an underground test probably would be) by the 'national means' which are still all the Soviet Union is prepared to discuss.[16]

It would not be unfair to say that during the sixties the super-powers have colluded in presenting to the world a series of insignificant agreements, and that these have been turned into insignificant treaties at very considerable expense of international time and trouble and breath. Not only has no significant agreement been reached, but the central problem, which is how to substitute the security of certainty for the insecurity of weapons, and on which the super-powers disagree, has gone quite undiscussed.

The arrival of the Chinese at the UN is likely to dissolve the super-powers' monopoly of the main disarmament and arms control agenda; whether verification or disarmament in general will be more systematically dealt with remains to be seen. A proposal to examine the general desirability of a World Disarmament Conference, a matter on which Russians and Chinese hold incompatible views, had to be settled by the acclamation of the 1971 General Assembly instead of in the usual way by a vote.

14. See David Carlton and Nicholas Sims, 'The CS Gas Controversy', *Survival*, October 1971, p. 328.

15. See John Erikson, *Soviet Military Power*, Royal United Services Institute (Defence Studies), 1971.

16. But see *The Problem of Chemical and Biological Warfare*, vol. V, *The Prevention of CBW*, published by the Stockholm International Peace Research Institute, November 1971, where a more optimistic view of CB disarmament is expressed.

Part Two: Hunches

9

What is Truth?

So far, I hope I have been able to document my argument. In the next two chapters I shall be advancing not so much arguments as a couple of hunches about political 'climates' – one macro-climate, one micro-climate. These are that we do not, substantially enough, consider the role and effects of implicit philosophical structures, or of prevailing intellectual fashions, on the conduct and interplay of international relations.

The first arises from a sense that, in discussions and negotiations about disarmament, Russians and Americans much of the time do not speak the same language. Discussing and negotiating reveal a bedrock of implicit, and opposed, philosophy on two types of occasion: (1) when the nature of truth and how it may be ascertained is at issue; and (2) when the agreement in view tends towards a new international system. Very substantial differences then appear, the product of the philosophical traditions of the two parties, service in whose administrations selectively and confirmingly attracts those who most wholeheartedly accept that tradition, part ethic, part political theory, part epistemology. The problem of verification is never just about how many inspectors and how many on-site inspections, but, quite simply, what is truth? How may the truth be ascertained? What is evidence? How can it be established? Criteria prevailing in East and West (or at least in Russia and America) are obviously very different. Nor will a practising Marxist, in terms of his own logic, happily seek to construct a new international system along with capitalists and capitalist states whose days he believes are numbered.

The second hunch concerns the role of intellectual fashion, particularly in the United States, where a self-sustaining growth of political and other beliefs and expectations tends to be influenced rather by its own internal developments than by developments outside. In the United States intellectual bandwagons abound: the view is always retrospective, and tends to anachronism.

The Russian theological tradition I take to be one of acceptance of the word of God as revealed and expounded by his church and by the Tsar, and endangered by heresy and heretics, a tradition into which Soviet Marxism settled quite comfortably for reasons of its own. Autocracy, bureaucratism, censorship and a secret police, combined with eccentric conservatism in high places have provided the perennial grounds of public complaint. The American tradition is a belief that God rewards the virtuous, which allows you to read back virtue from success and happily let the devil take the hindmost. On the assumption (which I shall not argue here) that the human race has a theological faculty, which never goes unused, and which in the absence of a 'God', will devise a substitute, each of the old theological traditions recently invested in 'science'. 'Science' is a form of theology in that its pursuit is identifiable with the perennial human search for certain knowledge, and in that it rests on a (theologically normal) faith in the existence and attainability of such knowledge: 'scientific' proof is commonly held to be a more proved kind of proof than ordinary proof. This natural desire for certainty, and for denoting it, and a rather naïve faith in its presence in 'science', have in the West recently been overflowing into adjacent fields, particularly into 'social science' and 'political science'. Because science is at its most pure and most potent in mathematics, the use of mathematical symbols, and even of the word 'scientific', is now used much as the sign of the cross used to be.

I believe a science of government or of ongoing international relations to be a chimera: an artificial beast made up of mutually repugnant elements. Just as there can be no science of ethical behaviour nor a science of aesthetic response (because ethical and aesthetic events – I-now events – are unique and cannot be verified or replicated or refuted) so there can be no science of the actual making of political decisions, national or international, though there can be sound histories; nor of the criteria by which they should be made, though there can be fruitful political theories; nor even of the matter concerning which, or for the sake of which, political decisions are made, though there can be, and is, a vast number of partial and limited and overlapping appreciations of what is happening, a manifold patchwork of understandings built up of report, research, analysis, insight, prejudice, history, personality, experience, philosophy, chance, fashion, prevailing climate and weather of opinion. There can never be more evidence than that which is present at the actual moment a decision is reached; that evidence can never be better understood than it happens to be; nor can it be better judged in relation to the ungraspable totality of fact and event that it is.

The governments both of Russia and of the United States have sought to stiffen these taxingly finite uncertainties with 'science', and each has drawn it into the very image that it has and presents of itself. In America the image shows signs of wear.[1]

1. During the last half century in England and North America, philosophy has been done very much in minimalist style: an amiable, desultory and respectful fingering-over of the scientists' gear. Ethics – and consequently politics – have been out of fashion and dismissed as some minor branch of aesthetics. A. J. Ayer put the matter most classically and precisely: 'For in saying that a certain type of action is right or wrong, I am not making any factual statement, not even a statement about my own state of mind. I am merely expressing certain moral sentiments. And the man who is ostensibly contradicting me is merely expressing his moral sentiments. So that there is plainly no sense in asking which of us is right. For neither of us is asserting a genuine proposition.' (*Language, Truth and Logic*, Penguin Books, 1946, pp. 142–3. First published 1936.) A hunger to go on 'asserting... genuine propositions' may help explain the recent growth of so many bastard 'sciences' whose practitioners might in fact have done better to examine the fallacies in the original judgement. The existence of a generation of teachers, which has been fed on Ayer and Ryle and Hampshire, may account for the combination of political illiteracy, destructive suspiciousness, and aimless warm-heartedness, that hit our universities a couple of years ago. Such an eventuality was, interestingly enough, forecast by R. G. Collingwood, also in Oxford in the thirties. Ethical concepts of course are still with us: 'Responsibility' (as among scientists), 'relevance', 'commitment'. The appropriate words, 'moral', 'ethical', 'good' are now used otherwise: 'moral' means 'moralistic'; 'ethical' refers to some types of pharmaceutical products; 'good', by and large is too embarrassing a word to use seriously.

The Russian Government affirms that the necessary superiority of its system over all others derives from its foundation in Marxism–Leninism, which, being by definition scientific, is therefore true. Here, recognizably triumphant, is the ontological argument for the existence of God.[2] The American establishment used to see a demonstration of the superiority of its system in its evident success and might and power, which were indeed the result of natural science applied in peace and war as never before, and to which at one time it saw no end. Here was the argument from design, laced with a touch of utilitarianism. Affirmation of revealed truth, of course, is invulnerable to the kinds of failure the Russian Government might have become aware of in Czechoslovakia and Poland and in its relations with China, but these are seen not as facts about the truth of Soviet Marxism, but about imperialists, or hooligans, or Mao Tse-tung. 'The Defense of Socialism is a Supreme International duty.'[3] There is no tradition of liberty to suggest otherwise. The United States' self-evident failure in Vietnam and in the burning ghettoes on the other hand was widely felt retrospectively to refute a whole national hypothesis.

The crisis in Soviet Marxism derives, says Marcuse, from the

2. Shortly after writing this (surely overstated?) opinion, I came on these remarks by Professor Ye. D. Modrzhinskaya in a critique of Daniel Bell's *The End of Ideology*, broadcast on the Moscow Home Service (26 July 1971): 'The interests of the working class fully coincide with the objective course of social development. Therefore the party-minded and class-rooted nature of proletarian ideology is in no way unscientific. On the contrary, it is rooted in science and demands a scientific approach. Thus Marxist ideology is scientific, and Marxist science is ideological. It cannot be otherwise . . .' She went on to speak of a lecture broadcast on the 'Voice of America' in which Professor Talbot Perkins [*sic*] of Harvard 'tried to deny the scientific character of Marxism–Leninism by asserting that it was no more than the Soviet political religion. At the same time he praised bourgeois sociology, the sociology that is unscientific and hostile to Marxism–Leninism, which he recommends for socialist countries as a substitute for Marxism–Leninism. . . . Our social science is objective and scientific, yet party-minded and ideological.'

3. Title of the immensely long *Pravda* article which justified the invasion of Czechoslovakia, 22 August 1968.

'attempt to reconcile the inherited body of Marxian theory with a historical situation which seemed to vitiate the central conception of this theory itself, namely the Marxian conception of the transition from capitalism to socialism'.[4] Marx himself considered his writings to be works of 'free scientific enquiry' in 'the domain of political economy',[5] his forecasts to be erected on a foundation of the best social statistics then available and therefore, implicitly, open to refutation – or at least improvement – should better social statistics become available. Some of his followers have revised his forecasts in the light of new evidence, but the Soviet authorities from Lenin on have preferred in practice to try changing the status of these forecasts. In Lenin's view, 'The sole conclusion to be drawn from the opinion held by Marxists that Marx's theory is objective truth is that by following the *path* of Marxian theory we shall draw closer and closer to objective truth (without ever exhausting it): but by following *any other path* we shall arrive at nothing but confusion and lies.'[6]

Moreover, the very success of the Revolution will depend on how closely the true path of Marxian theory is followed. Other revolutions have failed, destroyed from outside or sapped from within. If Marx's theory were not 'objective truth', the Revolution would have no certain function nor communism a certain future; the sacrifices would have been in vain. The failure of events so far to coincide with Marx's theory caused one whole set of ideas in Russia (ideas about 'objective truth') to be shifted out of the 'domain of political economy' where Marx left them into something like God's will in a theocracy. The standards which Marx considered appropriate in his studies – solid evidence,

4. Herbert Marcuse, *Soviet Marxism*, London, 1958, Introduction, pp. 12–13.
5. See author's preface to the first edition of *Capital* (ed. cit.), p.XVIII, where he also praises the commissions appointed by the British Parliament 'armed with . . . plenary powers to get at the truth' and the English factory inspectors as highly 'competent . . . free from partisanship and respect of persons'.
6. V. I. Lenin, *Materialism and Empirio-Criticism, Collected Works*, vol. 14, Foreign Language Publishing House, Moscow, 1962, p. 143.

respect for the facts, common 'scientific' inquiry and practice, have been kept on *de jure*, but provided, except in the physical sciences, with *de facto* religious functions, radiating qualities of orthodoxy[7] rather than inquiry. The system has left itself with no means of political self-criticism and self-renewal, because it admits no criteria other than those 'of a class nature' which it generates within its own orthodoxy and in terms of that orthodoxy. A perhaps unfairly rustic example of how 'free and scientific enquiry' has shrunk from the sense in which Marx used the phrase comes from the report of its secretary to the Azerbaijani Party Congress: 'Our scientists still do not rebuff bourgeois falsifiers with sharpness and good arguments. . . . Now, as never before, all our ideological weapons must operate faultlessly.'[8] A less rustic example is the Philosophical Society recently set up under the Academy of Sciences to 'further creative development of philosophic research, propaganda of Marxist–Leninist ideas, struggle against idealistic and revisionist ideas' and promote contacts with philosophical societies abroad.[9]

The uncriticizable acceptance within public discussion in the Soviet Union that Marxism–Leninism is 'scientific' and irrefutable now stretches beyond current and past events in the Soviet Union and the national interests of the Russian people, to cover the interests and concerns of other governments and peoples within the ill-defined, but certainly Moscow-led, socialist community; it has been enshrined as dogma in the Brezhnev doctrine of 'proletarian internationalism' and is being embodied in the organization of the Warsaw Pact and of the Council for Mutual Economic Aid (CMEA). The purpose of the former is integration among the armies of member countries,[10] of the latter among the economies of member countries, on the principle of the inter-

7. 'It will be possible to carry out the wish of many Communists that on the Party card there appears a picture of the founder and leader of the CPSU, Vladimir Ilyich Lenin,' Mr Brezhnev promised the 24th Congress in March 1971. 'From 1 October, when the new ideological year begins . . .' Moscow Home Service, 30 September 1971, SU 3803/B/1.

8. Aliyev's report, 10 March 1971, SU 3642/C2/6.

9. Tass in English, 24 December 1971, SU 3876/B1.

10. See p. 45.

national division of labour.[11] Negotiations (as the Americans are finding in the Paris Vietnam negotiations, and the Chinese in the Peking negotiations about the Sino-Soviet frontier, and the West Germans over Berlin) tend to be conducted as a process during which it should dawn on the other side that the Russians, or the Russian-supported party, is right.

As far as arms control is concerned the problem of verification emerges as an outcrop of the underlying assumptions about the nature of truth. The purpose of arms control and disarmament I take to be the maintenance or the enhancement of national and international security at a lower level of expenditure, by substituting the certainty of knowledge and control for the uncertainty of fear and weapons. The Soviet view is that verification for arms control is to be done by 'national means', and that anything open-ended and not pre-permitted is espionage and a violation of national sovereignty. This view has continued throughout the last quarter of a century – except during the brief periods when Mr Khrushchev accepted in principle the possibility of some specifically occasional inspection on Russian soil. Uncorroborated government statements after all are what the Soviet system itself accepts in its own political life, for the well established reason that

11. Not all member states of CMEA interpret its purposes thus: President Ceausescu of Romania has declared that integration 'does not affect national independence and sovereignty and does not lead to a superstatal form of organization' (13 July 1971, EE 3734.i). Their alarm may well be whetted by Soviet statements, like that of Mr Grishin, of the CPSU Central Committee Politburo (4 November 1971) during the October Revolution celebrations: 'The volume of capital investment in the years 1971–5 will exceed the sum of the capital investments directed to the national economy during the first 45 years of Soviet power.' Where will that investment come from? Albanian propaganda maintains it is to be appropriated from the Comecon countries, in Marxist terms that the Russian exploiters will be appropriating the results of the productive activity of the working classes of other countries. The leaders of the other Comecon countries would probably, in state terms, agree with Marx himself who considered that 'the division of labour offers us the first example of how . . . man's deed becomes an alien power opposed to him, which enslaves him instead of being controlled by him.' *The German Ideology* (1943) Moscow, Progressive publishers, 1964, p. 44, quoted in *The Good Society*, ed. by Anthony Arblaster and Steven Lukes, Methuen, 1971, p. 176.

what ought to be true must be held to be true, or truth will have no meaning. To quote Marcuse again, '. . . their verification is not in the given facts, but in "tendencies", in a historical process in which the commanded political practice will bring about the desired facts.'[12] The Russian Government is expecting no more faith from the rest of the world's governments that it requires of itself and its own people.

The prospect is, however, that as long as the Russian Government retains intact this sense of Truth as the Great Affirmed, this belief that verification – and certainty – can be achieved and accumulated by special kinds of national affirmation, rather than by observation and inquiry, there will be little arms control, and no disarmament: are other governments mistaken, and will they change their view that, in matters which concern their national security, uncorroborated Russian government statements cannot be accepted as sufficient?[13]

There are of course Russians who do not accept this view of truth (Tolstoy, who eventually did, disliked them as much as his Tsar did), who feel with us that what is or is not true (or beautiful) cannot be determined by what has been agreed ought to be true (or beautiful), and who feel with us that conventional Russian epistemology is passing off as 'knowledge' (and 'art') what is not necessarily any such thing. Who in this case are 'we'? The heirs at large of the European tradition, including, on this occasion, most Americans and many non-Soviet Marxists (including perhaps the Chinese Marxists).

The range of theories of knowledge to which we in the European tradition give assent, those in which we in practice have faith, overlaps but partially with that which today operates in the Soviet establishment. However, Russian physical scientists (as such, though not necessarily as anything else – citizens, members of the reading public, etc.) do operate within a theory of knowledge which they share with Western physical scientists; they too are heirs of Western science. It is on this area of overlap that the

12. Marcuse, op. cit., p. 87.
13. See an egregious example, pp. 80–81.

Pugwash movement grew up and that the unusually open discussions between Russian and American space scientists have occurred.[14] In this small area Russians and Americans really can 'speak the same language' – they share not only words and meanings which an experienced interpreter can translate, but the essential philosophical underpinning of their professional activity: an habitual awareness that the state of knowledge is always, but always, provisional, and that creative genius in science, and elsewhere, is always, but always, providential.[15]

The freedom and the 'neutral non-class positions of bourgeois science', as they are called, are a perennial threat to the official view that Marxist–Leninist philosophy gives a 'scientific answer to the supreme questions of our time ...'. Once in a while the limitation of the truth of class-truths is hinted at ('The scientific truth about the destructive nature of a world war is undoubtedly not of a class nature itself, any more than mathematical or physical truths');[16] but this is rare, even though Soviet biology, such as Lysenko provided for Stalin, did not work as well as Mendel's.[17] The Lysenko supremacy lasted so long partly because the possibility of the inheritance of acquired characteristics would naturally be sympathetically received by believers in the material perfectibility of man. But also what Lysenko appeared to offer, Stalin found preferable to what his opponents offered. That the Lysenko lesson has not been learnt appears from, for instance, what passed at the two-day All-Union Students' Rally, which Mr Brezhnev addressed on 19 October 1971. One student delegate,

14. There is a feeling within the American space community that this co-operation may be about to diminish; serious 'action' exchanges no longer appear to take place at Pugwash meetings.

15. See academician Peter Kapitsa's contribution, on *Rutherford and Creativity in Science*, to the History of Science Congress held in Moscow and reprinted in *New Scientist and Science Journal*, 16 September 1971, p. 639.

16. A speaker, Morilov, on *Marxism–Leninism on World War*, Moscow Radio in Chinese, 7 June 1970. S U 3409/A3/7.

17. There is a legend that Stalin would have preferred something more Soviet than Einstein's (Jewish bourgeois) relativity, but that, when told he had to choose between nuclear weapons and a more Soviet science, chose the nuclear weapons.

A FAREWELL TO ARMS CONTROL?

from Leningrad, referred[18] to the 'further development of public-political activity of students as one of our main tasks. For this purpose a system of public political practice is being introduced in our university this year. Every student will now have entered in his dossier, with his other marks, a note on the results of his socially-useful extra-curricular activity.' Mr Brezhnev himself had said to them:

You are preparing to become specialists in your field. . . . The Soviet specialist today is a person who has mastered well the foundations of Marxist–Leninist teaching. . . . I should like to stress especially, dear friends, that to master one's speciality in a creative manner, to become an active participant in the new communist construction . . . one must master Marxist–Leninist theory, which is the foundation and an inalienable component part of the knowledge of the specialist in any field. . . . The granting to Party organizations of higher educational establishments of the right of control over the activity of the administration increases their role in the life of the high school. Not one principal question of the work of the higher educational establishment must remain beyond the field of vision of Party organizations. The compositions of academic work and student leisure, the organization of scientific research, social work and sport – all this must be the concern of Communists in higher educational establishments.

So the Solzhenitsyns may not be going to higher educational establishments in future.

The horrible niceness of choosing between the good party man and the inconveniently talented heretic must perpetually confront the Russian authorities. Academician Sakharov must be the single most alarming character to them, because he is an exceptionally brilliant and useful physicist – reputed 'father' of the Russian H-bomb – because many of his colleagues in the Soviet Academy of Sciences admire him and will stand up for him, and because of his publicly expressed, and probably haunting, view that the country's in some ways sluggish and unreliable economy results from the lack of common freedoms and will only revive when such freedoms are allowed.[19]

18. Moscow Home Service, 21 October 1971. S U 3819/B/1.
19. That outstandingly wise and acute journalist, Mr Muhammad Hasa-

Mr Brezhnev's directives – they were, unusually, signed by him, as Secretary of the Party, alone – for the new five-year plan (and approved by the Twenty-Fourth Congress in March 1971) show how very far the present establishment is from considering the injection of 'freedom' into the system – and how wrong are American forecasts of the 'convergence' of the two systems, communist and non-communist, at least in the short run. What is intended is a state system fully 'automated' with computers, for information and planning and control, able to 'reinforce state discipline at all stages of the national economy' and eventually to result in 'the bringing up of a new man'.[20] In Canada, Mr Kosygin even talked about 'solving' the problem of the 'improvement of man's biological nature'.[21] The doctrine of 'proletarian internationalism', 'Marxism–Leninism's dialectical law for the integration of national and internationalist tasks within the world socialist system'[22] is to carry the system into the

---

nayn Heykal, President Nasser's close friend, wrote in *The Times*, in a series on *The Shifting Balance of Power*: 'The Soviet Union has also to cope with upheavals inside Russian society. Workers there as elsewhere are today different. It is no longer just their muscle that counts. We have to deal with people who make decisions in front of a computer – decisions based on their own judgement. Such a worker must be given freedom, and he cannot have freedom to react to a complex machine and at the same time be denied freedom in Society.' 5 April 1971.

20. *Draft Directives*, broadcast Moscow Home Service, 14 February 1971, S U 3611/C/367. See also below, p. 156.

21. Speech by Mr Kosygin at Government Dinner in Vancouver, 24 October 1971, M. Debré (Revue de Défence Nationale, January 1972, p. 13) refers to measures being taken to maintain the birthrate of the Slav group proportionately to others in the Soviet Empire.

22. 'A major yardstick for measuring loyalty to proletarian internationalism is the capability and readiness to subordinate national to internationalist interests. Naturally a certain amount of sacrifice is inevitable.' Moscow in Standard Chinese, 28 March 1971, S U 3648/A3/3. Talk by Slepov, '*Proletarian internationalism is a dependable weapon in the hands of the working class.*'

'All the CMEA countries are working together to compile a programme for the development of socialist economic integration.' N. Kosygin's Election Speech, 9 June 1971 (SU 3706/C2/II).

Warsaw Pact and CMEA. In such a world dissent becomes 'not only a political crime, but also technical stupidity, sabotage, mistreatment of the machine'.[23] The achievement of maximum production (and maximum national security) is to be the criterion by which all activities, including science and the arts, are judged.[24] The 'new man' will, in the language of Mao Tse-tung, be taught to put economics first.

Russian Marxist–Leninists are not unaware of the antithesis building itself up against their own thesis.[25] The problem is that the Russian Marxist system cannot do without that antithesis, science proper, because it provides them with so much that is necessary to that system, particularly of course in military hardware. However they may wish to avoid 'ideological coexistence'

'Our party is obliged to and must wage a decisive struggle against nationalist prejudices, against chauvinism wherever it may appear in our state, in whatever group, a struggle against the non-class understanding of the problem' . . . 'the sovereignty of our Czechoslovak State in the class sense of the word is fully assured.' Gustav Husak's speech to the 14th Congress of the Slovak Communist Party, 5 May 1971. EE 3686/C6 and C4.

'Mr Brezhnev's talks in Belgrade have thwarted the attempt by the enemies of socialism to sow mistrust and discord between the peoples of the Soviet Union and Yugoslavia, and have laid bare the slanderous fictions about the so-called "doctrine of limited sovereignty" and other similar rumours and lies.' 14 October 1971, SU 3814/A2/1. *Pravda* article by V. Zhynavskiy: 'A firm basis of friendship and brotherhood.'

23. Marcuse, op. cit., p. 85.

24. Medicine too: a new oath was in April this year approved by the Presidium of the Supreme Soviet. Doctors will now swear to 'devote all their energies and knowledge to the protection and improvement of human health and the treatment and prevention of disease and to work conscientiously in whatever field the interests of society require'. It is these interests presumably which may require a doctor to certify inconvenient dissenters as insane – people, that is, 'who have committed socially dangerous acts in a state of derangement' as *Izvestia* put it, 10 October 1971.

25. 'The Scientific Council on Questions of Alien Ideological Trends of the USSR Academy of Sciences held an extended session on 11 May to consider the further development of criticism of the ideology of anti-communism.' Moscow Home Service, 11 May 1971.

with non-class science, they cannot: every Russian scientific achievement is the fruit of ideological cohabitation with it.

Official Moscow's dislike for the 'neutral non-class positions' of bourgeois science is not the only impediment of principle to East–West agreement about disarmament and arms control. There is also the matter of coexistence, desire for which is a necessary (though hardly sufficient) condition for disarmament. In Marxian theory, capitalism is logically previous to socialism, and Lenin and his successors wrestled staunchly with the fact that the theoretically obsolete system, which should already have reached terminal disintegration, in practice was increasingly producing more than the new and truly contemporary system. To most of us in the West, despite the momentum of past events, the future is open, is something we are making; indeed is something that it is *not* open to us *not* to be making: we are its parents, not its midwife. The future which is in process of formation includes a continuously developing system of international relationships, of coexistence and cooperation between quite equally existent national and other political and social units. Part of that coexistence and cooperation will be shaped and determined by arms control and disarmament negotiations.

But the orthodox Soviet Marxist should believe that coexistence with non-communist entities is, by definition, no more than a temporary state of affairs. In his view, whatever may be being negotiated, in Geneva, in Helsinki or Vienna, in New York, is not the 'better' international system which is enshrined in the United Nations Charter, because 'the inevitable triumph of socialism' is already in process of development, and this involves the supercession of capitalism in all its forms. To the orthodox Soviet Marxist, capitalism is a contemporary anachronism. Although Lenin indeed advocated, and his successors today accept, that socialist states should use and acquire all they can in the way of capitalist expertise and techniques and cooperation, and indeed credits and investment, this should be exclusively economic: the kind of 'bridge-building' that President Johnson sought to start up in 1966, is as welcome to the Russian Government as grappling irons put out from a sinking ship.[26]

After all, after the downfall of capitalism and 'the universal victory of socialism it would become quite pointless to speculate about war'. This quotation comes from an interesting article by N. Goryainov, 'Lenin on weapons of mass destruction and the problem of elimination war',[27] which seeks to show that Lenin's understanding of contemporary advances in science (including work on relativity and radioactivity) was such that he foresaw the development – and political effects – of the unprecedentedly powerful weapons that unprecedented sources of energy would make available. Goryainov quotes Lenin's wife, N. K. Krupskaya, whom Lenin told in 1920–21 that he 'had had a conversation with an engineer who said that a device was now being invented which could destroy a large army at long range. This would make war impossible.'[28] Later, in 1921–2, she recalled, Lenin told her he 'did not reject the idea of this device, and indeed agreed with it'. Mr Goryainov provides evidence for Lenin's interest in atomic energy itself,[29] and continues:

If one reflects on the words of Krupskaya written more than thirty years ago, few though they may be, it becomes unmistakably clear that they reveal not only Lenin's remarkable ability to see tens of years ahead, but also his programme of action to meet the conditions he correctly anticipated. These conditions were as follows. Firstly, weapons

26. See p. 95. *Pravda*'s immediate comment on the bridge-building speech was that it was 'hard to imagine that Washington should be so poorly informed of the foundations of Soviet foreign policy as to proceed seriously from such a premise'.

27. P. 20 in *Articles on Disarmament from USSR Academy of Sciences* I, Glagolev (English version duplicated by Columbia University 1963).

28. Op. cit., p. 22, quoting N. K. Krupskaya: '*The Leninist Line in the Field of Culture*', Moscow Partizpat, 1934, pp. 137–50 (1st edition).

29. Particularly from the reminiscences of E. Drabkina, published in *Novy Mir*, December 1961 and from the contents of Lenin's library. He may have got the idea from H. G. Wells, who foresaw the military application of nuclear energy in *The World Set Free* (1914). See M. Hammerton, 'The Military Predictions of H. G. Wells', *Journal of the Royal United Services Institute for Defence Studies*, December 1971, p. 72.

of terrible destructive power which could wipe out whole armies at long range might make their appearance while there still existed armed forces and armies. This presupposes in its turn the continued existence of imperialist countries in the world and a world not yet free from the threat of possible wars launched by these countries; it also implies that the imperialists would try to use these new scientific and technological achievements primarily for military purposes. From this it also necessarily follows that the *appearance of new weapons of tremendous destructive power was expected within the next few decades* since the capitalist system itself was doomed to perish within a few decades as a matter of historical inevitability. The second condition is that the world's progressive forces, headed by one or several socialist countries, would inevitably become so powerful that they would be able not only to prevent the imperialists from using the new weapons for launching destructive wars, but also to compel them to agree to general disarmament and the banishing of war from human society. It may be assumed that Lenin was able, to some extent, to hope for the common sense of soberminded capitalists, who would not be so foolish or so blind as to will their own destruction or that of their own and other countries and peoples. [Goryainov's emphasis.]

If the 'world's progressive forces' were indeed to seek to become 'so powerful that they [would be] able to . . . compel the [imperialists] to agree to general disarmament', the 'imperialists' (or even the Chinese, or the inhabitants of the third world) might have other views, not themselves having any reason for accepting Russian victories as inevitable or tolerable. There is little place left in such a forecast for any new system of international coexistence and cooperation, joint construction of which by East and West together is implicit in any comprehensive arms control negotiation and explicit in any actual arrangement. Mr Goryainov's account[30] of Lenin's forecast not only fails to accord with the pleasant American view that economic development, enlightened self-interest, and the instructive responsibilities of super-power status are leading to the 'convergence' of the Russian and the American systems; it also fails to accord with

30. Which still appears completely orthodox today: see for instance A. Shevchenko, 'Disarmament: a Problem that can be solved', in *International Affairs* (Moscow), no. 5, May 1971, where a precisely similar Leninist argument is advanced.

any reasonably peaceful future for any of us, be we European, American, Chinese, or whatever.

Today, Mr Goryainov's scenario is part a plausible one for Russian policy, part not: the Soviet Union is certainly becoming very powerful in terms of weapons, but it is no longer unquestionable, in the 'vanguard of progress'; as the Chinese know only too well, it is not at all 'pointless to speculate about war' within those areas of the world where 'socialism has triumphed.' But even so, there is no sign that the Russian Government is yet contemplating any systematic non-Leninist long-term coexistence and cooperation with 'capitalism' or even with alternative forms of socialism. Certainly, as Lenin recommended, it is encouraging the import of investment and expertise from the monopoly capitalists to develop – some might say to colonize – the vast nineteenth-century empire that it inherited from the Tsars.[31] But Mr Brezhnev's speech of 30 March 1971 to the 24th Congress, reported in the West for its general mildness and for its concern about raising living standards in the Soviet Union and for its 'peace' initiatives, in fact gave a highly unsystematic and confused picture of Russian foreign policy,[32] torn as it is between two conceptions of world affairs: the global confrontation of the 'two world systems' on the one hand and 'coexistence with countries belonging to a different social system' on the other:

The total triumph of socialism is inevitable. . . . We believe that an improvement of relations between the USSR and the USA is possible . . . the monopolies . . . intensify the exploitation and oppression of the working people . . . the liquidation of colonial regimes must be carried out in full. . . . We cooperate, of course, on mutually advantageous terms with Italian, Japanese, British and other firms. . . . An unprecedented growth of militarism in the capitalist countries. . . . The CPSU will . . . promote the further activation of the anti-imperialist struggle . . . the strengthening of the unity of all participants in the combat . . .

31. When China is thought (probably wrongly) to be contemplating allowing 'the US monopolies' to develop Chinese off-shore oilfields this 'adds up to a betrayal of the people's interests'. Radio Peace and Progress in Chinese, 12 October 1971.

32. Perhaps a country which rewrites its history cannot have a coherent foreign policy.

the maintenance of normal ... relations with the countries belonging to a different social system. ... We have no territorial claims on any-one. ... To utilize fully opportunities which emanate from the present sharpening of the general crisis within the capitalist system ... and to implement consistently a policy of unity and international solidarity with the workers' movement in the capitalist countries. ... The imperialists try to resurrect the myth of a Soviet threat.

... Soviet foreign policy is honest and open, as are its aims. We have no territorial claims on any state in the world.

Except for the last (from Mr Gromyko's speech on 4 April) these quotations are all from Mr Brezhnev, whose primacy, both in internal and now in external affairs, was fully confirmed by M. Pompidou's reception of him as heir of the Tsars and successor to Peter the Great.[33] The foreign policy parts of the speech in fact come in two main sections, one hard-line ideological, and the other, unrelated to it, indeed quite discontinuous with it, full of pragmatic self-interest and offers of détente. The latter part was well reported in the West, welcomed, and responded to by the commentators. But the ideological parts went virtually unmentioned, largely, I suspect, because most of our commentators are now so bored with the jargon of communist ideology that they selectively ignore it, as one learns to ignore other forms of 'noise' deemed irrelevant. They now skip and extract only the genial and, hopefully, true message.[34] However, there are many messages in the noise and I have seen nothing in them which suggests that under Mr Brezhnev 'convergence' is on the way, or that ideology has been downgraded (the cold war with China is carried on half in military, half in ideological terms), or that the philosophical underpinnings of Russian home or foreign policy are in process of

33. *Le Monde*, 27 October 1971.

34. Influenced perhaps by the recollection that Robert Kennedy did just this during the Cuba crisis: he extracted and hung on to a negotiable strand of argument in Khrushchev's reputedly incoherent letter to President Kennedy, and thereby saved the day. There is also a tendency to fall over backwards to avoid 'cold war attitudes'. See, for instance, Professor Marshall Shulman, who is able to refer today to 'the residual ideological commitment of the Soviet Union'. 'What does security mean today?', *Foreign Affairs*, July 1971, p. 614.

change. On the contrary.[35] It is noticeable that wherever the common interests of the world at large collide with the national

35. The last section, entitled 'Improvement of Control and Planning', of Mr Brezhnev's 'Directives of the Five Year Plan for the development of the National Economy of the USSR for 1971–5' (the whole of which took four hours to broadcast on the Moscow Home Service on 14 February 1971) conjures up a not altogether attractive future for 'Soviet man':

'With a view to improving the planning of national economy and management, large-scale use must be made of economical and mathematical methods, electronic computers, and organization techniques and communication media. Work must start on the creation and introduction of automated planning and management systems in industries, in regional organizations, associations and enterprises with a view in the future to forming an automated state system for the collection and processing of information essential for control, planning and management of the national economy, on the basis of the state system of computer centres and of the single automatic communications system of the country as a whole. In doing this, the application of the principle of organizational, methodological and technical unity of the system must be ensured from the start. To introduce widely automated systems of control of technological processes in enterprises; consistently to expand and constantly to improve the system of training and retraining personnel and organizers of production at all levels, including senior managerial staffs, first and foremost in the sphere of Marxist–Leninist economic theory. . . . To reinforce state discipline in every way at all stages of the national economy. . . . Verification of the fulfilment of Party and Government directives must be the centre of attention of Party and Soviet bodies and of the people's control organizations, as this is becoming particularly urgent under the present conditions of production. . . . Every Soviet man, through his labour, brings the triumph of communism closer. . . . A purposeful struggle for more efficient production must become in deeds a most important condition of socialist management of the economy, and the main content of the socialist competition of all production kollektivs and millions of working people. . . . The trade unions are called upon . . . to inculcate by their practical experience socialist discipline in the masses, a communist attitude to work and public property . . . and strictly to control the observance of the Labour Code.'

The directives conclude with the statement that 'The five year plan will ensure the further growth of the defensive might of the Soviet Union' (about which Chapter 10 discusses) and ends with an expression of 'firm conviction that the working people of the Soviet Union will make every effort not only to fulfil but also to over-fulfil the tasks of the new Five Year Plan'. As these included 'the transformation of nature', the Western mind tends to boggle. Perhaps the whole thing is a wild structuralist dream.

interests of the Soviet Union, the latter win the day:[36] thus the Soviet Union is taking a very small part in preparing for the UN Conference on the Human Environment; explicitly disapproves of the proposed 1973 Conference on the Law of the Sea, which might seek to enhance the common interests and rights at sea and limit national ones, and takes a negative line in the UN Seabed Committee. It did, however, in June 1971, submit to the UN General Assembly a draft treaty concerning activities and property on the moon.

Under Khrushchev things were moving, but he was ousted in 1964, a casualty perhaps of Cuba, and therefore, as we shall see in the next chapter, of the McNamara/Kennedy strategic misconceptions. How Mr Brezhnev's increasingly inflexible ideology at home will cope with the emergence of China, Japan and Western Europe into the big world will be the history of the seventies. Meanwhile, détente and the 'peace offensive' are uncomfortably like a bunch of shop-bought cut flowers, in no way rooted in the domestic soil of the Soviet Union.

In the underlying structure of American political practice there is the same basic range of epistemologies as is usual in the European tradition, but a far wider acceptance of success as the criterion and indicator of rightness: if something works well, it will have been right to have done it; but otherwise, perhaps not.

The contortion of the verbs' tenses suggests inherent confusion. The question after all is how to know at the time that A is the better course and that B is wrong: later is by definition too late, either in politics or in private life. Results and consequences are never there to help, nor really can they be man-handled into existence to provide retrospective justification. In arms control, American non-proliferation policy was powered, during the Kennedy and the first Johnson years, by a conviction that it could successfully be imposed by a combination of lesser policies and gambits, and thereby eventually be proved to have been right in the first place. General de Gaulle's ability to prevent any such imposition was felt far more deeply than can be accounted for in

36. See Part Three, Chapter XII.

terms of a policy even brutally interrupted. It was the inherent rightness of the policy that was endangered by his attitude, not merely its possible success. The confusion of tenses was evident in the already quoted phrase of a State Department official who claimed at the time of the Multilateral Force discussions (itself one of the lesser anti-proliferation gambits) that 'the secret of leadership is the *fait accompli*': *have* done it and then you *can* do it.

With the United States' new found imperial role it became supremely urgent to solve this problem of uncertainty, to remove the deadly inconvenience of the future not being confirmingly to hand when decisions were being taken: A. J. Ayer must be improved on; political judgements must be *made* to have 'validity'.[37] Two solutions offered: one was to treat political affairs as if they were a physical science – a kind of study where forecasting was most effective and practicable; the other derived from the various kinds of simulation in which computers can be used.

During the early sixties there were brought into the American political–military establishment a number of highly influential physical scientists, mathematicians, and theoretical economists. The economists contributed a character not unlike 'economic man' in his amazing simplicity; and the others provided analyses of the numbers and types of nuclear and other weapons which would or would not deter this character from wiping civilization from the face of the earth or from doing anything else that Washington disliked. Some of the 'political science' that was being done (and probably still is) almost passes belief: thus at North Western University, Department of Defense funds went to finance an 'Inter-Nation Simulation' which (in the words of one of the participants) 'has enabled scholars of international relations to control, manipulate, and replicate phenomena that previously could only be studied after the fact, or, in the case of non-occurring events, not at all'.[38] Even Albert Wohlstetter, a

37. Cf. A. J. Ayer, op. cit., p. 145.
38. D. Druckman, 'Ethno-centrism in the Inter-Nation Simulation', *Journal of Conflict Resolution*, March 1968, p. 45.

man of proven insight in the fifties, could write in 1968 that 'it is a paradox that we can do better in analysing the potential outcomes of some sorts of conflict that have never occurred than we can do with conflicts of the sort that have been endemic for ages.'[39] As a 'not trivial' example he cited the 'estimate of the second-strike capability of the first generation French nuclear force'. The example was wholly trivial because he did not mention the actual strategy behind the French force, which is evidently quite other than he was suggesting, but one of the things which are not publicly discussed by American strategists, or mentioned only to be dismissed. Myopic complacency became a veritable industry, turning out obfuscating books and graduates and policy papers and calculations, on a scale which in part accounted for the tragedy of the Vietnam war.[40]

At that time, before the days of ecological stocktaking, science seemed capable of providing so much, and the joyous feeling was abroad that surely it could now provide a foolproof political calculus along with everything else. Gone be the slipshod and murky politics of yesteryear: on with games theory and Nation A and Nation B.[41] The sense of euphoria that imbued the Kennedy years was seen truly crowned when the Cuba Crisis of October 1962 confirmed and justified, or for a time appeared to justify, all that Albert Wohlstetter (physicist), Herman Kahn (physicist), Tom Schelling (economist), Walt Rostow (economist) had foretold about the oscillations of the delicate balance of terror and the

39. Albert Wohlstetter, 'Theory and Opposed-Systems Design', *Journal of Conflict Resolution*, September 1968, p. 311.

40. Anatol Rapoport came near to elucidating the national category mistake in *Strategy and Conscience* (New York, 1964); in this fine book he opposed 'strategic thinking', which 'assumes that decision problems have rationally defensible solutions', to 'conscience-inspired thinking'; and rejected the former. My own view is that 'strategic thinking' can be useful provided it is subordinated to 'conscience-inspired thinking'.

41. The Pentagon at one point in 1965 began to finance a project called 'Camelot' to measure the prospects for left wing insurgency in developing countries. $4–6 million, 3–4 years, a staff of 20 were intended, and $300,000 were actually spent before local protests and complaints from Congress and from ambassadors on the spot caused its cancellation.

merits of thinking unflappably about the unthinkable. They appeared not to notice that in the heat of the crisis President Kennedy had reverted to Dulles-like threats of massive retaliation.[42] In fact the crisis was released by the purely political nous of Robert Kennedy, who discerned a negotiable strand in Khrushchev's communications, and negotiated it, ignoring the rest. As we shall see, the crisis had been largely self-administered by President Kennedy and Mr McNamara, with the second strike counterforce strategy which to them appeared so rational and to the Russian Government so immediately threatening. The scientists and economists went on to calculate just how much pressure must make North Vietnam 'hurt' enough to give in, ignoring the lessons of wartime London and Hamburg or of the 'emergency' in Malaya.

Clio, her altars all untended, her priests from office all suspended, was no doubt vowing vengeance, and in Vietnam it came, proving at last that everything had been a mistake all along.[43] Paediatricians and professors of linguistics sprang up to declare America wholly diseased, when what had happened was that two presidents had, vaingloriously, continued too long to suppose themselves well advised by dangerously mistrained men who promised a rational heaven and secured a nightmare. President Nixon has sensibly chosen an historian for his special adviser for national security affairs. There is no substitute for politics.

The singular run of failures in Vietnam and at home, ample proof that Washington did not understand the outside world, positively encouraged the growth of the second technique for depoliticizing politics. This was 'simulation' or 'gaming',[44] and it derives from the kinds of systems analysis which are indeed rewarding in cases where the elements can properly be quantified

42. See fn. 27, p. 179.

43. The only astonishing thing about the 'Pentagon Papers' is that anyone should have been astonished by them.

44. Andrew Wilson's book *The Bomb and the Computer* (London, 1968) is a fascinating history and critique of war-gaming. Russians by and large were not impressed with the new-fangled intellectual tools. Recently however (i.e. since Mr Brezhnev's conversion to the computer) a principal American

and conclusions mathematically expressed can make sense. For evaluating what *cannot* be quantified it is generally recognized that the human mind is a preferable tool. 'Games' were devised to make use of that for purposes of prediction and intellectual acclimatization.

The controller of a 'game', official or semi-official, relating to some plausible situation or crisis, will construct in detail an hypothetical scenario, using the very best advice and information and including if necessary high security material;[45] he also selects the most appropriate cast possible to act out the various human roles. Mr McNamara is said to have regularly participated in 'games' when he was Secretary of Defense; presumably he played himself. The game then happens, the controller from time to time injecting extraneous events. When it is over the various performances and outcomes are dissected and conclusions drawn. The effect hoped for is that the participants will be better 'sensitized' to the scale and scope and variety of the problems likely to arise from that particular situation or crisis, when, or if, it or ones like it occur in real life.

That the activity can be useful as part of a 'decision-maker's' training, a kind of group intellectual gymnastics, is obvious. That it has serious limitations as part of a 'decision-maker's' decision-making is equally obvious. Just as a computer is only as good as its data, a 'game' is only as good or as apposite as its participants, and as its scenario writers, and as its controller. If, which is not unlikely in Washington, they all share even a few

---

exponent is understood to have had a great personal success in conducting a 'game' actually in the Kremlin.

45. Information reached the Pentagon in substantial quantities. UPI reported for instance (*International Herald Tribune*, 27 September 1967) that it would 'soon have a world-wide communications capacity for transmitting six hundred million words a day. That is the equivalent of 40 million punched cards, and is equal to 22,222 words a day for each of the 27,000 persons who work in the Pentagon. The communications system involved is called "Autodin", for Automatic Digital Network.' Or for suicide by noise?

false assumptions, these will be reinforced three times over.[46]

American policy in the last twenty-five years has probably failed most often through insufficient insight into the mentality of non-WASP, non-American peoples and individuals. The courage and intelligent pertinacity of the North Vietnamese as a people and of General de Gaulle as an individual are two exemplary albatrosses round official Washington's neck which did not go 'ungamed' before they were shot at.

To the extent that 'games' are an attempt to synthesize experience and understanding of unfamiliar things and people from home-grown materials, they have at least to fail; they are very positively dangerous if they make the 'decision-maker' feel that he understands a person or a situation when he does not, if they encourage him to mistake simulated understanding and synthetic eventuality for the real thing. The only proper attitude in a decision-maker is one of alert, well informed, open-mindedness. In all forms of moral activity, which certainly includes the conduct of international relations, presumption that one's own knowledge and understanding are sufficient or that they are superior to any-one else's – the sense that one doesn't depend on what used to be called God's grace – is certainly and simply a mistake. Self-satisfaction and arrogance are, politically, accident-prone, as Chairman Mao has often pointed out;[47] their harbourer adopts, as Sir Karl Popper put it, an 'authoritarian attitude in the realm of opinion'[48] and eventually he is tempted, perhaps impelled, to impose his view by force or violence. I suspect that the rival ideologies of the sixties have each had as foundation this kind of

46. I think it was Sir Robert Thompson who remarked of American activity in Vietnam that whenever the effort was doubled, the error was cubed. That many people in Washington sensed that the prevailing 'scientific' methods were inadequate for doing defence and politics was revealed by the growing use of words and phrases like 'charisma' and 'gut feeling'.

47. In a 1943 essay entitled 'Some questions concerning methods of leadership' Chairman Mao emphasized how important it was to 'eliminate once and for all, the theory that the leadership is highly efficient'. The essay is being much quoted again now. See FE 3731/B11/1.

48. See K. R. Popper on 'Utopia and Violence' in *Conjecture and Refutations*, London, 1963, p. 357.

fantasy of certainty and superiority: too much of official Washington – administration, congress, press, consultants, academics, the lot – has believed that the more money spent = the better research = the superior understanding = the duty to lead = the right to leadership and to respectful and unquestioning assent from others. (The equivalent Russian fantasy being that the party leadership makes no mistakes because Marxism is a science and therefore guarantees prognosis or justifies the tailoring of eventualities.)

None of this is to suggest that government should not call upon real science in aid; on the contrary. The true nature of scientific activity I take to be (again in Popper's words) 'systematically to search for our mistakes, for our errors'[49] (and in Francis Bacon's) 'the love making or wooing of truth'.[50] Any scientist, and any scholar, knows that what he is pursuing, if he is indeed a scholar, is the 'Truth'. He also knows that his sense of the propriety and desirability of doing this is not itself a scientific fact, because it is not open to challenge and it is in no way provisional. This knowledge, and knowledge it is, can never be refuted because the only possible refutation would itself be done in the name of truth – '. . . truth, which only doth judge itself'.[51] Even the determinist does not defend his contention by claiming that it is the only response he is able to make.

Optimistically, one might say that the last quarter of a century has seen Western Europe almost fully occupied 'systematically searching for our mistakes, for our errors' – rather than 'love-making' with the truth. At the present time, apart from Portugal's continuing imperial pretensions, and the trade in arms, no Western European government is conducting its foreign relations other than reasonably and harmlessly. France's imperial days

49. 'Conversations with Philosophers' (Sir Karl Popper talks about some of his basic ideas with Bryan Magee), *The Listener*, 7 January 1971. Probably both Khrushchev and Eisenhower would have agreed that this activity is desirable also in statesmen.

50. Francis Bacon, *Essay on Truth*.

51. Francis Bacon, op. cit.

seem hardly regretted, and conservative nostalgia in Britain is never likely again to crystalize into Suez-type folly. For the most part, governments are conducting their foreign relations in the light of developing events, and in terms of an adjustable sense of national interest. The results are not brilliant, but for the most part they are decently constructive and alert and nowhere murderous. The foreign policy questions that arise are in fact more like the internal problems of larger units than the kind of thing ambassadors extraordinary and ministers plenipotentiary used to deal with in the old days. I am thinking of the problems of spaceship earth's environment, those posed by the fact and behaviour of the multinational companies, by the needs of developing countries, even of regional economic relations. In dealing with these, European governments do not seem hampered or hamstrung by old theologies or new scepticisms.

Nor, interestingly enough, do the Chinese. About theory the Chinese government is extraordinarily explicit: indeed, it has recently been putting its people through a massive course in practical philosophy, in favour of 'Mao Tse-tung thought', against 'idealistic *a priorism*', and particularly against Kant. Any day now, Hegel will be given a great toss; and even Lenin, as theorist, may eventually be found wanting. (See the passage quoted from *Materialism and Empiro-Criticism*, p. 143). The purpose of the cultural revolution's great shake-up was, I have argued, to recall to each of China's hundreds of millions of individuals his own responsibility: in the first instance, if the United States launched nuclear war through North Vietnam into China, and then if the Russians did so from the North. Today the individual's responsibility is the development of the national economy, and Chairman Mao's teaching *On Practice*, which is ceaselessly repeated in the press and on the air in so many words, and in the form of stories and examples, precepts and mottoes, is this:

If a man wants to succeed in his work, that is, to achieve the anticipated results, he must bring his ideas into correspondence with the laws of the objective external world; if they do not correspond, he will fail in his practice. After he fails, he draws his lessons, corrects his ideas to make them correspond to the laws of the external world, and can thus turn failure into success. This is what is meant by 'Failure is the mother of success' and 'a fall into the pit, a gain in your wit'.

Another Mao precept is: 'Discover the truth through practice, and again, through practice, verify and develop the truth.'

Man's correct ideas come from social practice, and from it alone, and they can turn into a material force only through social practice. . . . The revolutionary movement of the proletariat is the source of Marxism–Leninism, and Marxism–Leninism is the compass for the proletarian revolutionary movement . . . the reason Marx, Engels, Lenin and Stalin were able to work out their theories 'was mainly that they personally took part in the practice of the class struggle and the scientific experimentation of their time'; we attach great importance to the role of Marxism–Leninism, not because its founders were 'prophets', but 'solely because it is the science which leads the revolutionary cause of the proletariat to victory', and it has proved itself correct in our struggle.[52]

Chairman Mao is the only leader of a major state who has himself sought to train his people in philosophical method, to get them to ask themselves, on a national scale, 'where do correct ideas come from?' and to ask them to answer that question with modesty and prudence, and to avoid 'pride and complacency'. Whether this is how it works out will not be clear until far more travellers have brought news out of China. If the result of the cultural revolution is a nation of philosophers, the world will never be the same again: we shall have an answer to '*Quis custodiet ipsos custodes?*' Perhaps the lap of the gods is vast enough.

There are certainly implications for arms control in Mao *On Practice*: Chinese declaratory policy on arms control, as we have seen, is coherent and reasonable, but so far it has been expressed only in very general terms. One cannot forecast how much of Mao Tse-tung's thought will survive Mao's death, or how Chinese governments then will address the two base problems of arms control: that of ascertaining and demonstrating that what is

52. *Red Flag* on Mao's criticism of 'Idealist Conception of History', 10 November 1971, P E 3837/B/II/6. There is no suggestion that if it ever fails to prove itself correct 'in the social practice', it will not itself be corrected 'to correspond to the laws of the external world'.

said is so, and that of devising cooperative coexistence. Today, prospects for both are reasonably good, provided Mao-thought survives Mao: although apparently so highly personalized, it is not a hierarchic or class doctrine, like the Brezhnev doctrine of 'proletarian internationalism', the hub and nub of which is the CPSU's pre-eminence in rights and duties.

Among the more indicative Sino-Soviet bones of contention is the right size for enterprises, the Russians yearning for novelty and magnitude, the Chinese for convenience without waste. Mr Brezhnev's desire to computerize the economy of the Soviet Union, and perhaps CMEA and the Warsaw Pact, and run everything from Moscow, is an ambition no ruler of eight hundred million people would dream of envisaging: Mr Brezhnev's plans are alarming not because they will succeed, but because they will fail, and chaos in a country as heavily armed, as nationally diverse, and as politically inexperienced as the Soviet Union is an alarming prospect. International life with China should not be half so difficult – unless China is, as some China-watchers today believe, in the invisible throes of yet another phase of the inevitable revolution. Meanwhile Chairman Mao's message for 1972 begins: 'Affairs of the world require consultations. The internal affairs of a country must be settled by the people of that country, and international affairs must be settled by all concerned through consultation. They must not be decided by the two big powers.' (*Peking joint New Year's Day Editorial*. 31 December 1971. FE 3877/C2/1.)

10

Fashion: The Changing View from the Bandwagon

(i) *1961–2 The Missile Gap and Cuba*

Particularly in the United States, defence and foreign policy evolve within a rapidly changing climate of opinion. Shifts in this climate seem to be the result of internal changes at least as much as of changes in the outer world the opinions purport to be about. A precise metaphor is hard to find: there is something of the ebb and flow of the tide, there is something of seasonal change; there is also a delay mechanism, the perception of one particular situation only coming into full effect when that first situation has already been overtaken by another. Thus the cold war climate in the United States survived Stalin into Khrushchev's reign when détente and agreement, hindsight suggests, were not impossible. Now, when détente, in the sense of unfettered mutual interaction at all levels, appears, for a variety of telling reasons,[1] to be the last thing the Soviet Government wants, the prevailing climate, except among the very alert and well-informed, holds that détente is perfectly feasible provided the West rejects 'cold-war' attitudes.

During the last ten or twelve years, the opinion shift-about has particularly affected American views about the nuclear arms race. Such shifts take place in that residue of information and understanding and forgetting into which the news settles as it reaches one day by day; it colours that news and only too often distorts it, or at least misplaces or misfiles it. A nutshell of the shift-about is that ten or so years ago one very seldom saw an article published in a non-radical American periodical which argued methodically

1. Some of which we have examined in the last chapter.

that the Russians were not hell-bent arms-racing; and that in the last two or three years of the sixties it was just about equally unusual to see the view put in such a place that the United States was not hell-bent arms-racing. The sump of public consciousness, which retained residual cold war sludge long after Khrushchev had denounced Stalin, now retains residual thaw sludge long after Khrushchev has gone and the Soviet system has begun, ideologically and militarily, to freeze up again. Some news travels slowly.

In this chapter I shall be examining a few occasions and attitudes from the period before President Johnson's foreign policies collapsed. My argument is that that collapse was due as much to the beer available on the intellectual bandwagon of the time, as to the ruts in the road it travelled.

In 1960 John F. Kennedy fought and won the presidency on the issue of a Missile Gap dangerously in the Soviet Union's favour, and although it was confirmed by the first reconnaissance satellite that there was no such thing (and Mr McNamara admitted as much in a press conference)[2] the new President chose to allow the misconception to stand. Indeed, during spring 1961 he increased the Minuteman order, among others, and of course the defence budget as a whole, and appointed General Curtis LeMay, the Commander of SAC (Strategic Air Command) Air Force Chief of Staff – whom Eisenhower had kept well away from the levers of power. The misconception about the missile gap effectively stood in the public mind until the Cuba crisis, when the fact of America's vast nuclear preponderance was branded there, perhaps for all time, along with a renewed awareness of America's own, quite physical, vulnerability to Russian military attack. The desperate disillusionment with President Kennedy's idealized gendarmism[3] that the United States suffered in President Johnson's last year, and the huge defence monies that were being

2. See Hanson Baldwin, *New York Times*, 12 February 1961. The missile gap had apparently been known by the CIA not to exist the preceding summer. Allen Dulles, who had been Director of the CIA at the time, in March 1963 admitted the overestimations.
3. See fn. 1, p. 12 for a telling passage from his inauguration speech.

poured into Vietnam during the late sixties, tended to mask the fact that American strategic nuclear forces were no longer expanding and that the Russian forces were expanding very fast indeed. Now, in the arms control field, the few who in the early sixties had been pressing for American restraint, and those many who out of closeness to the Kennedy administration did not so press but have subsequently felt they erred, have gone on pressing for American restraint[4] without noticing that the post-Khrushchev Russians have become as zealous arms-racers as President Kennedy and his appointees had been in 1961–2. The 'New Left' unrest in the universities, and Black Power, anti-Draft and Peace Movements, all Gene McCarthy and Bobby Kennedy's nationwide constituencies, gave politically powerful backing and reinforcement to the change of mind and consciousness of guilt of a number of conspicuous and vocal Kennedy appointees. The rather specialist arguments and convictions of these latter became nationally and internationally important partly because of this mass backing, partly because of the pandemic of doubt and suspicion in which the Johnson presidency ended, and partly of course because Congress too wanted to rewrite its contribution to the débâcle.

This body of opinion (which though diminishing still exists) has sought to lay the blame not only for the Vietnam war but also for the uncertainty and the alarm which so much power the arms race exclusively on American administration shoulders. Those who in Washington and the universities had earlier accepted that America was the greatest, did not change their basic proposition: they merely added 'threat to world peace' and went on assuming their country all-powerful.

What was blameworthy is, in fact, rather precise. Before the days of accurate photographic information from satellites, there was room for very considerable disagreement about what nuclear and other forces the Russians actually had deployed, and even

4. An attitude much praised in Russian propaganda, which for instance claimed at the time of the Chappaquiddick incident that Edward Kennedy was being vindictively prosecuted for dangerous driving on that occasion because of his opposition to the Safeguard A B M programme.

more about what they might be in process of acquiring. The situation was basically asymmetrical – and is still – because while a great deal of precise information about defence matters is publicly available in the West very little indeed is available in the East. It is clear that some parties to assessment in the United States were taking gross advantage of the prevailing uncertainty to press wild claims to a larger share of resources. This was the 'military industrial complex' which President Eisenhower referred to in his farewell speech.[5] The scare of the 'bomber gap', discerned in the mid-fifties by the United States Air Force, was founded on a fly-past near Moscow at which wave after wave of bombers passed overhead, assiduously being counted by the air attachés. The Americans present apparently did not consult their watches, which would have alerted them to the possibility that not very many bombers were flying round and round and round and being counted again and again and again. The attachés were able to report alarming, most satisfactorily alarming, figures. It was later 'discovered' that the Russian bombers had indeed been counted more than once, but by that time new orders for American bombers had been approved. This is the version recalled, straight-faced, in terms of exclusively Russian duplicity, in *Strategic Power and Soviet Foreign Policy*, by A. L. Horelick and Myron Rush,[6] a book concerned, not very successfully, with 'documenting' Khrushchev's 'grand deception of the West'. Such a judgement holds no water – the deceivability of the deceived was too culpable and energetic – but it was quite generally accepted when it was being advanced in the early and mid-sixties. It was then succeeded by the view, which Mr McNamara came to hold, that secrecy was a true strategic concern of the Soviet Union, justifiably, or at least understandably, used to counter-balance Ameri-

5. He also warned against the build-up of a technical-scientific complex which might seek to exercise actual power, instead of just tendering advice to those whom the people had elected.

6. A Rand Corporation Research Study, Chicago University Press, 1966. Having reviewed this book rather sharply in the *Bulletin of the Atomic Scientists*, I was interested to hear that the authors' friends were describing me as a 'Limey Communist'.

can nuclear plenty; a judgement which was certainly fair – if short-sighted – during the mid-sixties.[7]

However, increasing nuclear parity has not led to any reduction in Russian secrecy, and seems unlikely to do so for the political, quite non-strategic, reasons we have seen. Nevertheless, in the recent American dispute[8] about whether the Soviet Union is digging pits to put new and yet larger missiles into, or whether the pits are for a hardened version of the already gigantic SS9 missile, the secretiveness of the Russian Government has not been mentioned as the actual occasion of the dispute. The Pentagon, in well-informed leaks from inside the official machine, has been blamed for exaggerated pessimism, the CIA reported counter-blamed for precocious optimism. It is likely that the quality of the evidence for the time being precludes firm judgement; but actually to discuss the problem of Russian secretiveness at all seriously would raise the subject of verification, a dog that optimists in the American arms control scene prefer to leave sleeping.

By and large we must, I think, pin total responsibility on the Soviet Union for not making public matters which in the West are rightly acknowledged to be the public's close concern, and for the consequent uncertainty and pessimistic interpretations of their activities in the world's defence establishments. The grounds for their aversion to making things public is neither here nor there: to my mind it is undoubtedly the prime fuel for the continuation now of the arms race, and for the dim prospects there are for arms control and disarmament.

It is also necessary to pin subsequent responsibility on the American services and defence industry, and in the case of the 'missile gap' on President Kennedy and Mr McNamara, for exaggerating and prolonging the Russian-created uncertainty. The original responsibility was Russian; it was compounded in

7. A time when it was becoming rather acceptable in leftish academic circles to believe that the Soviet Union, being a super-power too, must, or at least ought to be, or at least could be assumed to be, very like the United States. People were beginning to draft their 'convergence' books.

8. March–October 1971.

Washington, the better to pursue the arms race, which in the early sixties almost all establishment people, countrywide, considered only patriotic and right. Such was the climate of opinion in 1961 and 1962 that several of today's most prominent doves, particularly but not only among the scientists, retained their very close connections with the Kennedy administration in spite of its unprecedented and obvious acceleration of the arms race.

Mr McNamara made the major speech of his career at Ann Arbor at the University of Michigan on 16 June 1962. In this speech he announced a new strategy for the United States:

In future, to the extent feasible, basic military strategy in a possible general nuclear war should be approached in much the same way that more conventional military operations have been regarded in the past. That is to say, the principal military objective, in the event of a nuclear war stemming from a major attack on the alliance, should be the destruction of the enemy's military forces, not of his civilian population. The very strength and nature of the alliance forces make it possible for us to retain, even in the face of massive surprise attack, sufficient reserve striking power to destroy an enemy's society if driven to it. In other words, we are giving a possible opponent the strongest imaginable incentive to refrain from striking our own cities.

He also made clear that in his view the United States did have the capability to do exactly this. The speech, which was one of a series by Mr McNamara and his aides in the Pentagon which stressed the astonishingly vast nuclear and other forces being acquired by the United States, was greeted by the political and scientific intelligentsia inside the United States as announcing a more rational and humane strategy than President Eisenhower's administration had professed.

A few individuals considered it quite misconceived.[9] In the Soviet Union it was read, as it could not but be, in conjunction

9. Including Henry Kissinger in the United States and Wayland Young in the United Kingdom. In Whitehall the new strategy seems to have been disliked, but principally on the rather parochial grounds that it dismissed small independent nuclear forces as mischievous.

with the hardware deployed and on order,[10] as a first strike policy to go with a first strike force: if the US Government believed its forces, even *after* a 'major attack,' to be capable of the 'destruction of the enemy's military forces', of what did they not consider them capable *before* such an attack? The Russian nuclear capability for hitting the United States at the time the Kennedy administration came in was, according to the ISS *Military Balance*, 35 ICBMs and 185 long-range bombers: the threat implicit in Mr McNamara's speech was not provoked by any headlong Russian nuclear procurement. According to Deputy Secretary Gilpatric,[11] the new strategy was the result of 'an earlier period of study and debate which made it possible for the new administration to move forward on its defence programme with speed and confidence in 1961. Issues such as survivability, non-nuclear options and controlled response had been extensively examined for several years prior to 1961.' There was no effective objection to the new strategy, which had been sketched out to NATO allies some months before; there was no anticipation of any particularly troublesome reaction to it on the part of the Russians. It is even possible that the implicit threat had not been perceived in Washington: Marquis Childs reported[12] that Mr McNamara was wounded and surprised at anyone interpreting his Ann Arbor speech as 'implying that the United States might ... strike first to knock out an enemy's bases'.

Just a few weeks later, an unusual number of ships were noticed passing through the Dardanelles and making their way towards Cuba. In September and October it became clear that Russian medium-range missiles were being set up in Cuba, such as would certainly 'spoil', by confusing, any attempted American first strike against the Soviet Union. President Kennedy is reported by

10. On 2 May 1962, Mr McNamara's Deputy Secretary, Roswell Gilpatric, had explained that when completed in 1965 this force would comprise 950 long-range bombers, 800 air-to-surface missiles (like Hound Dog and Skybolt) and 1,500 intercontinental missiles, including Atlas, Titan, Minuteman and Polaris. This would be double the 'alert weapons' and double the megatonnage of 1962.

11. *Foreign Affairs*, April 1964, p. 375.

12. *Washington Post*, 13 July 1962.

Adam Yarmolinsky to have not regarded the 'placement of missiles in Cuba as a military problem. It was a political problem.'[13] At the time, and for several years afterwards, his management of the Cuba crisis was looked on as quite masterly, and full justification of all the labour of the strategic community. The very topic of 'crisis management' acquired special glamour, and even six years later a reviewer in the *Times Literary Supplement* could write of the 'sober, Churchillian self-confidence of Kennedy' and declare that the judgement of the day, that 'the President scarcely put a foot wrong', can now be fully confirmed.[14]

Mr McNamara did not include the text of the speech which launched the Cuba Crisis in the collection of speeches and Reports to Congress, which he published in 1968 under the title *The Essence of Security, Reflections in Office*.[15] He may well have come to feel about that speech, indeed about the whole period, as Mr Fulbright has come to feel about the Tonkin Bay Resolution. In the epilogue to his book Mr McNamara wrote, 'Man does have the unhappy ability to stare at the obvious, and then deliberately to retreat into escapist dreams'; he does not identify any 'obvious' that he himself may have 'deliberately' retreated from. Rather oddly, Mr McNamara, who remained deeply involved with the Vietnam war almost to the end, and one of whose last announcements as President Johnson's Secretary of Defense was for an area Ballistic Missile Defence of the United States, was largely exempt from the ferocious anger that Kennedy Democrats have heaped on Lyndon Johnson and Dean Rusk and Walt Rostow. (The publication in 1971 of the 'Pentagon Papers' tarnished his image for a while.) The exemption derived partly perhaps from the fact that that part of the military which most distrusted or disliked Mr McNamara's methods and his computers and whizz-kids have not stopped recalling his mistakes (the TFX 111 – or F 111 – aircraft business in particular is still very much alive), and

13. *War/Peace Report*, December 1968, p. 7. Mr Yarmolinsky was one of McNamara's brightest, closest, and least apolitical whizzkid appointees.

14. Anonymous reviewer, *Times Literary Supplement*, 11 June 1967.

15. Hodder and Stoughton, London, 1968.

the enemy of the military can hardly be the enemy of the doves. Also, his last major speech as Secretary of Defense, given in San Francisco on 18 September 1967, not only announced an ABM programme directed against a possible Chinese attack, but was also something of an *apologia pro vita sua*, and something of a collective recollective fudge of the issues in which the Kennedy people had been closely implicated.[16] About 1961, he said – and this speech *is* included in the 1968 book – 'the blunt fact remains that if we had had more accurate information about planned Soviet strategic forces, we simply would not have needed to build as large a nuclear arsenal as we have today.'[17] Earlier in the speech he even claimed that that arsenal was 'greater than we had originally planned', but there had been no sign in 1961 and 1962 of any original plan to which the Ann Arbor strategy was a regretted alternative. Indeed, its absoluteness was to be the beauty of the doctrine and of the policy. On the certainties of that time, and on the confidence in their own rationality that the Kennedy administration displayed, possible Russian actions and reactions seemed to have no bearing at all. The climate of the day was all-pervasive, impenetrable and even the Cuba crisis, self-inflicted, dangerous, and unnecessary, swiftly acquired a frosting of myth from the general headiness of the atmosphere.

16. He also participated after his retirement in the work of a committee which published a pamphlet, under the authorship of George W. Rathgens (late of the Institute for Defense Analysis and of the United States Arms Control and Disarmament Agency). This pamphlet, *The Future of the Strategic Arms Race*, appeared in the very early days of the Nixon administration and was the foundation document of the Kennedy Democrat campaign against the American ABM programme. It must have been at this time too that he commissioned the top secret study of Pentagon papers, parts of which have recently been published by a series of American newspapers. The political purpose of this gathering of documents and the identity of its compilers are, at the moment of writing, still obscure. As Richard Harwood puts it, writing in the *International Herald Tribune* on 30 June 1971, 'The substance and sometimes the precise details of virtually everything the *Washington Post* and the *New York Times* have printed from the *Pentagon Papers* is ancient history. It was nearly all published while it was happening. And it was largely a futile enterprise; neither the public nor the Congressional politicians were listening.'

17. op. cit., p. 58.

(ii) *1964 The Bay of Tonkin*

America's doves of today have not always been doves. In August 1964, when Mr Johnson was seeking a reason for bombing North Vietnam, Mr Fulbright, already Chairman of the Senate Foreign Relations Committee, willingly accepted a story that North Vietnamese PT boats had attacked a couple of American destroyers which happened to be in the Bay of Tonkin (close to China and North Vietnam) and that these events justified not only immediate retaliatory bombing, but also the equally immediate issuing of Mr Johnson with a blank cheque from the Senate for military action in the whole of South East Asia. The events took place on 2 and 3 August and a collation of Mr McNamara's public statements at the time showed that the reputed sequence of events was highly implausible and that the North Vietnamese attack was not only not confirmed, but quite possibly had not happened.[18] It was also clear that 'retaliation' had been not only authorized, but also administered, before Washington's 'prior warning' and ultimatum could have been received in Hanoi. The climate of opinion in Washington and the country at the time was such that Senator Fulbright and the Senate did not think twice before voting a carte-blanche resolution (with precisely two dissentients),[19] an earlier text of which President Johnson is said to maintain had actually been drafted by the Senate leadership itself.[20] Senator Fulbright remarked in 1971 that 'the great tragedy of the Johnson administration was its subversion of the constitutional war-making responsibilities of the Congress by false information and deception. The fault of Congress including this speaker was in believing the President of the United States, in having too much confidence in a man and neglecting to insist upon the full exercise of the constitutional powers of the Congress.'[21] He is still Chairman of the Foreign Relations

18. See Wayland Young, *Guardian*, 11 August 1964.
19. Senators Wayne Morse of Oregon and Ernest Gruening of Alaska; both failed to be re-elected the next time they stood.
20. *Newsweek*, 28 June 1971.
21. *Guardian*, 19 April 1971.

Committee, and obviously, and explicitly, deeply regrets his folly in August 1964. But he also claims to have been guiltless at the time, to have been misled by a wicked administration instead of having been blameworthily, if fashionably, credulous.[22] Senator Fulbright is now unwilling to believe the new administration's word, and is seeking to enlarge the foreign and defence responsibilities of the Senate, and particularly of his own committee. However, compunction to save America from another Tonkin Bay Resolution is not in itself a guarantee of sound judgement, any more than Anthony Eden's determination to protect the world from another Hitler proved his judgement right at Suez. Mr Fulbright's opinion of other governments seems to remain quite relaxed (the Russian Government's professions he appears still to take at face value); his conduct of hearings on anti-ballistic missiles suggests that he does not much believe in the recent expansion in Russian nuclear capability; he has even, although no friend to government censorship at home, been urging the administration to discontinue support of Radio Free Europe, which pierces government censorship in Eastern Europe, on the grounds that it offends the Soviet Government.[23] When

22. Shortly after the Tonkin Bay affair, Professor Thomas Schelling, whose stylish and rather sado-masochist writings had brought him many admirers among students of international affairs, wrote: 'A good way to describe the American response is that it was unambiguous. It was articulate. It contained a pattern. If someone asks what the United States did when its destroyers were attacked in the Gulf of Tonkin, there is no disagreement about the answer. One can state the time, the targets, and the weapons used. Nobody supposes that the United States just happened to have an attack on those North Vietnamese ports planned for that day; and nobody is in any doubt about precisely what military action was directly related to the attack on the destroyers. When a dog on a farm kills a chicken, I understand that the dead chicken is tied around the dog's neck' (*Arms and Influence*, Yale University Press, 1966, pp. 145–6). We have had the theatre of cruelty. This book was the politics of cruelty – another conceptual casualty of the Vietnam war: the Vietcong have not been 'compelled' by being hurt, as, according to the then prevailing theory, they had to be.

23. I hold no brief for what I am told are the cold war opinions of Radio Free Europe; but I would prefer to see it put out of business by the abolition of censorship in Russia and Eastern Europe than by the act of the American Government.

long-term loyal Kennedy administration men like J. K. Galbraith continue to warn the American public against that military-industrial complex whose doings they went along with while in office,[24] one is put in mind of a horse bellowing 'bolt the door' as it gallops off, far, far away from the stable.[25]

The disclosures in the 'Pentagon papers' seem to confirm that the conduct of the Vietnam war was throughout in civilian-appointee, rather than military-industrial hands. By 1969, secret research for the Department of Defence in universities was already down to half what it had been two years before, and amounted to about $10 million out of the more than $5 billion the United States was altogether spending on research that financial year. The great defence firms were already doing not too well. *Newsweek* ran a big story on them on 9 June 1969. 'Their profit on each dollar of defense sales was 4.2 cents versus an average for all United States industry of 8.7 cents . . . annual earnings on each dollar of invested capital, slipping steadily over the last decade, averaged 7.3 cents versus 10.1 cents for industry as a whole.' Wall Street's attitude to defence stocks was, said *Newsweek*, 'lukewarm: "Sure, they're cheap. But who's to say they won't stay cheap?"' Private stockbroking advice compilations were discouraging investment in the defence-related industry, except, and then only for the long-sighted investor, in those firms which were diversifying into civil and military submarine technologies. Employment in the aerospace industries decreased from well over 1,400,000 in 1967, to about 950,000 in 1971, i.e. by one third.[26]

24. J. K. Galbraith, *How to Control the Military*, NCLC Publishing, London, 1970. Professor Galbraith was President Kennedy's Ambassador to India.

25. I am not suggesting military follies are no longer being committed, only that whereas ten years ago to question the strategic intelligentsia was, among intellectuals, *lèse majesté*, recently academic opinion has held it to be virtually *de rigueur*.

26. *Aviation Week and Space Technology*, 12 July 1971.

(iii) *1967–8 The ABM Debate*

THEORY

It may seem excessively severe to examine the 1968–9 ABM debate in terms of fashion and climate. It is useful to do so because that debate illustrates the complexity with which a decision, in itself politically not too abstruse, can be invested by the participation in it of people who are in the toils of an intellectual or a political fashion.

The decision about ABM that President Nixon and the Senate had to take was agitated by strong gales of disagreement. At issue were the following questions:

To what extent and in what configurations was ABM technically possible?

To what extent and in which configurations was ABM relevant to the American military posture versus the Soviet Union and versus China, and to its relations with its allies and client states?

How, and again in which configurations, did United States ABM relate to arms control and disarmament issues?

To what extent and in which configurations was ABM budgetarily significant within the United States Government expenditure?

To what extent was it important in American party political terms?

The language of strategic analysis cannot at this point quite be avoided. How real a language this is, in the sense of how well and how fully do its users realize and accept all the implications of the words and concepts they use, is difficult to say. It seems indicative to me of its *unreality* that during the Cuban missile crisis (the nearest the super-powers have ever come to nuclear exchange), when the new strategic language and concepts had been in theoretical use for several years, President Kennedy should have reverted to the theoretically long rejected Dulles language of massive retaliation.[27]

27. In his broadcast on Monday, 22 October, he warned the Soviet Union that if 'any nuclear missile' were fired out of Cuba at any nation in the

The accepted analysis of *nuclear balance* is roughly speaking this:[28] *deterrence* is *stable* and in balance when each side knows that his *first strike* attack will trigger *second strike* retaliation, either *countervalue* against his own cities or *counterforce* against such forces as he may not have used in his *first strike* or both. The possession of a *second strike counter force capability* necessarily implies the possession of a *first strike counterforce capability* (an undamaged whole being larger than a remaining part).

Cities tend to be *soft* targets, because they are easier to hit, being well known and large and more vulnerable than *counterforce* targets, which are, comparatively, *hard*, being smaller and more difficult to hit, and easier to protect and hide.

Hitting cities is considered the ultimate *escalation*.

If an aggressor believed himself able to disarm his opponent by destroying his *retaliatory* forces in a *counterforce first strike*, he might be tempted to try, or to threaten, to do so.

It is therefore important for *stability* that both sides' strategic forces should be as *invulnerable* to a *first strike* as possible by being as *hard* as possible.

Moreover, any offensive forces which are not *hard*, are open to being interpreted as intended as *first strike only* weapons and as such are *destabilizing*.[29] As part of a national *catalytic* system, small vulnerable strategic forces may have a political or military function for lesser allies as mitigant to the monopoly in decision-making of a super-power ally. The super-power will consider them destabilizing. See Chapter IV.

The *nuclear balance* then is *stable* – and stability is the best that can reasonably be hoped for in a world of nuclear powers – when each of the two sides understands that it cannot with impunity launch a major attack because the other side has an *assured des-*

Western hemisphere, this would '[require] a full retaliatory response upon the Soviet Union'.

28. This analysis is only applicable to an effectively bipolar world, such as that of the 1960s, to which a lot of the current conventional wisdom is decidedly over-geared.

29. An example of such a force was the American missile *Thor* which used to be deployed in Eastern England and which was so very vulnerable to attack that it made no sense as part of a retaliatory system.

truction capability. Each side will of course watch the other to see if it is becoming technologically able for any reason to develop a *first strike capability*. This it might do in either of two ways: 1) by acquiring weapons in enough numbers, weight, accuracy, or speed[30] to destroy the other side's *second strike forces* and so preclude retaliation; and 2) by setting up an *anti-ballistic missile area defence* system, *thick* enough to absorb and destroy the other side's retaliatory *second strike forces* before they can reach their targets.[31]

The side which fears that its opponent is acquiring a *first strike capability* can react in several ways:

1) by acquiring more *second strike* weapons;

2) by making these *second strike* weapons better able to *penetrate* the other side's *ABM area defences*;

30. Speed: bombers can never have the speed to participate in a *first strike* though they can in a *second strike*; except perhaps against certain naval targets. See fn. 3, p. 131.

31. *Civil Defence* also has a place here, in the *first strike* posture, because its likely efficacy is strictly proportionate to the time available to put it into effect. The party launching a *first strike* necessarily has longer to set its civil defence arrangements, such as evacuation, in motion than the party suffering a *first strike*. There is a very substantial *civil defence* programme in the Soviet Union which, when it was set up in its new form in 1967, Marshal Chuikov referred to it as 'a major type of strategic safeguard' (*Soviet News*, 20 June 1967). It is compulsorily taught to 'the population' as well as in schools which are supposed to have a 'military lecture room' and a 'military equipment room'. In the 'ninth form' the subject is allocated '35 hours', according to Minsk Radio, 25 December 1970. Evacuation is also practised by factory workers and their families: and according to the Soviet First Deputy Chief of Staff for Civil Defence: 'Our country possesses everything necessary for the successful implementation of measures for evacuating the population. A planned national economy, extensive territory and well-managed transport all make it possible to carry out evacuation measures quickly.' (Moscow Home Service, S U 3263/B/2, 22 December 1969). 'A month-long programme of films about civil defence began in towns and villages of Kirghizia on 15 March ... last year more than 600,000 young people had participated in mass defence work ...' (Frunze Radio, 15 March 1971). After a brief spurt of enthusiasm in the United States in 1961, the topic has been virtually dropped. John E. Davis, U S 'Civil Defense Director', was quoted (*U S News and World Report*) in March 1970 as saying: 'In the absence of an international crisis, civil defense does not stir public interest.'

3) by making them more likely to survive a *first strike*. This last can be done:

(a) by putting them in submarines, where they will be both mobile and difficult to locate;

(b) by making them mobile on land;

(c) by further physically *hardening* their launching pads;

(d) by giving them *hard point ABM defences*.

The first and second of these possibilities would be no different from any other acquisition of more or more effective offensive weapons. Such acquisition therefore could be interpreted by the other side's strategic planners, whose job, as Mr McNamara has pointed out, is to 'prepare for the *worst possible case*',[32] not as a justifiable reaction to a perceived threat, but rather as an attempt to gain some new margin in the nuclear arms race. It would be provocative.

In the third group of reactions, (a) and (b) would probably involve the construction of new delivery systems and therefore, like 1 and 2, would be open to pessimistic interpretation as being of offensive significance. All these, 1, 2, and 3 (a) and (b), would necessarily be destabilizing and provocative. On the other hand, 3(c) (more steel and concrete etc. in silos), and (d) the local deployment of a number of nuclear missiles of such demonstrated range and character as not to allow them to reach the other side's territory, are not open to pessimistic interpretation and consequently are not destabilizing or provocative.

ABM defences appear in this analysis in two places: they can be used either (1) as part of a *first strike posture*, when they are intended to provide *area defence* against the anticipated retaliation of the other side's *second strike* forces; or (2) they can be part of a *second strike posture* when they are deployed to protect *second strike* retaliatory forces. The suggestion sometimes made that increasing the invulnerability of retaliatory forces alters the balance and therefore must be destabilizing is wrong: any reduction in either side's *first strike capability* cannot fail to improve overall stability. This distinction between *area defence ABM* which is part of a *first strike posture*, and *ABM hard point defence*

32. op. cit., p. 58.

which is part of a *second strike posture* should be kept in mind during our examination of the ABM debate of 1967–9.

So should the essential asymmetry of the *worst possible case* calculations concerning the two types of ABM deployment. A party contemplating launching a *first strike* must calculate that the other side's *hard point ABM*, which his *counterforce strike* has to *penetrate* if his strike is to be successful, will perform at effective capacity, which could be as low as sixty per cent or even thirty per cent.[33] Equally, he must assume in his calculations that his own *area ABM defences*, that is those which are to protect his own society, will perform at minimum capacity. From this it follows that *hard-point ABM defences* can have a dissuasive effect against a *first strike attack* even if they are not technologically first rate; *area ABM defences*, on the other hand, to encourage a *first strike attack* must positively be technologically first-rate. In fact, of course, neither the United States nor the Soviet Union has been able to test *anti-ballistic missile defences* of either type with any high degree of verisimilitude. This means that uncertainty obtains, and neither side can count on having correctly calculated. Seeing that the success of a *first strike* is more dependent on correct calculations than is a *retaliatory strike*, in this case uncertainty contributes positively to *stability* – that is, it contributes to deterring either side from launching a first strike.

A third distinction concerns the implications of ABM for other members of an alliance. *Area defences* protect exclusively the areas protected, which are likely to be (and in the case of the Sentinel programme which Mr McNamara announced in September 1967 were) exclusively the super-power's national territory. *Hard point defences* protect those forces which deter attack not only on the super-power's national territory, but on that of its allies as well.

As we have seen in 1962 the Russian Government, not unreasonably exercising '*worst possible case*' type pessimism, seems to have interpreted Mr McNamara's new doctrine, coupled as it

33. Harold M. Agnew, director of Los Alamos Scientific Laboratory in testimony to Senate Armed Services Committee quoted in *Aviation Week and Space Technology*, 26 April 1971.

was with massive procurement of strategic weapons, as a declaration that the United States was acquiring a *first strike capability*. (In the explicitly declared American *second strike counterforce* capability there was necessarily implicit a *first strike counterforce capability*.)

It is fairly clear that as a result of this discomfiting insight the Russian Government not only sought immediately to install short-range strategic weapons in Cuba, but also set about reaching at least parity of nuclear capability with the United States as soon as possible; and has now, by and large, done so. The 1970 *SIPRI Yearbook* notes that the Russian rate of increase in ICBMs deployed, from 1966 to 1969, was about the same as that in the United States from 1961 to 1963.[34] One may assume that between 1962 and 1966 the new Russian weapons were being researched, designed, tooled up for, and tested: at a VE Day 20th Anniversary Parade on 9 May 1965 several of them were displayed for the first time.

In 1968 and 1969 the time came for the United States Government to judge whether the Soviet Union was intending with its new deployments to achieve nuclear parity with the United States, or nuclear superiority: the theoretical blueprint of the requirements of nuclear stability had to be compared with actual events. There was now, thanks to observation satellites, pretty fair certainty about actual numbers of Russian weapons deployed and some certainty about their size and weight-lifting capability. There remained almost complete uncertainty about what might be on the Russian drawing boards, or in the production pipeline, or inside the missiles, or being tested underground; or of course what might be in the Russian Government's minds, now or in the future, about final numbers and purposes. As in 1961 when the last lot of major American strategic decisions were taken, there remained great scope for subjective interpretation of what was actually known of the situation on the Russian side of the hill: as for the future, to quote SIPRI again, 'it is impossible to say

34. *SIPRI Year book of World Armaments and Disarmament*, 1969–70, p. 41. From these figures it is clear that both Eisenhower and Krushchev each in his day successfully reined in their arms race enthusiasts.

what policy as regards the acquisition of strategic weapons the Soviet Union will follow.'[35] This has allowed hectic alarm to be expressed by the 'hawks', angry complacency by the 'doves' and puzzled distress by the 'owls' – if these are the wise birds of the political aviary.

What was agreed about the situation was that in deployed forces the Soviet Union was catching up with the United States in numbers of land-based missiles, and was overtaking it in deliverable megatonnage; that the Soviet Union was deploying a new class of nuclear submarine (capable of launching sixteen missiles) which it could build at a rate of about eight a year; that the largest Russian missiles were much larger than anything the United States had; and that their launchers were also capable of putting a nuclear 'bombardment system' into orbit.[36] There had been observed Russian tests of multiple re-entry vehicles, which were thought to be individually but not independently targetable. The Soviet Union also had some sixty odd ABM sites set up round Moscow and there was another line of anti-aircraft defences, the radar installations of which some people thought might have, or come to have, an ABM function. What might be the eventual scale of any of these programmes was of course not known. Some of them were seen to stop and to start again, but whether for technical or other reasons was also not known.

All figures about the strategic arms race derive ultimately from information made available by the United States Government, whether they are subsequently published in the *ISS*'s annual *Military Balance*, or in the *SIPRI Yearbook of World Armaments and Disarmament* – the two most handy sources, both highly respected. But in a sense these figures about actual deployment, though instructive, are also necessarily misleading. What is more instructive, if it can be known, is the momentum, the manpower, the money, the quality, the intentions behind the figures, what in fact can place them in context and endow them with meaning. Mr McNamara, referring to the Russians, was quoted in April

35. op. cit., p. 54.
36. Known in the West as FOBS, for Fractional Orbital Bombardment System; Russian references omit the word 'fractional'. See p. 103.

1965 in *US News and World Report*: 'I'm simply saying that there is no indication they are in a race at this time . . . their rate of expansion today is not such as to allow them to equal, much less exceed our own 1970 force.' The following month, on 9 May, Mr McNamara could have changed his mind: the Soviet Government put on display for the first time a solid-fuelled intercontinental ballistic missile similar to the American Minuteman, a mobile medium-range solid-fuelled missile, and a 'large cylindrical device claimed to be an anti-ballistic missile';[37] a film probably three years old was shown in which an anti-missile missile was seen to intercept an ICBM, and a missile was seen launched from underground.[38] A very large three-stage ICBM was also shown. Mr Brezhnev commented later that, 'with every year that went by, the Soviet Union was developing quite a few new and formidable types of up-to-date military equipment which can be used to cool down any overweening aggressor'.[39] The Russians did in fact overtake the United States in numbers of landbased ICBMs and in total deployed megatonnage by 1970.[40]

Habitually the nuclear balance is discussed in terms of numbers of means of delivery or of warheads, rather than of the explosive capacity of what can be thrown, and this too may be misleading. The habit was formed in the early sixties when American experts were convinced that large nuclear weapons were not strategically interesting; a view with which their Russian opposite numbers evidently disagreed.[41] Meanwhile, of course, public discussion of

37. *The Military Balance 1965–6*, ISS, November 1965, p. 1.

38. *Missiles and Rockets*, 17 May 1965.

39. *Soviet News*, 5 July 1966, quoting Mr Brezhnev's speech of 1 July. See p. 150 for the current state of the nuclear balance.

40. President Nixon told C. L. Sulzberger in an interview on 9 March 1971 that the Soviet Union 'now have three times the missile strength' of the United States. It was made clear two days later that the President was indeed referring to megatonnage. *International Herald Tribune*, 11 and 13 March 1971.

41. The 56 megaton Soviet test of September 1961 was considered in McNamara circles to be technically wrong-headed. Mr McNamara was quoted as saying: 'It's clear to us that 30 warheads of one megaton each offer far more offensive power than does one 30 megaton warhead.' (*Missiles and Rockets*, 12 April 1965.) Equally, General Malinovsky's claim in October

the nuclear balance has been carried on in terms of the American convictions rather than the Russian. My own belief is that numbers and megatonnages of weapons should both be kept in mind, and also the configuration and course of their deployment.

There is nothing in the current Russian weapons policy that can allow one to forecast its limits; nor is there in the kind of foreign or domestic policies expressed by Mr Brezhnev. The Warsaw Pact invasion of Czechoslovakia in August 1968 was virtually bloodless, but it inserted into that small country rather more Russians than there were at the time Americans in Vietnam. The retrospectively legitimating Brezhnev doctrine was elaborated that autumn; the Sino-Soviet border dispute flared up the following March, accompanied by Russian nuclear sabre-rattling and, eventually, by hints of a pre-emptive strike on Chinese nuclear facilities. In all this, and in the continued expansion in weaponry and in far-flung military activity, there is nothing that accords with the hopes and expectations of the Kennedy defence intelligentsia of the early and mid-sixties, that the Russians were likely, were almost bound, to engage at least tacitly, in 'parallel action' on nuclear matters with the United States because of the extent of their shared concerns. Russian actions parallel rather Mr Truman's ideological expansionism of the post-war years, than the rational restraint urged in McNamara's last utterances.

On 18 September 1967, just after the United States and Soviet Union had jointly presented their draft non-proliferation treaty to the world, Mr McNamara announced, at the end of the apologia-like speech we have referred to above, that the United States was setting up a thin *area defence* ABM system, against the foreseeable nuclear threat from China in the mid-seventies and against accidental launchings from elsewhere. This system was named Sentinel, and was described as 'relatively inexpensive'. Maps were produced showing how the whole United States could

---

1961 that the Russians had 'solved the problem of destroying rockets in flight', that is with Ballistic Missile Defences, was dismissed as at the time simply not credible. The Orbital Bombardment System, which the Russians have been testing since 1967 seems only recently to have been accepted by American experts as an important weapons system.

be protected against a 'light attack'. It was open to the Chinese to see this as a promise to maintain the American *first strike capability* against China (to which Mr McNamara had explicitly referred) well into the eighties, and to the Russians to notice that any *thick area defence* could not but start as a *thin area defence* of the very configuration now announced. The decision appeared moreover to be of just that arms-racing kind that Mr McNamara had warned against in the first part of his speech: a destabilizing action which would elicit further destabilizations in reaction. The actual decision was assumed to be President Johnson's rather than Mr McNamara's and to be partly due to the maturing of the American ABM programme – the *ripe plum* syndrome – and partly because there were still in those days powerful hawks in Congress who required military meat of this sort to keep them happy. There was little sense that a cool study of the outside world lay behind either the ABM decision, or the Apologia.

Mr McNamara's exit from office that winter, Mr Johnson's own suddenly announced withdrawal from political life, the national despair which overflowed from Vietnam to disgrace the whole military thing, all resulted in a large number of people, informed and uninformed, fastening on to the ABM question during 1969 as if it contained all folly, all arms race, all guilt for previous connivances. Oppose the ABM and your sins will be forgiven you. The fashion changed, the bandwagon was in quite another rut.

(iv) *1969–70*

ABM POLITICS

When President Nixon arrived in the White House in January 1969 one of his first decisions concerned ABM. His National Security Adviser was Henry Kissinger, one of the few defence academics to be an historian by training, a European by birth, and a man unaffected by the intellectual bandwagons milling around him. By now, with Johnson administration Democrats joining Kennedy and MacCarthy Democrats off the leash, and with the anti-war movement for them to latch onto, anti-military fashion in general and anti-ABM fashion in particular were ready for take-off.

By early 1969 the Russian build-up was still further advanced. If the Soviet Union had felt obliged to obey President Kennedy in 1962 and withdraw its missiles from Cuba when the United States had a numerical advantage in delivery vehicles, and a throw-weight advantage in megatons,[42] the Soviet Union could reasonably accept as a working hypothesis that the ratios of superiority then obtaining could be as coercive on the United States as they had been on the Soviet Union. If President Kennedy found those ratios convenient, would not a Russian leader? The evidence before the President did not allow him to dismiss the possibility that some such thoughts were in circulation among the Russian leadership, and on 17 March he announced, not the cancelling of all American ABMs, but a fundamental modification from the *area defence* system of the *Sentinel* programme (which we have seen above was logically part of an offensive posture, and therefore provocative) to 'a measured construction of an active defence of our retaliatory forces'[43] to be called *Safeguard*, the system to begin with the deploying in 1973 of *hard point ABM defences* at two missile sites[44] (a configuration we have seen above to be part of a defensive posture and therefore not provocative). Mr Laird was quite explicit about this: '. . . the *Sentinel* system was ambiguous at best. It was interpreted by some as the beginning of a "thick" defence of our cities against Soviet attack. In fact, it could have been used for precisely that purpose.

42. See Chapter 11, p. 204, for the 1962 'balance'. American medium-range missiles at that date were deployed within range of the Soviet Union; Soviet MRBMs were not deployed within range of the United States. American megatonnage superiority seems mainly to have lain in the long-range bombers. However, there is a serious lack of public information on megatonnages.

43. President Nixon's statement on the US Antiballistic Missile Programme, 14 March, 1969.

44. Secretary of Defense Laird's statement before Senate Armed Forces Committee, 19 March 1971. It was clear from this that *Safeguard* would, optionally, have a limited area-defence capability, against 'accidental or small' attack.

It could also have been constructed as a system designed to protect our cities from surviving Soviet missiles after a surprise attack by the US.' He called it 'provocative' and 'an escalation of the arms race'.[45] Further American ABM deployment, the President said, was to be 'subject to modification as the threat changes, either through negotiations, or through unilateral action by the Soviet Union or Communist China'.

The concerned intelligentsia was not impressed: books and articles on the *Sentinel* programme were in manuscript or in the publishing pipeline, and nothing is more difficult than to chase after one's own expressed ideas to adjust them to a new situation. Pamphlets and collections of articles came out whose lists of authors and acknowledgees read like a Who's Who of the Kennedy administration. *The Future of the Strategic Arms Race*[46] was one of these: a pamphlet, very widely read and influential, by George W. Rathgens, making Mr Laird's points again and again. Mr McNamara (thanked for his cooperation in the preface, along with others) was reputed to have been closely concerned with its writing and indeed it opened with some very carefully worded paragraphs suggesting that in the early sixties 'pressures' to 'expand' the counterforce capabilities of the American strategic forces had been 'resisted' by the administration, and 'the line held'. Several other statements were as historically porous, including the statement that 'the Cuban missile crisis was resolved as it was because the United States was prepared to intervene with conventional strength that the Soviet Union could not match and that the existence of strategic forces for both sides served simply to deter escalation.'

A footnote, on page 14, mentioned that 'references to ABM [i.e. in the pamphlet] are to systems designed exclusively or primarily to defend population and industry' (that is to say, to *area defence* ABMs of the *Sentinel*, that is McNamara type).

45. Mr Laird's statement of 21 March 1969 before a sub-committee of the Senate Foreign Relations Committee on International Organization and Disarmament Affairs.

46. George W. Rathgens, *The Future of the Strategic Arms Race: Options for the Seventies*, Carnegie Endowment for International Peace, New York, 1969. See footnote 16, p. 175.

hardpoint, *Safeguard*-type, ABM was mentioned only in an appendix. Most of the people acknowledged in the preface went straight on to oppose the *Safeguard* programme, many of them contributing also to a paperback collection of articles, commissioned by Senator Edward Kennedy.[47] This appeared in May 1969, that is two months after the hardpoint ABM decision was announced, and claimed to refer to that decision; in fact the arguments marshalled applied almost exclusively to the McNamara, 1967 sort of ABM. This logical gap was bridged with the suggestion that there was no change except in the 'deodorant code-name'.[48]

One of the articles in the Kennedy collection, '*The Effect of ABM on US–Soviet Relations*', by Professor Marshall Shulman of Columbia University, was subtitled 'How will the Soviet react to the US decision to deploy the ABM?'[49] In his article, Professor Shulman stated his belief that *Safeguard* 'is designed for area defence' and as such might be expected to alarm them. However,

47. '*ABM, an evaluation of the Decision to deploy an Antiballistic Missile System*', ed. Abram Chayes and Jerome B. Wiesner, Signet Broadside, New American Library, 1969.

48. The experts who contributed to the Rathgens pamphlet and the Kennedy book went on, in the next year or so, to testify against *Safeguard* before various committees in both Houses of Congress. In September 1971 a committee of the *Operational Research Society of America* published in its Journal a report on the quality of the expertise that had been displayed by the Pro-and Anti-ABM scientists. The confrontation was between Albert Wohlstetter (now of Chicago University and late of RAND Corporation, the US Air Force California think tank) who had fathered the ORSA Committee's report, and who favoured the *Safeguard* ABM system) and Jerome Wiesner (now of MIT and late Scientific Adviser to President Kennedy) who was against. The anti-ABM scientists were accused of a number of faults of scholarship; and these accusations they returned, adding the knobs-on opinion that the committee had been reverting to McCarthyism attacks on their civil liberties. Both groups of scientists were excited and very highly 'motivated'; no politician in his senses would any longer be able to rely on their advice. Science, the great will o' the wisp hope of puzzled administrators and legislators, was being sucked back into its own, limited, category: in politics, there is no 'scientific' alternative to political judgement, of men, or of issues; in science, political motivation is self-defeating and the good scientist will not succumb to mixing his categories.

49. Op. cit., p. 153.

he did not provide the historical background to Soviet views on ABM or on their own deployment of area defence ABMs around Moscow. In the event, Russian reactions to the Safeguard decision itself appear to have been largely determined by the anti-ABM campaign in the United States. Certainly there was a volte-face on the previous stand.

Probably not all moments of the arms race are equally 'disarmable', or equally conducive to, even compatible with, agreement. It has always seemed that the arms race being in a comparatively stable phase would make agreement more feasible, either for arms control or for actual disarmament. Moreover, if current stability can be considered a conducive condition, the prospect of future instability and of a new and appallingly expensive round of rearmament could be assumed a positive inducement to agreement. Sending nuclear forces into the deep sea, which currently is a not distant prospect, could be such an expensive round. This given state of the arms race is part of the necessary background against which to judge the deployment of ABM, a type of weapon which Russian leaders and commentators had always, until mid-1969 and the anti-*Safeguard* campaign in the USA, seen as unprovocative, as stabilizing the arms race, and even as contributing to securing the disarmament process itself by way of the 'Gromyko umbrella'. This idea of an agreed transitional minimum deterrent had originally been conveyed to the Russians by American participants at the December 1960 Pugwash Conference in Moscow – among others by the same Jerome Wiesner who edited the 1969 Edward Kennedy book, who then was already known to be President John Kennedy's choice for his Scientific Adviser. The idea showed every sign of being the necessary, perhaps the sufficient, link between Russian and American concepts of the disarmament process: it was clear at that time that any Russian Government would accept inspection only of disarmament itself and not of any retained forces; equally that an American Government would not accept a Russian Government's mere word concerning the numbers and types of forces it retained, particularly of nuclear forces. Consequently the idea of an agreed, limited, invulnerable strategic nuclear force made particularly appropriate sense: it would be maintained during the highly sensitive transition from arms race to general and comprehensive disarmament, and would be a standing insurance against cheats and errors. A couple of years later, the idea was officially advanced at the UN General Assembly by Mr Gromyko as a Soviet initiative; a later elaboration made clear that in the Russian view the retained transitional force should include defensive as well as offensive missiles. In 1965, an article by General Talensky, an eminent and authoritative Soviet strategist (and a Pugwash participant), put the official Russian view on ABMs very clearly:

The main objection to antimissile systems, as seen by Western politicians and public figures, is that they tend to upset the nuclear balance, thereby undermining the system of mutual deterrence through nuclear rockets, that is, the system of 'deterrence through fear'. To prove their point they ignore the obvious facts and resort to verbal tricks instead of convincing arguments. . . . In other words, antimissile systems are defensive but, as the West insists, they upset the mutual deterrence based on the threat of a nuclear strike. This gives rise to the question: Who stands to gain and who is faced with 'serious difficulties'? . . . It is obvious that the creation of an effective antimissile defense merely serves to build up the security of the peaceable, nonaggressive state; . . . A country not willing to abandon its aggressive policy will naturally not be too happy about such a state of affairs . . .

It is said that the international strategic situation cannot be stable where both sides simultaneously strive towards deterrence through nuclear-rocket power and the creation of defensive anti-missile systems. . . . I cannot agree with this view either. From the standpoint of strategy, powerful deterrent forces and an effective antimissile defense system, when taken together, substantially increase the stability of mutual deterrence. . . . In any case, there is the question: Which is preferable for security as a result of the arms race, a harmonious combination of active means of deterrence and defense systems, or the means of attack alone? An exhaustive analysis of this can be made only on the basis of highly concrete military and technical data, but at any rate the side which makes a spurt in the means of attack will instantly expose its aggressive intentions, and stand condemned as the aggressor with all the negative political consequences that this entails. . . . As I have said, antimissile systems are purely defensive and not designed for attack. It is quite illogical to demand abstention from creating such weapons in the face of vast stockpiles of highly powerful means of attack on the other side. Only the side which intends to use its means of attack for aggression purposes can wish to slow down the creation and improvement of anti-missile defense systems. For the peaceloving states, anti-missile systems are only a means of building up their security. . . . There is one reasonable alternative to a race in antimissile systems, and it is the early implementation of general and complete disarmament. The elimination of nuclear-rocket means of attack will automatically result in the elimination of the means of defense against them.[50]

On 10 February 1967 Mr Kosygin answered a question off-the-cuff at a London press conference:

What weapons should be regarded as a factor making for tension – offensive or defensive? I believe that the defensive systems, which prevent attack, are not the cause of the arms race, but constitute a factor preventing the death of people. Some argue like this: What is cheaper, to have offensive weapons which can destroy towns or whole states, or to have defensive weapons which can prevent this destruction? At present the theory is current somewhere that the system which is cheaper should be developed. Such so-called theoreticians argue as to the cost of killing a man – 500,000 dollars or 100,000. Maybe an anti-missile system is more expensive than an offensive system, but it is designed not to kill people but to preserve human lives.

Views of this kind about ABM sank suddenly, quite without trace, in 1969.

In the United States, opinion about ABM was quite different. Originally plain incredulity about the possibility of ballistic missile defences prevailed, and I. F. Stone has nailed the recently developed belief that it was in reaction to fears of Russian ABM that American MIRV was set up.[51] In October 1961 John

50. N. Talensky, 'Antimissile Systems and Disarmament', *Bulletin of the Atomic Scientists*, Chicago, February 1965.

51. In the issue of the *New York Review of Books* of 27 March 1969, I. F. Stone refers to this purported relationship between Russian ABM and American MIRV, and quotes an answer Senator Mansfield elicited from Dr John S. Foster Jnr, Director of Research in the Pentagon during the Senate Appropriations Committee Hearings on the Department of Defense Budget for fiscal 1969 (90th Congress, 2nd Session, Part 4, p. 2,310 – which may

Maddox, now editor of *Nature*, was reporting in the *Guardian*
that a claim by Marshal Malinovsky 'that the Russians have
"solved the problem of destroying rockets in flight" was not
considered in the West to amount to a credible claim to have
developed a system for shooting down ballistic missiles; rather,
that the art of doing this was unlikely to be more advanced in the
Soviet Union than in the United States.' And the Americans
weren't doing at all well. Two years later, just after the Partial
Test Ban Treaty had been signed, President Kennedy was assuring the world in a press conference that 'the problem of developing a defense against a missile is beyond us and beyond the Soviet
technically.'[52] During the mid-sixties the Russians did indeed
deploy an ABM system round Moscow, the efficiency of which

account for its unfamiliarity). The Senator's question was: 'Is it not true that
the US response to the discovery that the Soviets had made an initial deployment of an ABM system around Moscow and possibly elsewhere was to develop the MIRV system for Minuteman and Polaris?' Dr Foster's answer
(minus some official deletions) was, unexpectedly, this: 'Not entirely. The
MIRV concept was originally generated to increase our targeting capability
rather than to penetrate ABM defenses. In 1961–2 planning for targeting the
Minuteman force it was found that the total number of aim points exceeded
the number of Minuteman missiles. By splitting up the pay-load of a single
missile [deleted] each [deleted] could be programmed [deleted] allowing us to
cover these targets with [deleted] fewer missiles. [Deleted] MIRV was originally born to implement the payload split-up [deleted]. It was found that the
previously generated MIRV concept could equally well be used against
ABM [deleted].'
    The 'action reaction' theory of the arms race formed a great part of Mr
McNamara's September 1967 *Apologia* and Professor Rathgens of MIT has
sought to document the hypothesis ('The Dynamics of the Arms Race',
Scientific American, April 1969, p. 15). The case is not made out because
until 1969 the evidence does not support it. What the evidence *does* support
is the theory of the 'ripening plum', which holds that what can be done, will
be done if the money is available, and that a good reason will be found when
the project is ripe for deployment. The case Mr Laird made for the *Safeguard*
ABM system is probably the first genuine example of 'action-reaction', no
doubt because only in 1969 had the two arms racers got really close to each
other. Of course, the theoretical possibility of Russian ballistic missile defences may very well have been in the minds of those who took the decisions
to proceed with MIRV research in the late fifties.
    52. 2 August 1963.

Americans cried down, and the United States continued research and development. A breakthrough came with the idea, not of 'hitting a fly in space' as Mr Khrushchev had once put it, but rather of using a large nuclear warhead to release a burst of radiation, outside the too absorbent atmosphere, and strong enough to destroy incoming missiles. The Russians tested something of the sort in 1961. When Mr McNamara announced an area ABM defence system in September 1967, American general opinion was not immediately either alarmed or elated.[53] Nor was Russian, except insofar as NATO allies were all expected to want it too. ('According to preliminary calculations forty anti-missile ships[for the NATO allies] will cost about two milliard dollars.'[54]) The Albanians and Chinese opined that 'while trying hard to achieve a limitation of ABM missile systems against each other, the USA and the USSR are taking concrete steps to establish ABM systems against China.'[55]

Eventually it was in the United States itself that opposition to ABM blazed up. During 1968 anti-military sentiment, which the failures, lies and obscenities of the Vietnam war had at last fanned into ardour, finally consumed President Johnson, and the reputation of his administration. Where, ten years before, national security studies had been the pride of institutes, universities and publishers across the land and the ambition of brightest graduates, now all was bane, shame and contempt.[56] Seldom can a new

53. A 1964 survey, reported in *Missiles and Rockets* (16 August 1965) was said to show that 71 per cent of American citizens believed the US did have an ABM system deployed and that 59 per cent thought the Russians had.

54. Moscow Home Service, 27 September 1967.

55. Albanian Home Service, 21 September 1967.

56. How things had come full circle can be seen from an article contributed by the long-term and eminent defence scientist, Herbert F. York, to the August 1969 issue of *Scientific American*: after mentioning the 'futility of searching for technical solutions to what is essentially a political problem, namely the problem of national security', he went on to seek to 'deal with the problem of national security in a more rational manner'. Ten years earlier, liberal scientists and politicians had been seeking in science and technology a 'more rational manner' than politics provided for dealing with the very problem of national security. This had been the *raison d'être* of the Pugwash meetings.

president have faced such a dispiriting prospect as Mr Nixon did: the public deeply and increasingly disillusioned, the armed forces professionally demoralized, the higher ranks of the foreign service still enfeebled by the MacCarthy purges of the fifties, and the rest of the world alarmed and disgusted to the extent that nothing American survived the contagious disrepute. The only conviction that seemed to survive intact from the early sixties was the belief among the anti-ABM opposition that the United States was all-powerful: if the United States withdrew from Vietnam, the war would stop.[57] If the United States stopped its ABM, so would the arms race itself be stopped.[58]

As the anti-military and anti-establishment feeling continued its slow explosion in 1969, the Soviet Government may well have been tempted to see in it the prophesied death throes of capitalism. During the summer hawkish Russian views were surfacing among the military, and Mr Nixon's suggestion that SALT should start in August went unanswered. The sober praise that Talensky and Kosygin had given to defensive missiles was hushed. Russian spokesmen began to give overt support to the 'more realistic forces' in the United States, to the domestic opposition, particularly to opponents of the ABM. High praise was given to Senator Edward Kennedy, Averill Harriman, Professor Morgenthau and others, in terms which would have been the kiss of death even a few years before. Even after the SALT had opened, there was clearly still some hope in Moscow that American ABM might be unilaterally given up without any international curb being put on offensive weapons.[59] There may even be those who advocate

57. The view was even expressed, by Mary McCarthy, in the *New York Review of Books*, that there wouldn't be a blood bath in Vietnam if the Americans pulled out even suddenly: there hadn't been one in France when they left in 1966.

58. During the heyday of British unilateralism, there was some discussion about whether this politics was not part of a post-imperialist syndrome. CND supporters certainly felt it was important that Britain give the world a lead and an example; some thought it would even be effective, particularly in the case of France.

59. And perhaps still is: an *Izvestia* article on SALT on 8 July 1971 was reported by Tass as 'emphasizing that the question of anti-missile defences represents the key to the problem'. (SU 3731/A1/1.) Mr Nixon continues

waiting until the next presidential election to see if agreement in SALT is really necessary.

At any rate, in March 1970 the *New York Times* reported Washington 'officials in various government agencies' as saying that 'in the last few weeks Russian diplomats have been busy privately lobbying with certain Congressmen and their aides against a *Safeguard* expansion.'[60] This coincided with a vigorous attack in *Pravda* on 7 March on official American attitudes and on its negotiating position in SALT: Defense Secretary Laird's description of current Soviet missile deployment was described as 'generously spiced with references to a mythical Soviet threat'. The Soviet Union was after all merely keeping up with the United States. Even now Soviet leaders will suggest the threat is an illusion. Mr Kosygin, according to Senator Church, told a group of 'prominent Americans' in July 1971 that 'He was inclined to think that mistrust is being artificially created. . . . Those who want to prevent agreements use mistrust as a smoke screen. They manufacture and manipulate mistrust . . .' When Senator Church countered that 'a primary cause of mistrust' between the United States and the Soviet Union was 'the immensity of our respective arsenals', Mr Kosygin was not to be deflected. 'It was his opinion that propaganda was largely responsible for creating mistrust, through the press, radio and TV. He had seen, during his visit to the United States (in 1967) the scale of the propaganda campaign against Russia. If this were reversed, it would be a giant step towards restoring confidence in our relations, he said.'[61] My own impression is that Russian propaganda has, both in 1967 and since, been more virulent than American. In October 1971 a commentator was even telling listeners to the Moscow Home

firm in his belief that there can be no agreement except on both offensive and defensive weapons. (Press Conference, November 1971.)

60. *International Herald Tribune*, 10 March 1970. In September, the columnist Joseph Kraft noted that Giorgi Arbatov and academician Millionshchikov had been suggesting on visits to Washington that 'Russia was still holding back [in SALT] because of pressure tactics on the ABM.' *International Herald Tribune*, 29 September 1970.

61. *International Herald Tribune*, 21 October 1971.

Service: 'In actual fact, there is no case of Soviet espionage, *as there never has been.*'[62] (emphasis added).

The Soviet Union still provides no details about the numbers and capabilities of its nuclear, or other, weapons, and the world's information continues to derive entirely from American sources, mainly from the observation satellites.[63] The photographic evidence is sometimes highly obscure, as when it appeared that intercontinental range missiles were in early 1970 suddenly being 'installed in complexes that previously housed only medium-range missiles pointed at Western Europe'.[64] Was this, Mr Beecher quoted his official sources as wondering, connected with the fact that the latter missiles were being excluded by the Russians from detailed discussion in the SALT talks? From time to time there was a 'pause' in Russian deployment. Did it signify? What did it signify? 'Doves' interpreted such pauses as intended to give the SALT a fair wind, and Russian scientists occasionally implied as much to American colleagues. The Administration itself received no public or private hints that the pauses had any such meaning. Anyway, the weather might have been bad, or there might have been technical difficulties or trouble at the factory, or perhaps a decision to go for something else altogether. In spring 1971 a new and larger kind of hole in the ground was discerned: indicating what?[65] It could indicate substantial hardening of new sites for old-type missiles, which would be good news – hardening is part of a defensive posture; it could be the deployment of a missile yet larger than the SS9, which would be bad news: part of an offensive posture.

On the bandwaggon, ABM is no longer the chief topic; it has

62. 10 October 1971, S U 3810/A1/1.
63. Past, as well as present. The Nixon administration has made news of Russian weapons deployment public quicker and more substantially than did the Johnson administration, and has also made public for the first time information acquired during both the Johnson and Kennedy administrations – about for instance the original test-sightings of the SS9 missile, and the kind of radar associated with the ABM launchers deployed round Moscow.
64. William Beecher, *International Herald Tribune*, 12 February 1970.
65. See below, p. 215.

been joined by the withdrawal of American troops from Europe and the setting of a date for American withdrawal from Vietnam, regardless of context and inherited responsibilities and economics. The sense of exhilarating righteousness is beginning to fade. Senator Muskie, a possible democratic candidate for the presidency next time, returned from a journey to Europe and the Soviet Union, aware, as evidently not before, of the interconnections of things: particularly how the American withdrawal from Empire is not only important to Americans.

Part Three: Salt, Esc, Etc.

11

The Arms Race

The actual present state of the strategic nuclear balance is usually a matter of dispute: some people look at who now has how many of what; others look at who now can throw what at whom; some look at the rate at which one side or the other is getting how many in the way of which, or how much in the way of what. Types, numbers, weight, accuracy, range, ability to penetrate defences, all matter. Intentions and the psychology of nations and rulers matter. Views on the usability or the non-usability of nuclear weapons, on the usability of nuclear threats, of the effects or the effectiveness of the existence or presence or possession of nuclear weapons, matter.

The quality of the evidence about the Russian side is still inadequate for firm judgement; about things American it is rather better, except in matters psychological (some kind of dégringolade has occurred and may or may not be continuing) and political (presidential and other elections are always in prospect).

It is easy enough to cite round figures of ICBMs and of SLBMs for each side, or MIRV or ABMs, and compare these; easy but misleading. Because there are other things to keep in mind I propose to glance rather more panoramically at the general body and pace of the arms race, and of the current set of proposals for curbing it. The evidence is all American; the estimates of weapons are all western; the disputes about the evidence are almost all western; a few of the comments and several current proposals are Russian. In a sense, the purpose is to enumerate and list for disposal some of the objects in two rooms, in one of which the light is on and there already are lists, and in the other of which the light is off and the objects are concealed, into which we may not go, but only watch from a distance through curtained windows.[1] Michel Tatu, *Le Monde*'s highly percipient Soviet-ologist, doubts even if the inhabitants of the unlit room actually know what may be the total sum of the objects it contains.[2]

At the time of the Cuba crisis, when President Kennedy was able to stare down Mr Khrushchev, the bare bones of the strategic balance were something like this:

Category	United States and Allies	Soviet Union and Allies[3]
ICBM (2,000+ mile range)	450–500	75+
MRBM (700–2,000 mile range)	250	700
Long range bombers (5,000+ miles range)	630	200
Medium range bombers (2,000+ miles, including carrier based aircraft)	1,630	1,400

plus a few submarines on either side capable of launching nuclear weapons. It was particularly in ICBMs, and in the long-range bombers with their huge thermonuclear bomb cargo – probable 4×25 megatons – that American superiority lay.

It seems likely that Mr Khrushchev's successors have been more interested in Mr Kennedy's 'stare down' capability at that time than in the oddly boy-scout claims of Mr McNamara to have an actual second strike counterforce capability and therefore,

1. Among the results of the twenty-four months of SAL Talks between Russians and Americans has evidently *not* been the exchange of precise information, at least about Russian capabilities or programmes: this is clear from the confusion and uncertainty displayed in Washington concerning the spring 1971 'holes', which are discussed below, p. 215.

2. Comparing the SAL Talks negotiators, M. Tatu has written about the 'compartmentalization of knowledge and of secrets, particularly on the Soviet side: each expert knows strictly only that which he has to know, and it is not certain, according to the Americans, that Mr Semionov himself has any precise idea of his country's stockpile of thermonuclear weapons' (3 November 1970). Mr Semionov is the chief Soviet negotiator at the talks.

3. *The Military Balance 1962–3*, ISS, November 1962.

effectively, an actual first strike capability, against the Soviet
Union and all its allies. The threat to launch nuclear war is now
unpersuasive: the nuclear-backed stare may not be. Certainly
Mr Laird only muddied current discussion when he suggested, in
March 1969, that with the SS9 the Soviet Union must be seeking
a first strike capability against the United States. The implausi-
bility of the opinion (which Mr Laird subsequently said he did
not hold – he had intended merely to say that the SS9 was a
counterforce-type weapon) has been perhaps incautiously over-
used as grounds for deriding actual information provided by Mr
Laird and his department.[4]

The situation now appears, and is, very different. The comparable barebone figures are these:

	United States	Soviet Union[1]
ICBMs	1,054	1,510
SLBMs	656	440 (plus some 310 other missiles surface-launched by subs)
MRBMs	nil	700
L-R Bombers	500	140

1. Military Balance 1971-2. IISS, p. 55.

But these figures are not at all simple. The figures for *launchers*
hide *numbers of warheads* (and the United States has gone in for
multiple warheads, many and small); and hide *megatonnage*
(which the Soviet Union has gone in for, particularly with the

4. The extreme of this derision came perhaps in autumn 1971 when an
American Air Force statement that the USSR had deployed FOBS was
being felt by some Western commentators virtually to be evidence that the
Russians had not deployed such a system. The Russians themselves have
been mentioning it for some years (see p. 212), and Mr Laird had confirmed
its non-novelty only a few days before (14 October 1971).

Warheads Total	Warheads Strategic	Numbers 1967	Numbers 1971	TYPES	LOAD	Megatonnage Strategic	Megatonnage Total
		150	140[5]	Long range Bomber	3×?MT		
				Long range Bomber	?		
			220[5]	SS7 & 8 ICBM	1×5 MT		
5662[1]	2500[3]	520 ICBM	280[5]	SS9 ICBM or DICBM or OBS[4]	1×20–25 MT or 3×5 MT or 6×?	7940[1] MT	230000[1] MT
			950[5]	SS11 ICBM[4]	1×1 or 2 MT or 3×? KT		
			60[5]	SS13 ICBM	1×1MT		
				ICBM[6]			
		130	320[5]	SSN6 SLBM[7]	1×? MT		
			78[5]	SSN5 SLBM	1×? MT		
			42[5]	SSN4 SLBM	1×? MT		
			355[5]	Shaddock Cruise Missile	1×? MT		
			67[5]	ABM	1×? MT		
				ABM[8]	1×? MT		
				SLICBM[9]	1×? MT		

Megatonnage Strategic: inbetween 5 & 10 times the thermonuclear capacity we have[10]

Megatonnage Total: 4 times 1965 megatonnage; 2½–3 times U.S. megatonnage[9]

3 times Russian total[2]					
7502[1]	520	505	Long range Bombers[11] with SRAM	4×? MT / 20×60 KT	
	54	54	Titan 2 ICBM	1×5 MT	1900[1] MT
	1000	1000	Minuteman ICBM 1 & 2	1×1 or 2 MT	
5700			3	3×60 KT	
	656	160	Polaris SLBM[12] A2	1×800 KT	5200[1] MT
		432	A3	1×1 MT or 3×200 KT	2/5–1/3 of S.U. total; 46% of 1965 megatonnage[9]
		64	Poseidon SLBM	10×40–50 KT	
			Safeguard ABM Spartan	1×? MT	
			Sprint	1×? KT	
			Hibex	1×? KT	

Note: these figures, which are about the best publicly available, are not mutually consistent. Additions do not result in sums.

KT = Kiloton
MT = Megaton

⊠ = programme not completed
☐ = tested but not operational

1. *Military Balance I.S.S. 1970–71* p.89.
2. *U.S. News & World Report* 10 Oct.1970, quoting "Pentagon Officials".
3. *International Herald Tribune* 4 May, 1972.
4. *International Herald Tribune* 16 Dec, 1970.
5. *Military Balance I.S.S. 1971–72* p.55.
6. *International Herald Tribune* 24 April, 1972, this is larger than SS9.
7. 16 missiles carried in each Y-Class submarine; 43 submarines in being or under construction, March 1972.
8. A new "advanced" ABM *International Herald Tribune* 11 Oct, 1971.
9. Secretary of Defence Laird; Senate disarmament sub-committee, 20 May, 1970.
10. Stewart Alsop *Newsweek* 1 Nov, 1971.
11. Soon to be armed with short range attack missiles (SRAM)—about 20 per bomber.
12. *Poseidon* is to replace *Polaris* on 31 out of 41 boats; each boat carries 16 missiles.

SS9); they hide puzzlers like the Russians' *Depressed Trajectory ICBM* and *Orbiting Bombardment System.*[5] The chart on pages 206-7 is in many ways preferable. That this chart is still not at all satisfactory (though the middle is better than the sides) is in part a fact about available published evidence. The figures and proportions given on the left, for numbers of warheads, do not begin to agree with each other and neither do the figures and proportions for megatonnages on the right.

The figures about bombers are not satisfactory either: the megatonnage carried by American long-range bombers at one time may have been as much as 4×25 MT bombs, for B52s, but this is certainly not compatible with Mr Laird's (and other administration) statements on current relative megatonnages; American bombers now presumably carry something smaller in the way of bombs and/or of air-to-surface missiles; some, used in South East Asia, are for the time being probably denuclearized.[6] To the Russian long-range bombers the *ISS Military Balance* regularly allots a smaller maximum *load* than to the American bombers.

Equally unsatisfactory are the number of ⊠▷ (signifying incomplete programme), particularly of course on the Russian side: even *Poseidon*[7] has a limited number of boats to go into, and *Safe-*

5. Nothing seems to be available about the warhead type or yield of this latter. In 1963 there was mention of a satellite from which rockets could be launched by Col. Glazov, in an article in a series in *Red Star* beginning 2 April 1963; reproduced in *Soviet News*, 8 April 1963.

6. See *US News and World Report*, 27 December 1971: 'Latest Worry: Plight of Nation's H Bombers'.

7. Either '*Poseidon*' itself which would have a range of 3,000 miles, or an 'extended *Poseidon*', or ULMSI (Undersea Long Range Missile System) the range of which would be nearer 5,000 miles. (*Aviation Week and Space Technology*, 1 November 1971.) This may eventually be followed by an altogether new ULMS II, which would go in a new submarine, for which the 1973 Defense Budget will include over $900 million for a start on the construction programme for the new submarine. (President Nixon, *State of the Nation Message* 20 January 1972.) The new system might be ready for deployment in the late nineteen seventies – failing an agreement on submarine numbers in SALT.

guard is on a short leash. No one has the least idea of the final figures for SS9, for SS11 or 13, or for SSN6, or of the state of play with the SS12 which may be short range and may or may not be deployed operationally; or the SS14, which is mobile and may be in the medium range; or a new SSX2, also mobile and probably in the intermediate range.[8] Recent Russian military parades have been uninformative. The chart also leaves out programmes in an early stage, like the American Underwater-Launched Missile System (ULMS II) now being researched; this system which President Nixon has just boosted[9] would include not only inter-continental range submarine-launched missiles, able to reach the Soviet Union from American territorial waters, but also a new, very quiet, very deep-diving and rather large submarine for carrying it. The Soviet Union has already tested a new naval missile with a 'potential 5,000 mile range',[10] but is not known to have a submarine appropriate for carrying it. The United States is developing a new supersonic bomber, which is running into trouble in Congress; the Russians have tested one.[11]

Over the years, American (and other Western) commentators, on the one hand, have been interested and impressed by numbers of warheads, while, on the other, Russians appear to have been interested and impressed by size of warheads and preponderantly have conducted larger yield tests than the Americans.[12] Thus after the explosion of a 50–60 megaton device in its 1961 series of nuclear weapons tests, Russian spokesmen from Khrushchev

8. *Military Balance, 1970–71*, ISS. Notes, p. 109.

9. See footnote 7, p. 208.

10. *Newsweek*, 11 January 1971.

11. *Aviation Week and Space Technology*, 13 September 1971.

12. Overall total of reported tests up to 1970: United States 539, Soviet Union 236, United Kingdom 25, France 37, China 11 – but of the United States tests 280 have been of lower yield than 20 kt, compared with 25 by the Soviet Union. 18 US tests have had a yield greater than 1 megaton, compared to 44 for the Soviet Union. With the United States, at every yield the lower, the more tests; with the Soviet Union, with every yield the greater, the more tests. See R. R. Neild, *The Test Ban*, SIPRI Research Report, 1971, p. 19 and table I. By no means all tests have been reported; this would not necessarily be the picture if they had been.

on and down referred, with approval, first to 'warheads of 50 to 60 and more megatons' that were being 'perfected',[13] and then to the 100 MT bombs that Soviet scientists 'have worked out'.[14] In the United States General Curtis LeMay (President Kennedy's Air Force Chief of Staff, and later on George Wallace's ticket for Vice President) was almost alone in considering such things desirable.[15] The Pentagon's Director of Research and Engineering, Harold Brown, agreed with the general strategic community and dismissed them as appearing not very important for the United States.

This sensible argument, that the Russians having a particular weapon is not in itself a reason for the Americans to have it too, is sometimes stood on its head: it then goes: 'after the United States itself has discarded something as impractical, there is no cause for alarm from the defense establishment' if the Russians do acquire it. The quotation is from a report in the *International Herald Tribune*[16] and refers to (evidently dovish) sentiments that a currently-testing Russian satellite inspection, or anti-satellite, system which had the observed ability to intercept and destroy Russia's own satellites, should give no cause for alarm because the United States abandoned just such a programme more than ten years ago. In fact this system, which is non-nuclear, may threaten both early warning and command and control communications satellites.[17] Even I. F. Stone, whose logic is usually

13. Marshal Birynzov, Commander of Rocket Forces, quoted in the *New York Times*, 11 December 1962.

14. N. Khrushchev, *The Times*, 16 January 1963; Marshal Sokolovsky, Moscow Home Service, 2 February 1965, etc.

15. *New York Times*, 22 March 1964.

16. 29 April 1971.

17. It has been pointed out that 'at present U S A F lacks adequate measures for knowing whether its satellites have been intercepted.... There is fear that in the event of hostilities a foreign power's first act would be to deny U S A F access to ballistic missile early warning information from satellites' (*Aviation Week and Space Technology*, 8 November 1971). Well, perhaps. Such early warning satellites have recently been put up, to give information of an I C B M launch within 3–4 minutes of it happening, and therefore some 15 minutes warning. Another system warns of S L B M launches which would give 5–10 minutes warning to bombers to take off, which is barely enough: they take 6–10 minutes to do so. Work is proceeding 'to develop a satellite

admirable, falls for this chauvinistic argument to dismiss the SS9 – a very large, and variously capable launcher – as 'cumbersome and inefficient',[18] without admitting that it is as a second strike weapon that it is faulty, not necessarily as something else. Which of course raises the question again, what do the Russians want such weapons for?

The American Strategic Community, including I. F. Stone, are disinclined to believe in questions to which they themselves have no answer. President Kennedy's Scientific Adviser, Jerome Wiesner, was still saying in 1968 (after Russian A BM deployment, after FOBS) that 'One of the things you have to remember is that very frequently the Soviets are following our lead';[19] and Zbigniew Brzezinski, then recently of the State Department, expressed the opinion in December 1969 that the SALT at least 'will help to provide the more moderate members of the Soviet Establishment with the needed information about the complexity of the nuclear relationship'.[20] This view of Soviet naïveté and ignorance Mr NcNamara not only shared, but seems to have believed must absolutely be the case, even if evidence pointed the other way. Thus when a type of weapon such as the United States had decided against, the liquid-fuel 25 megaton SS9, first appeared in the Soviet Union in 1965 and began to be deployed, he kept the fact quiet: they should be given the opportunity of knowing better. . . . Equally, he was 'not concerned'[21] when the Soviet

---

communications system which will have the same degree of survivability from a nuclear attack as the strategic weapons systems of the United States' (*Aviation Week and Space Technology*, 27 September 1971). It won't be ready for testing until late 1973. Joseph Alsop, a very hawkish journalist, suggests the Russians must have spent 'well above $2 billion' on the anti-satellite system. (*International Herald Tribune*, 23 November 1971.) Several times in the strategic arms race the Russians have surprised the Americans by taking a sort of Knight's Move: *Sputnik* was a surprise because the Americans expected bombers, the Cuba deployment was a surprise; a non-nuclear anti-satellite satellite would be a surprise.

18. *New York Review of Books*, 4 June 1970, p. 17.
19. *War/Peace Report*, December 1968, p. 8.
20. *Newsweek*, 29 December 1969.
21. *US News and World Report*, 11 November 1967.

Union tested its Orbiting Bombardment System: his view was that it had no use. He described it firmly as a Fractional Orbiting Bombardment System (FOBS) – a concept a little less offensive to Strategic Reason; the Soviet Union went on referring to its 'orbital' and 'global' rockets as it had been doing since the early sixties, and did not qualify them as fractional. Here was one aspect of the strategic Realism (in the philosophical sense of the idea being more real than its instances) of the Kennedy period – a realism whose banner Edward Kennedy is still keeping aloft: 'It is important', Senator Kennedy writes in the foreword to a recent book,[22] 'that in dealing with others, we seek to understand how they view a problem, and make every effort to alter their perception.' Such beliefs and attempted practice helped direct his brother's administration straight into the quagmire of Vietnam.

It is more instructive (and probably safer) to interpret one's fellow mortals' actions in their own terms; certainly there is no reason for judging Russians (or North Vietnamese) as a special kind of mistaken American. If Russians believe in the strategic significance of 25 megaton warheads and anti-satellite systems and manoeuvrable orbiting bombardment systems, it is the commentator's job to elucidate the strategy if he can, not to declare it wrong-headed (although it may be), nor to pretend it doesn't exist. If he can't elucidate it, he must still not declare it wrong-headed, or pretend it doesn't exist. My own guess is that the hunter satellites would indeed seek to damage the American retaliatory systems in their current Achilles heels high up in the sky,[23] and that OBSs might be handy against nuclear-bomber-bearing aircraft carriers[24] on a second, perhaps fractional, orbit, a first orbit having been used for exact targeting. Or perhaps not. The Soviet Union has no aircraft carriers and until recently has

22. Roger Fisher, *Basic Negotiating Strategy*, Allen Lane the Penguin Press, 1971.

23. 'The Pentagon hopes to begin development of an experimental "survivable communications satellite" during fiscal 1972.' *Aviation Week and Space Technology*, 5 July 1971. See footnote 17, p. 210.

24. Aircraft-carrier buffs believe it is possible to develop methods whereby even very large surface vessels may be 'hidden' for days on end.

not been thought to be acquiring any.[25] What I believe to be quite clear is that if the Soviet Union has decided to acquire and deploy a system which the Americans have decided against, this is interesting, but not an indication that the Russians do not understand their own military business. It is noticeable that in the SAL Talks so far, the Russians seem to have made two proposals: one in late 1970 concerning ABM, more recently another concerning Multiple Re-entry Vehicles but not for anything which would limit their own current deployment programmes either for submarines or launchers. The chart on pages 206–7 shows how far the United States is presently going in the substitution of 600 and 200 kiloton, and even 50 or 40 kiloton warheads for its earlier 1 or 2 megaton warheads. The Russians on the other hand are staying with megaton and multi-megaton warheads.[26] The prevailing American assumption has been that this is due to technological backwardness, which may be so. But it does not dispose of the weapon system, or vitiate the strategy into which it is now incorporated: weapons are not necessarily ineffective because they are technologically inelegant. However, the unofficial (often ex-official) arms control community in the United States is largely convinced that, failing a Strategic Arms Limitation Agreement, the next event of the arms race is likely to be a new round of ABM and MIRV action-reaction, and that the Russians must still be following the American lead. As we mentioned in the last chapter, Russian ABM was not the trigger to American MIRV: this was self-triggered: the plum ripened; nor can the three war-headed version of the Russian SS9 have been a reaction to Mr McNamara's *Sentinel* 1967 ABM programme because that was to protect cities, not missile sites; and SS9s, with MRVs, which can perhaps be pointed at groups of three Minuteman missile sites, were available for testing in 1969,

25. A very large vessel is understood to be under construction at a Black Sea ship yard, which may be an aircraft carrier. *International Herald Tribune*, 20 January 1972.

26. Moscow broadcasting to the Chinese People's Liberation Army: 'But the pitiful theoreticians forget that . . . a 50 megaton nuclear bomb can cause the complete destruction of an area from 1,500 to 3,000 sq. km.' SU 3281 A32, 13 January 1970. This may be mere propaganda.

when the *Safeguard* programme was being decided. SS9s MRVs *may* have been triggered by Russian awareness of, or expectation of, or anticipation of, American development of a hard-point defence capability, but that is 'worst case pessimism', not 'action-reaction'.

However, each SS9 MRV is thought to carry a 4–5 megaton warhead,[27] which is gigantic, and very different in kind, and probably in purpose, from an individual *Minuteman* III or *Poseidon* MIRV. The smaller, *Minuteman*-size, SS11 has apparently been tested with three re-entry vehicles,[28] but the reports suggest that two of the three were concerned with penetration aids, not with miniaturized warheads. Russian interest, in fact, does seem to remain with very large warheads, and any Russian proposal to limit the deployment of MRVs would fall, just as would an ABM freeze, far more heavily on American arrangements than on Russian. This may well be the way to grasp the American head of the hydra. But the arms race is two-headed and only a limitation on size and on numbers of launchers (or a combination of size and numbers) will seize hold of the Russian head. A moratorium on ABM and MIRV, such as some people in the United States have suggested,[29] if it did not also freeze bigness and numbers of missiles, would merely license the Soviet Union to continue its own kind of build-up.

What actually is Russian nuclear strategy, what are the intentions of the Russian Government? Are they seeking superiority to the United States and China combined, as Mr McNamara sought against Russia and China combined? What was the meaning of the turn-about on ABM? If they are seeking a 'stare-down' capability, what would this be and how could it be recognized? How do arms control and disarmament fit in with such a capability? After all, along with the plethora of new weapons has come, in the last few months, a plethora of nods and becks and conference calls, to which we shall shortly come.

27. I have no figure for the rumoured 6-re-entry vehicle warhead.
28. Michael Getler, *International Herald Tribune*, 7 July 1970.
29. Including Hubert Humphrey, who still has presidential ambitions.

The argument about what the Russian build-up is for has of course taken place mainly in America, and much of it since the SAL Talks began in November 1969. President Nixon conducted a general review of American defence policy in early 1969, and only in June that year announced his government's readiness to start SALT in August. The Russians, who in the first quarter of the year had been expressing *their* readiness to start, became silent. A number of hawkish, anti-disarmament articles peaked in the Russian military press, and the general press followed the anti-ABM campaign in the United States very closely. Only after the Senate had approved *Safeguard*, if only by a tiny margin, did it become clear that the Soviet Union would decide to participate. Perhaps if the Senate had thrown out *Safeguard*, the Soviet Union would have sat back and waited for the United States to disarm itself, to the satisfaction of both hawks and doves in the Kremlin. In the event, the preparatory meeting for SALT, to draw up ground rules, opened on 17 November 1969 in Helsinki.

Two particular Russian weapon programmes have been largely mentioned in the context of the SAL Talks: the SS9 ICBM and the Y-class submarine about whose numbers (operational or under construction) the evidence has been ambiguous. Pauses in site construction of SS9 silos have been seized by the (sometimes unilateralist) opposition as tacit signals that the Russians desire a deployment freeze; starts have been counter-seized by the Administration to show that pause could as well have been due to the cold weather, or to a technical hitch, or to a change of mind. Neither side knew for sure. Hints about a freeze had not been dropped with the Administration, though they had with the opposition. Chalmers Roberts, of the *Washington Post*, mentioning 7 March 1971 that work stopped on eighteen SS9 silos in October 1970 and had not resumed, noted also that 'efforts to draw out the Russians on the meaning of that halt have been unavailing.'[30] The same day, Senator Jackson, a hawkish Demo-

30. *International Herald Tribune*, 7 March 1971. The Americans have fairly certainly carried out more underground nuclear tests since the start of SALT; and the Russians more missile tests.

crat from the state of Washington,[31] and no doubt concerned about unemployment among his aerospace constituents, announced that new missile holes, larger than ever, had been observed and that the Russians were about to deploy a new weapons system, with missiles even larger than the SS9. A Pentagon spokesman was more cautious: 'We're not sure exactly what it is or what Soviet intentions are.' No mention can have been made of the new activity by the Russians at the SALT, but Mr Roberts revealed that ten of the new-type holes had been spotted in February, and Mr Nixon knew about them before he made his annual 'State of the World Report'; they were one reason why he rejected the Russian 'ABM limitation-only' proposal in the talks. After a period of bad spotting weather, there appeared to be forty;[32] after which Senator Jackson broke the news. Tass quoted *Pravda*'s New York correspondent on 21 March: 'the myth about a "Soviet menace" is being dispelled by life itself.' *Le Monde* commented: 'As if by chance, these pessimistic declarations coincide with the *Safeguard* debate . . .' The Administration appeared almost nonplussed by the scale of what it was disclosing: thus Mr Laird: 'I cannot say with certainty . . .'; Mr Rogers, the Secretary of State: 'We're not sure at the moment . . .' The *New York Times* headlined a leading article 'The Annual Spring Scare'.[33] By early May there were 66 holes: 17 big ones, 49 suitable perhaps for super-hardened SS11.[34] The relief that it wasn't 49 SS9s somehow turned 66 new silos, including 17 SS9-size holes, almost into good news. By August the figure was nearly 80; by October it was 90, with a new, third, type of silo sighted. The inner dimensions of all the three types were thought to be 'significantly larger than the ten-foot diameter . . . of the SS9'.[35] ABM building resumed round Moscow. On 24 April 1972, the *New York Times* confirmed a 12 foot diameter missile was ready for testing.

By contrast, the argument about the numbers of Y-class sub-

31. Also with presidential ambitions.
32. Chalmers Roberts, *International Herald Tribune*, 23 April 1971.
33. 23 April 1971.
34. 10 May 1971.
35. *International Herald Tribune*, 10 October 1971.

marines that the Soviet Union may be building is rather less hectic than the SS9 argument: the weapons are not as alarming, or at least not as provocative, and, because the more owl-like doves are ready to argue that the deep sea is probably the best place to deploy a retaliatory system, the ULMS, the development of which Mr Laird had accelerated in 1971, is not disputed like the *Safeguard* programme had been. The disagreement is about when the Soviet Union can be expected to catch up with the United States in numbers of nuclear-powered, missile-launching submarines, and whether this will matter if it happens. Uncertainty prevails here, as it does with the SS9, and with the new holes, and with the rest of the Russian military programme and policy. The principal nuclear submarine construction yard, on the White Sea, is reportedly being doubled in size.[36] In October Mr Laird said at a news conference: 'The production of [Russian] ICBMs, the production of ... *Polaris*-type submarines ... has gone forward at a pace that far outdistances the estimates which I gave to Congress in March in my defence report.'[37] He said parity in submarine numbers was now likely to occur in 1973, a year earlier than he suggested in March.[38]

Into this sea of uncertainty Mr Brezhnev launched a fleet of arms control 'initiatives' in the summer of 1971: a compromise proposal on biological warfare at the CCD, a new Moon Treaty, invitations to discuss force reductions in central Europe (MBFR), to discuss reductions in far-flung fleet movements, to establish a nuclear-free zone in the Levant, to hold a conference of the five nuclear-weapons powers or, alternatively, a world-wide disarmament conference outside the United Nations. What with an agreement on West Berlin (which would probably have arms control implications) already the subject of four-power negotiations, a European Security Conference the subject of a multiplicity of bilateral discussions, and a couple of suggestions for

36. *International Herald Tribune*, 10 October 1971.

37. 14 October 1971.

38. Senator Jackson, who broke the news of the 'holes' in March 1971, claimed on 21 November that the Russians were in process of assembling their 42nd Polaris-type submarine. The United States has 41 Polaris submarines.

negotiation in SALT, there was a great deal more being spoken of than could be discussed, and more being discussed than could conceivably be negotiated, let alone agreed.[39] There was – and is – still no underlying consensus about either the international system to which agreement would contribute, nor about how internationally to verify and to police (in other words, to institutionalize) whatever new system might come to be constructed; no one has proposed discussing these. That the Russians intimated nothing to the American Government either on the subject of the 1971 silo-building, or of the 1970 silo-building halt, suggests that they do not yet intend to substitute factual certainty – on which alone arms control can be developed – for the uncertainty concerning their military affairs that now obtains, and which is still the prime and most potent fuel for today's many arms races.

Meanwhile, moreover, despite the polite words of official spokesmen at Helsinki and Vienna about the 'serious atmosphere' of the SALT and of the 'goodwill' and the 'intent to agree', Russian comment for domestic consumption had become particularly destructive.

The Soviet view, put by Vasil Shestov in *Pravda* in February 1971, was that 'the military build-up which is being carried out by the United States is incompatible with a constructive approach to the settlement of problems being discussed at Soviet-American talks.'[40] There are forces in the United States 'which are only

39. It might seem that this list includes everything possible: in fact not. The Soviet Medium and Intermediate Range Strategic nuclear missiles, which could in one strike destroy all of Western Europe, have had no slot allotted to them: the Soviet Union has explicitly refused to discuss them in SALT, although Mr Nixon is understood to have originally assured his NATO allies that SALT would deal with them. (Henry Brandon, 'What Nixon said to Wilson', *Sunday Times*, 1 February 1970.) Mr Gromyko apparently has made equally clear that although American Forward Based nuclear Systems (AFBS) may be discussed in SALT or in the MBFR talks, nuclear weapons based in the Soviet Union may not be discussed in either. (Chalmers Roberts, 'The ABC of FBS and SALT and MBFR and CES (ESC)', *Washington Post*, 2 May 1971. It is not even clear that the Russians are prepared to consider limiting missile launching submarines.

40. 2 February 1971.

interested in casting aspersions ... and to stir up distrust of the Soviet Union's position'.

An article in the March number of *International Affairs* warned against confusing 'on the one hand the consistent and purposeful struggle of the USSR ... to put an end to the arms race and on the other the policy of the imperialist powers which have been steadily building up their military potential ...'. 'It is highly important ... to expose those who have tried to white-wash the imperialist powers ... and which have suggested the two super-powers are equally to blame.'[41]

In June, Igor Glagoliev, an arms control expert, declared that difficulties arose in SALT over the question of the limitation of offensive strategic weapons 'when the USA started to equip its strategic missiles with MIRV warheads, when it concentrated numerous means of nuclear weapons delivery in and around Europe, and began to build up [sic] the *Safeguard* ABM system. All that, of course, did not enhance the course of the negotiations.'[42]

In July in a series of articles on SALT in *Red Star*, the army newspaper, Colonel Kharich declared that the 'race in strategic weapons is being escalated in the United States to the accompaniment of chatter about a mythical "Soviet threat". .... Hysterical shouts about a "Soviet threat", accompanied by the policy of building up strategic armaments in the United States, are incompatible with a constructive approach to a solution of the problems which are under discussion in the Soviet-American Strategic Arms Limitation Talks. All this seriously prejudices the Talks.'[43] Colonel Kharich referred to the Soviet build-up rather obliquely: 'To any attempts by any party to ensure military superiority over the USSR, we shall reply with an appropriate increase in the military might which guarantees our defence.'

41. A. Shevechenko, 'Some lessons of the Disarmament Struggle', *International Affairs* (Moscow), March 1971.
42. Tass in English. Report of article by Igor Glagoliev in *Moscow News*, 16 June 1971. S U 3712/A1/1.
43. Reprinted in *Soviet News*, 20 July 1971.

These rather one-sided declarations have not found much resonance in the United States: after the announcement of Mr Nixon's trips to China, and to Moscow, together with the dwindling of the Vietnam war, Mr Nixon has become less vulnerable in foreign affairs. Moreover, for opponents to doubt the accuracy of the information Mr Laird gives them about the Russian build-up, would obviously raise unspeakable problems about verification, even of a SALT agreement. Anyway, this year economics are in. ... *Safeguard*, which had got through the Senate by one vote in 1969, went through 64–21 in 1971.

On 20 May 1971 the two sides simultaneously announced that they had agreed to reach a formal agreement on limiting defensive missiles, and that this would be 'accompanied by certain measures with respect to the limitation of offensive weapons'; the Russian text had 'followed' instead of 'accompanied'. According to *Newsweek*, which carried this story, the 'error' was 'rectified' as soon as it was animadverted upon. This 'accompanied' was the actual nub of the agreement: Mr Nixon had already rejected a limitation on only ABM which the Soviet Union had proposed earlier.[44]

The insouciance with which the Russians brushed aside the little Suez Canal arms control arrangement of August 1970[45] was

44. Mr Nixon confirmed in a press conference on 16 November 1971 that 'we cannot limit defensive weapons first and then limit offensive weapons. Both must go together. It will happen.'

45. According to Mr Riyad, the Egyptian Foreign Minister, in an interview on Cairo Radio on 6 October 1970, the ceasefire which started on 8 August included a weapons standstill, which specifically referred to 'not introducing missiles into an area extending 50 kms. from the Suez Canal and not establishing new missile sites there'. This was confirmed by the Director of Israeli Military Intelligence on 26 October. Trouble and dispute arose because although flying to within 10 kms. of the canal was permitted, no machinery was set up for considering the evidence of violations such flights might produce. U2s had been flying, as well as Israeli and Egyptian planes, and all parties, with credible circumstantiality, complained of violations. But as Mr Riyad said: 'We have a long list of Israeli violations, but to whom do we submit it?' He went on to say that he would not comment on or identify the 'mistakes and series of mistakes' in a United States list of Egyptian violations because 'it is not possible for them to learn the truth without our divul-

remembered. If such small and desirable birds in the hand as that cannot be kept alive, was there any hope for the implausibly grandiose and complicated creatures that Mr Brezhnev had been adumbrating in the bush? If the emperor's new birds are not there at all, the Chinese at the UN are now likely to say so.

The public problems remain what they always were: how may the truth be known, what is the good society and how may it be worked for?

The 'truth' about what is or may be happening gets coloured and transfused by what, formatively, happened before: Anthony Eden foreclosed on Hitler at Suez, Dean Rusk avoided appeasement in Vietnam, Senator Fulbright does not accept the Tonkin Bay story nowadays, the Kennedy academics stood fast against their President's *Minuteman* purchase of 1961 by opposing Nixon's *Safeguard* purchase of 1969. Deeply felt circumstance froze as a scar on their minds; but the actual world then, as now, was never circumstant, always circumfluent, never to be stepped into twice. Mr Brezhnev's arrangements cannot signify a return to domestic Stalinism, Mr Laird's missile counts cannot be a revival of the cold war. They are what is happening now. We expect repetition but it doesn't come.

What is coming? How much can we hope for out of the SALT, out of the European Security Conference, out of a World Disarmament Conference? The SALT have been going on for two

---

ging military secrets.' He claimed that all the new missiles had been emplaced, with great haste, in the three nights immediately before the ceasefire began on 8 August. The Israelis and the Americans disputed this. The Russians, in whose tacit 'parallel action' the Americans had obviously been trusting, by disowning any active part in the ceasefire and standstill agreement itself (according to Secretary of State Rogers it was only an 'oral agreement' – Mr Rogers's press conference, 7 May 1971) and by declaring the American reconnaissance flights which reported the violations to be themselves a 'gross violation of sovereignty of the UAR', sidestepped responsibility for the reported moving of what were certainly Russian-provided and, the Israelis claimed, Russian-manned missiles. Moreover, they said, if the moving had occurred it was justified because 'ground-to-air rockets and anti-aircraft artillery do not qualify as offensive weapons.' It was not suggested that the standstill exempted the introduction of defensive missiles.

years, the arms race has continued unabated, nothing has happened. The joint announcement on 20 May 1971 was no more than belated agreement about the SALT agenda, and Mr Nixon, perhaps rightly, has called it an 'historic breakthrough': there may be something for him to initial when he travels to Moscow in May. If there is agreement, either formal or informal, the question of verification will have arisen and in some way will have been answered. But verification, to whose satisfaction? By definition any agreement will be verifiable to the satisfaction of the United States and the Soviet Union. Russian verification of United States observance, the United States being an open society, will be partly by study of open sources (budget, congressional hearings, the press, etc.) and partly by the use of observation satellites and by more traditional forms of espionage. The Soviet Union being a closed society, the United States will depend far more exclusively on espionage and on the observation satellites which are now providing reliable figures for Russian missile deployment. The United States has, I believe, entered the SAL Talks convinced that its own national means of verification would be adequate for any agreement likely to be reached. (It is because reliance on national means would not be adequate for monitoring any ban or limitation on Multiple Re-entry Vehicles, that MRV as such will not figure in any SAL agreement.)

The Soviet Union has, in the UN Outer Space Committee, come very close to suggesting that photographing of foreign territory from satellites and aircraft for whatever purpose without the special permission of the governments should be considered an infringement of national sovereignty.[46] Certainly any attempt at prohibiting overflying by satellites would so reduce the scope of national means of verification as probably prevent any SAL agreement. However, satellite missile warning systems are now mentioned in the little US/SU agreement[47] on *Measures to reduce the risk of war*, and this must be assumed to legitimize them. But even if American observation satellites are accepted by the

46. Russian sensitivity derives in part from their apprehensions about uncensored television pictures reaching Russian screens.

47. Of 30 September 1971; see p. 131.

Soviet Union it is not only the United States and the Soviet Union who have a legitimate interest in this matter of the verifiability of a SAL Agreement. Article VI of the NPT refers to negotiations for the cessation of the nuclear arms race, and several of the near-nuclear signatories of the NPT (including Japan and West Germany) have made it quite clear that they would ratify the Treaty only when they were satisfied that the United States and the Soviet Union were actually in process of curbing the strategic arms race.

The question arises, how may they, and other powers without observation satellites, verify a SAL agreement? The Seabed nuclear non-emplacement treaty specifically (in Article III) enshrines the right of parties other than the technologically well-provided to seek and obtain certainty.[48] This right has so far not been mentioned in the context of the SALT, but it should not be under-estimated. Two kinds of solution to the problem of third-party verification suggest themselves: 1) that the contracting super-powers should themselves publish evidence verifying their observation of the limitations agreed, and 2) that the third powers should acquire and operate an observation satellite system of their own: many of the parts are on sale on the open market.

Possibly, some governments might accept the completion of the Test Ban (if this were to be agreed) as adequate indication that a limitation of strategic arms was in operation; more are likely to recall the large number of tests already carried out and to doubt if there is very much more to find out that way. How shall they be persuaded except by way of some kind of international verification system? Proposals for an international system for seismic monitoring are quite far advanced, and there is no reason to suppose that a satellite system would not also be negotiable among the interested third parties.

Any such proposal is likely to be found distasteful by the Russian Government, whose attitude to verification was, with perhaps short-sighted sympathy, acknowledged in 1967 by the Johnson Administration. An Under-Secretary of Defense, Mr

48. The 1971 Convention for banning biological weapons is much less permissive.

Paul Warnke, as part of the Johnson bridge-building policy, promised that in any talks the two powers might hold about limiting strategic missiles (and Mr Johnson was keen to start such talks), they could certainly 'avoid bogging down in the perennially difficult issue of international inspection'.[49] American 'unilateral verification', he made clear, would be considered adequate, even in the case of 'formal agreement' to level off or reduce strategic systems. This acknowledgement still obtains, and the relationship between the SAL Talks and the NPT's Article VI tends to be played right down by both Russians and Americans.

In his 1971 report on the work of the United Nations, U Thant recommended that progress in SALT should be reported to the CCD in Geneva and that the latter should acquire a third, unaligned, chairman to sit along with the permanent Russian and American. The Chinese have long expressed their disapproval of the monopolistic aspects of the SALT and other Russian American private arrangements, and their view may lend enough weight to U Thant's and that of the unaligned at Geneva for something to happen. Certainly there is little to be said for a privacy so complete as to permit no visible movement at all. Had we but world enough and time, this coyness, gentlemen, were no crime. As it is, all other possible agreement is in practice geared to this one: the NPT formally by way of its Article VI, informally by the caveats attached to their signatures by several near nuclear powers; the complete test ban, which has first to be accepted by Russians and Americans and then multilaterally negotiated to include arrangements for the peaceful explosions which some Russians and some Americans believe in; and even the European Security Conference, onto whose table SALT leftovers will have to fall (particularly of course the Russian intermediate and medium-range strategic missiles).

Since Mr Brezhnev's visit to Paris in the autumn of 1971, the proposal to discuss Mutual and Balanced Force Reductions (MBFR) in Central Europe has disappeared from Russian dis-

49. Paul C. Warnke, speaking at Detroit, 6 October 1967.

course – the French consider the issue unnegotiable – but the American Government, goaded by Senator Mansfield and his troops, will have, visibly, to insist: some meeting, some negotiation, Nato to Warsaw Pact, will have to occur. Another endless series of meetings, about the dismantling of the European blocs, seems not impossible. Would its writ reach into the Soviet Union where the Soviet missiles lie? MBFR would not, the Russians are said to say. Would the Pact's *alter ego* system of bilateral military and political agreements between its members be up for dissolution too? It is difficult to suppose so.

The Russians want the status quo formally accepted. Their Mr Arbatov, specialist in American affairs, told a *New York Times* reporter in November 1971 that three common interests could be advanced during Mr Nixon's visit to Moscow in May: the prevention of thermonuclear war, steps to curb the arms race, and an expansion of trade and scientific collaboration.[50] The same sort of confirmation of security coupled with passing goodies through the bars may be the strict limit of their hopes: the planned – or at least intended – integration of the Comecon countries cannot easily combine with economic détente; nor censorship and the persecution of intellectuals and nationalist dissidents with cultural cooperation.

The French Government sees the purpose of a European Security Conference as an 'interpenetration of the blocs'.[51] M. Schumann, the French Foreign Minister, recently called it the 'Conférence des Européens' which is perhaps new. For President Pompidou, Europe is 'fragile, petite, petite presqu'île menacée', and yet with 300 million people, who for the last five hundred years have made the history of mankind (he could have added, for good and evil), here is a unique reservoir of abilities, and economic power superior to that of all the Soviet world and not far from equal to that of North America.[52] Geography dictates what Europe should do; and arms control agreements for our

50. American official USIS comment on an Arbatov article in the November issue of the Russian periodical *USA*, 18 November 1971.
51. *International Herald Tribune*, 12 November 1971.
52. *Le Monde*, 26 June 1971.

continent are too serious to leave to the military blocs. 'Normal-ization requires the uninhibited flow of communications and free ideas.'[53]

Eastern Europe (each country – today bar Czechoslovakia – with its private heresy: Romania's independent foreign policy, Poland's return to Christendom, Hungary's decentralized near-capitalism, East Germany's economic efficiency, Bulgaria's Balkan ambitions) praises what could lift America off Western Europe and mirror-wise lift Russia off them. The European Security Conference is all things to all governments – even a dull bore to the British Foreign Office. What is negotiable?

The Chinese arrived at the United Nations, on 15 November 1971, objects of astonishment, delight, and plain alarm. Is there a revolution going on in China? Is the army decapitated? Have the local revisionists been 'peddling anti-Marxist black goods' with the international revisionists?[54] The language is opaque, but the posture at the UN is staunch and bland against the super-powers. On 18 November China conducted a 20 kiloton nuclear test in the atmosphere. Mr Chiao at the UN repeated the usual undertaking that China would never be the first to use nuclear weapons, and invited the other nuclear powers to reciprocate – 'This is not something difficult to do. Whether this is done or not will be a severe test as to whether they have a genuine desire for disarmament.'[55] He denounced the Russian proposed World Disarmament Conference as a 'permanent club for endless dis-cussion.'[56] If there is a World Disarmament Conference in 1972, where could it start? The great disarmament schemes Kennedy and Khrushchev published ten years ago refer to another world,

53. Of a kind that Mr Brezhnev on his visit to Paris may not quite have grasped – M. Pompidou told him at dinner at the Quai d'Orsay (*Le Monde*, 29 October 1971) that exchanges of books and films were 'ridiculously low' and that the purported level of Franco–Russian relations imposes 'the reci-procal study of history, language, literature and art'. Mr Brezhnev spoke contentedly of the already 'large cultural exchanges'.

54. Hunan Provincial Service, 5 November 1971.

55. *International Herald Tribune*, 17 November 1971.

56. *Guardian*, 25 November 1971.

with fewer weapons, fewer wars, fewer countries, fewer super-powers; and more illusions and more self-confidence. Neither the French nor the Chinese have taken part in any of the currently operating disarmament talks and negotiations; and neither so far has lied about the problems. But it is not true that a declaratory ban on the first use of nuclear weapons would be other than difficult for the United States and for the United Kingdom and France, facing, as they see it, the possibly irresistible conventional power of the Warsaw Pact; or even for the Russians facing as they see it, the endless hordes of China. They acquired and have deployed their nuclear weapons out of specific (not necessarily justified) fears. Deterrence cannot certainly be said not to work: if the emperor has no new clothes on, those clothes are still the ones he supposes himself to be wearing, and he certainly doesn't yet know how to take them off.

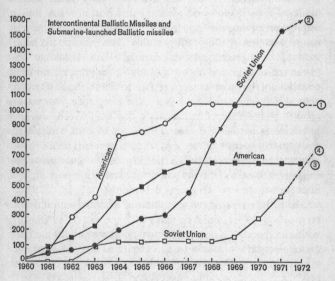

Intercontinental Ballistic Missiles and Submarine-launched Ballistic missiles

O ICBMS : U.S. ① Now new land based ICBM announced.
● ICBMS : S.U. ② Approximately 90 new silos under construction.
■ SLBMs : U.S. ③ 41 submarines in being each with 16 missiles.
□ SLBMs : S.U. ④ 43 submarines each with 16 missiles now in being or under construction.

12

And welcome to something else

The title of this book could properly continue like that. At one time, it seemed that apprehension of nuclear holocaust might compact mankind's political will. But mankind's political will continued diffuse, hectic and unimpressed, and international arms control evidently still seems optional. The great emotions and great ratiocinations of the late fifties and early sixties affected mankind's perceptions of nuclear war, but not the rate of acquisition of nuclear (and other) weapons which its governments went on finding indispensable. The perceptions which induced some governments to promote a ban on nuclear tests in the sea and in and above the atmosphere related rather to unacceptable environmental risks than to risks deemed unacceptable in continuing the arms race. The arms race goes on unaffected by the series of treaties and agreements which have been presented as partial or collateral measures of arms control. The treaty to ban nuclear and some other emplacements on the seabed may well be the last, as well as the most, insignificant treaty that the international community will agree to negotiate – its effect on even the negotiators was deeply depressing.

If it is the case that one condition of disarmament and arms control is certainty, and if certainty is the product of satisfactory verification and of a degree of actual consensus about the international system which is being substituted for the arms race system, an alternative to negotiated arms control may be growing up.

What is happening is the occupation, or illumination, of some areas, or fields, or elements, so that their use for military pur-

228

poses is reduced and discouraged. One might call it negative arms control or *de facto* arms control; it works on the same principle as a switched-on light works to prevent burglary. The reason for this development is the growing recognition which, in its effects could be revolutionary, that we are on the way to killing our planet. Governments are responding to the diagnosis by seeking to increase the information they have about what is happening; and by seeking to increase their powers to deal with what is happening. Both of these purposes increasingly involve international cooperation, and on an increasing scale.

In June 1970 the Canadian Government took remarkable, unprecedented, and stringent, powers under an Arctic Waters Pollution Prevention Act: the alarm had been set off by the discovery of the massive North Slope oil field and the risks of pollution attendant on getting the oil away. Under the act, exploitation, transportation, and waste disposal are all to be precisely controlled as to location, methods of operation, hardware, insurance, and so on, over an area reaching out 100 nautical miles from the Canadian coast-line. There is the possibility of outright prohibition of certain types of ship and certain types of equipment. Pilots may be required on board, accompanying ice-breakers may be compulsory. Exceptions, for instance for NATO warships, may be made, but certificates will be required. Pollution prevention officers have full powers of entry to all places and ships and may order the latter away or to anchor, or even, if 'dangerous', to be destroyed, seized, or forfeited. The law applies to the bed, body and surface of the sea, and it cannot but deter other governments in their military activities there. Under other legislation, 'innocent passage' in Canadian territorial waters is now controlled by regulations to prevent pollution. The Steamship Inspection Service operates 'regular aerial inspection flights to spot offenders'.[1] A system hitherto voluntary, now made official, regulates traffic along 400 miles of the St Lawrence,

1. *Canadian Ministry of Transport News – Nouvelles*, no. 5–71, 22 February 1971.

downstream from Montreal to where it is some eighty miles wide: every passing vessel has to be equipped to be in radio-telephonic communication with shore-based authority and under its orders.[2]

Several Latin American countries have declared their territorial waters extended to 200 nautical miles, and they are acquiring naval and air craft for policing them. China supports them. The US does not and has its fishing vessels seized. Iceland is to extend territorial waters to fifty nautical miles and will no doubt police that. Malaysia's territorial waters and Indonesia's now straddle the Malacca Strait, through which ninety per cent of Japan's oil travels. Regulation will follow. The United Kingdom and France are discussing a traffic system for the Channel. So will all the world's pollutable narrows – which is all the important ones – soon be policed. Moreover, full, and therefore policeable, insurance is becoming compulsory everywhere at sea.

The bed of the North Sea is being divided up between a number of commercial enterprises and so are other shallow, oil-rich, off-shore areas. Planning regulation will have to follow, and if The Queen's Peace is to be kept, so will far more positive policing arrangements than now obtain, as various sensitive or dangerous types of enterprises, each with increasingly expensive and complex gear, seek to coexist in limited space: fishing, dumping, shipping, mineral extraction, channel-dredging, oil and natural gas extraction, sea-farming, artificial islands, underwater containers. A degree of *de facto* arms control will operate on, in and under the shallow seas, the enclosed seas and the narrow seas.

The Soviet Union already claims to be using satellites to assist its fleets in finding fishable shoals. Satellite-borne radar can detect and monitor oil slicks. Heat-sensitive devices can locate not only natural sources of heat, but pollutant warmth and that which issues from submarines' propulsion systems. Electronic sensors can intercept wireless transmissions. Optical photography can 'distinguish . . . a light patch on a dark surface if the patch is some ten inches across and the camera . . . some sixty miles

2. *Canadian Ministry of Transport News – Nouvelles*, no. 38–71, 13 July 1971.

above it'.[3] Aircraft, using a variety of sensors, can locate and sample pollution of various kinds, identify natural resources, and even map sub-surface geology and interferences with it. Seismic monitoring can catch earthquakes and underground tests. The United Nations Peaceful Uses of Outer Space Committee's Scientific Sub-Committee (with the support of the United States, the Soviet Union, the United Kingdom and Japan) has even gone so far as to call for a working group to consider the question of the 'remote sensing of the earth by satellite'.[4] The early-warning satellites of the super-powers have a role in the little 1971 agreement on Measures to Reduce the Risk of War between the United States and the Soviet Union.[5] The combination of satellite-derived information of all kinds, international regulations concerning meteorology and pollution, together with policing and enforcement even by national means, cannot but have a large negative effect on the military deployments and activities of states, everywhere but in the deepest oceans. It is not likely that the 1972 United Nations Conference on the Environment in Stockholm will have these implications for arms control very actively in mind when it discusses world-wide monitoring systems, but the implications will be there, all the same. The United Nations Conference on the Law of the Sea, set for 1973, is likely to be more consciously alert to them.

Verification will be preceding agreement because it is a side effect of something else. Moreover, the 'science' which will be providing the evidence will all be of the 'bourgeois non-class' kind, and closed societies will have little choice but to accept that this is not espionage, but information publicly and properly acquired and presented by, or on behalf of, the world organization for purposes related to the world's survival. As usual, there are foreseeable difficulties, the more intractable again deriving from the currently held beliefs of the Russian Government. The Russian Government has always protested at overflying by air-

3. Neville Brown, 'Reconnaissance from Space', *The World Today*, February 1971, p. 70.
4. *International Herald Tribune*, 14 July 1971.
5. See p. 131.

craft, and during the operation of the Suez Canal arms freeze maintained that American reconnaissance satellites were violating Egyptian sovereignty by observing events on the Egyptian side.[6] The Soviet Union has put noticeably less effort into the preparation of the 1972 Stockholm UN Conference on the Human Environment than the other developed countries.[7] The only contribution of its two-man delegation to the Working Party on the Prevention of Marine Pollution was a *Statement on the Organization of Regional Control* which declared as a principle that 'the control of the extent of environmental pollution in territorial waters and on the continental shelf' must be 'undertaken on a national basis'.[8] As the national continental shelf may stretch to the middle of a shallow sea, such as the North Sea, such a principle would be counter-productive to the setting up of Regional Sea Regimes, which would need executive authority over just this sort of thing. The Russian attitude to the 1973 UN Conference on the Law of the Sea is bleakly cold.

The Soviet Government is in fact divided in mind about the whole issue of environmental pollution.[9] The idea may sit un-

6. An attitude which the Soviet Union had earlier taken up in the 1969 General Assembly: 'photographing foreign territory . . . from satellites and from conventional aircraft' is unlawful and a violation of national sovereignty. This seems incompatible with the Soviet Union's views on the adequacy of national means of verification of arms control agreements, with the Soviet Union willingness to accept American space photographs of Russian weather; and of course with the agreement mentioned above and on p. 131. See also footnote 46, p. 222. Russian photographic satellites appear to have been sent up specially to observe the progress of the Indo–Pakistan conflict, however.

7. And in January 1972 actually withdrew from a preparatory meeting, along with Czechoslovakia, after disagreements about the status of East German delegates to the conference proper. China's subsequent acceptance of an invitation to Stockholm may influence the Russian attitude.

8. A/Conf./A8/IWGMPI/5.

9. The American delegate to the UNESCO Executive Council in October 1971 charged the Russian Government with 'hiding the truth' about industrial pollution from its people, by deleting a large section of an article on Environmental Control and Economic Systems that dealt with pollution in Russia, in the July issue of the Russian language version of the UNESCO monthly, *Courier* (*International Herald Tribune*, 15 October

comfortably with the Labour theory of Value; such problems ought to be exclusively capitalist, but evidently are not.

Moreover, conservation of natural resources within the Soviet Union is one thing – and by now self-evidently necessary; conservation of natural resources outside is another. The Soviet Union, alone with Japan, continues hunting whales to extinction. The Russian (and Polish) Governments refused to attend a meeting in Norway in October 1971 to discuss the control of dumping toxic wastes in the North-East Atlantic and the North Sea.[10] Russian fishing programmes are among the most aggressive and least conservation-minded in the world: as a Russian trawler captain put it recently on Moscow radio, 'the fishing grounds will continue to recede from Soviet shores.'[11] The Russian Government, in short, is still tempted to dispute whether the world is one: the conundrum will perhaps be answered at the Stockholm Conference.

The difficulties erected in the West are of a different kind, and more familiar: sectional interests and hysterias (political, economic, and academic) vie and counter-vie. The right work is done at the wrong expense: an elite organization of industrialists commissions deep research at MIT,[12] and no developing nation will believe a word of it; experts in one field set up as experts in another and there is no one to knock their heads together; governments, whose function is to determine priorities in legislation and public expenditure, plead inadequacies of knowledge rather than admit another candidate for high grading in the priorities. The developing world notices post-imperialist 'do as I say and not as I did-ism' and the seductiveness with which international capital invites them to set up as dirt-havens.

1971). Domestically they do appear reasonably concerned about industrial and other pollution; Lake Baikal has been the locale for a great battle, which the environmentalists appear to have won.

10. Agreement was reached in January 1972 in Oslo.

11. 10 October 1971. S U W645/A/12.

12. The 'Club of Rome', which is seeking to foster a 'mass movement'. See 'Blueprint for Survival', *The Ecologist*, January 1972.

Still, slowly, the sense of one physical world, of one system vulnerable to misuse, is driving itself into more and more minds. The realization that the human race *could* kill off its civilization with weapons has not convinced enough people that a system as risky as the arms race should be changed. This time, and for the first time, the evidence is forcing itself into all our minds, governments and peoples alike, that the world is one, that this could be our last chance, and also, and therefore, that it could be our first.

Stop Press: 1 June 1972

Some of the questions posed on pages 221–4 about the Strategic Arms Limitation Talks are now answered: among much else, Mr Nixon had one treaty on defensive weapons and one 'interim agreement' and protocol on offensive weapons to sign when he visited Moscow in May 1972. They are to impose limitations in the form of future ceilings, equal for both sides for ABMs, higher for the Russians than for the Americans for offensive weapons (which presumably carries a message for the Chinese). 'Verification' is to be by 'national technical means', which is understood to mean observation satellites, which, thus defined, are now not only legitimated, but, specifically, not to be 'interfere[d] with'. Parties are also not to increase the current levels of 'concealment' of their strategic missiles. If the ABM treaty is not ratified by either side, the offensive arms agreement fails too.

Although Article VI of the Non-Proliferation Treaty is mentioned in the preambles to both the Treaty and the interim agreement, no mechanism is adumbrated whereby third parties may convince themselves either about the actual state of affairs or about Russian or American observance of their undertakings. There is also no mention, either in the Treaty or the agreement or in the joint communiqué issued at the end of Mr Nixon's visit, of any movement towards completing the Test Ban, which might provide an alternative way of internationally monitoring a reduction in the pace of the Russian/American arms race. However, a standing consultative commission is to be set up to carry on negotiating 'further measures aimed at limiting strategic weapons' in accordance with the principle of 'equal security'.

The texts were published in full in the Soviet press, and the

Russian people may well have been surprised to learn about the actual state of the nuclear balance. The ABM text, at first glance, appears sound: quite without the loopholes for word-twisting and technological developments with which the NPT is riddled. The offensive arms text is altogether softer: ambiguities and undefined terms abound. It is clear that the Russians have not confided their own figures to the Americans, and that the Americans know nothing about Russian intentions for the big holes or for the new bigger-than-SS 9 missile, whose warhead is currently being rumoured at 50 megatons. The language of the protocol which actually names figures for the prospective ceilings is even more opaque than the main text. Evidently agreement was not reached at all on limiting the size of silos; according to A.P., this was one of four, last-minute, problems.

The arms race itself is scarcely snaffled. Mr Laird, although he immediately halted work on all but one *Safeguard* ABM site, has now named the ULMS *Trident* and announced the first boat for 1978. The Russians appear to be building an improved type of nuclear submarine to carry their new SLBM, and are holding the gigantic new missile ready to test. All of this is fully compatible with the agreements. Chou En Lai, a Japanese visitor reports, sees them as having 'plenty of loopholes'. Whether the loop-holes in the interim agreement and protocol will delay American ratification of the ABM treaty remains to be seen.

Still, after two and a half years, the SALT mountain has at last given birth. The mouse may be small, but it is not ridiculous.

Initials

ABM	Anti-Ballistic Missile
BMD	Ballistic Missile Defence
CBW	Chemical and Biological (and Bacteriological) Warfare
CCD	Conference of the Committee on Disarmament
CMEA	Comecon, the Council for Mutual Economic Aid
CTB	Complete Test Ban
DICBM	Depressed Trajectory ICBM
ENDC	Eighteen-Nation Disarmament Committee
ESC	European Security Conference
FOBS	Fractional Orbiting Bombardment System. See OBS
IAEA	International Atomic Energy Authority
ICBM	Intercontinental-range Ballistic Missile (beyond 2,500 miles)
IISS	International Institute for Strategic Studies (after 1971, London)
IRBM	Intermediate Range Ballistic Missile
ISS	Institute for Strategic Studies (before 1971, London)
MBFR	Mutual and Balanced Force Reductions
MLF	Multilateral Force
MMRBM	Mobile Medium-Range Ballistic Missile
MRBM	Medium-Range Ballistic Missile
NPT	Non-proliferation treaty
OBS	Orbiting Bombardment System
PTB	Partial Test Ban
SALT	Strategic Arms Limitation Talks
SIPRI	Stockholm International Peace Research Institute
SLBM	Submarine-launched Ballistic Missile
SLICBM	Submarine-launched ICBM
SRAM	Short-Range Attack Missile
SRBM	Short-Range Ballistic Missile
TNDC	Ten-Nation Disarmament Committee

Index

Acronyms, e.g. SALT, are in strict alphabetical order; other groups of initials representing titles or names are at the beginnings of their letter sections.

'SU' means Soviet Union, 'US' means United States.

239